Mathematics Higher Level

for the IB Diploma

Exam Preparation Guide

Paul Fannon, Vesna Kadelburg,
Ben Woolley, Stephen Ward

CAMBRIDGE
UNIVERSITY PRESS

CAMBRIDGE
UNIVERSITY PRESS

University Printing House, Cambridge CB2 8BS, United Kingdom

Cambridge University Press is part of the University of Cambridge.

It furthers the University's mission by disseminating knowledge in the pursuit of education, learning and research at the highest international levels of excellence.

www.cambridge.org
Information on this title: www.cambridge.org/9781107672154

© Cambridge University Press 2014

First published 2014
3rd printing 2015

Printed in Poland by Opolgraf

A catalogue record for this publication is available from the British Library

ISBN 978-1-107-67215-4 Paperback

Cover image: Craig Jewell/Shutterstock

....

CONTENTS

INTRODUCTION

ABOUT THIS BOOK

If you are using this book, you're probably getting quite close to your exams. You may have started off as a bright-eyed student keen to explore international perspectives in mathematics and the nature of mathematical knowledge, but now you want to know how to get the best possible grade! This book is designed to revise the entire core (Paper 1 and Paper 2) material that you need to know, and to provide examples of the most common types of exam questions for you to practise, along with some hints and tips regarding exam technique and common pitfalls.

 Any common pitfalls and useful exam hints will be highlighted in these boxes.

 This type of box will be used to point out where graphical calculators can be used effectively to simplify a question or speed up your work. Common calculator pitfalls will also be highlighted in such boxes.

▶▶ If the material in a chapter involves maths outside of that chapter, this kind of box will direct you to the relevant part of the book where you can go and remind yourself of the relevant maths.

The most important ideas and formulae are emphasised in the 'What you need to know' sections at the start of each chapter. When a formula or set of formulae is given in the Formula booklet, there will be a book icon next to it . If formulae are not accompanied by such an icon, they do **not** appear in the Formula booklet and you may need to learn them or at least know how to derive them.

For Mathematics Higher Level, each of the first two papers (Paper 1 and Paper 2):

- is worth 30% of the final grade
- is 2 hours long (plus 5 minutes of reading time)
- has a total of 120 marks available
- contains 9 or 10 short questions and 3 or 4 long questions.

The difference between the two papers is that calculators are **not allowed** for Paper 1, but are required for Paper 2.

 In this book, questions which are designed to be done without a calculator are accompanied by a non-calculator icon.

 Questions which are only sensible to do with a calculator are marked with a calculator icon.

All other questions should be attempted first without a calculator, and then with one.

IMPORTANT EXAM TIPS

- **Grab as many marks as you can.**
  - If you cannot do an early part of a question, write down a sensible answer and use that in later parts or, if the part you could not do was a 'show that' task, use the given result. You will still pick up marks.
  - Do not throw away 'easy marks':
    - Give all answers exactly, or to three significant figures when a degree of accuracy is not specified. Each time you fail to do so you will lose a mark.
    - Do not use rounded intermediate values, as this can result in an inaccurate answer; store all intermediate values in your calculator.
    - Read the questions carefully and make sure you have provided the answer requested. For example, if the question asks for coordinates, give both x and y values. If the question asks for an equation, make sure that you have something with an equals sign in it.
- **The questions are actually worded to help you.**
  - Make sure you know what each command term means. (These are explained in the IB syllabus.) For example:
    - 'Write down' means that there does not need to be any working shown. So, for this type of question, if you are writing out lines and lines of algebra, you have missed something.
    - 'Hence' means that you have to use the previous part somehow. You will not get full marks for a correct answer unless you explicitly show how you have used the previous part.
    - 'Hence or otherwise' means that you can use any method you wish, but it's a pretty big hint that the previous part will help in some way.
    - 'Sketch' means that you do not need to do a precise and to-scale drawing; however, you should label all the important points and at the very least where the curve crosses any axes.
  - If the question refers to solutions, you should expect to get more than one answer.
  - Look out for links between the parts of a question, particularly in the long response questions.
- **Use your 5 minutes of reading time effectively.**
  - Decide on the order in which you will attempt the questions. You do not have to answer them in order and you might want to do questions similar to ones you have seen before first. You will almost certainly want to do some parts of Section B before the last few questions in Section A.

 Make sure you leave enough time for the long questions, some parts of which can be fairly straightforward.

  - For Paper 2, decide which questions can be done easily or checked effectively on the calculator. Do not be surprised if this is the majority of questions.
  - Try to classify which section of the course each question is about.

 Practise using the reading time when attempting your practice papers.

Most importantly, there is nothing like good preparation to make you feel relaxed and confident going into an exam, which in turn should help you achieve your best possible result.

Good luck!

The author team

1 COUNTING PRINCIPLES

WHAT YOU NEED TO KNOW

- The product and addition principles:
  - The number of ways in which both event A **and** event B occur is the product of the number of outcomes for each event.
  - The number of ways in which either event A **or** event B occurs is the sum of the number of outcomes for each event (if A and B are mutually exclusive).
- The number of ways of arranging (permuting) n different objects is $n!$.
- The number of ways of choosing r objects from n:

  - is $\binom{n}{r} = \dfrac{n!}{r!(n-r)!}$ when the order **does not** matter
  - is $^nP_r = \dfrac{n!}{(n-r)!}$ when the order **does** matter.
- When arranging objects:
  - If a number of objects have to be kept together, treat them as a single cluster. Arrange the whole group including this cluster and then arrange the objects within the cluster.
  - If two objects have to be kept apart, subtract the number of ways of arranging the whole group with the two objects together from the total number of possible permutations.
  - If there is a constraint, first put the constrained objects into their positions and then count the number of ways of arranging the unconstrained objects.
- Counting principles can be helpful when calculating probabilities:

  $$P(A) = \frac{\text{number of ways } A \text{ occurs}}{\text{total number of ways}}$$

⚠ EXAM TIPS AND COMMON ERRORS

- Deciding whether the order of the objects matters can be tricky. Choosing committees or teams and dealing cards are common situations where order **does not** matter. Forming words or numbers and the results in races are common situations where order **does** matter.
- When a constraint is added, the number of possible combinations should decrease. You should always compare your answer with the unconstrained number of possible combinations (which might have been asked for in an earlier part of the question).
- Make sure you know whether the question is asking for a number of arrangements or a probability.

1.1 ARRANGING OBJECTS

WORKED EXAMPLE 1.1

Mr and Mrs Singh and their four children line up for a family photograph.

(a) In how many different ways can they do this?
(b) How many ways are there if Mr and Mrs Singh are at opposite ends of the line?
(c) How many ways are there if Mr and Mrs Singh have to be next to each other?
(d) What is the probability that Mr and Mrs Singh are not next to each other?

(a) 6 people can be arranged in 6! = 720 ways.

(b) Either:

Mr Singh, _, _, _, _, Mrs Singh

Or:

Mrs Singh, _, _, _, _, Mr Singh

> Consider separately the two cases that result from the constraint.

In each case there are 4! ways of arranging the children.

So there are 4! + 4! = 48 ways in total.

> Apply the addition principle to one case OR the other.

> ⚠ Always check that your answer makes sense. The answer to this part must be less than the answer to part (a).

(c) With Mr and Mrs Singh next to each other, there are 5! ways.

Mr and Mrs Singh can be arranged in 2! ways.

> Start by treating Mr and Mrs Singh as one cluster, so we have a total of 5 objects to arrange.

So there are 5! × 2! = 240 ways in total.

> Apply the product principle, as we have Mr and Mrs Singh next to each other AND they can arrange themselves in 2! ways.

(d) The number of permutations where Mr and Mrs Singh are not next to each other is:

$720 - 240 = 480$.

P(Mr and Mrs Singh not next to each other) =

$\dfrac{480}{720} = \dfrac{2}{3}$.

> From part (c), we know there are 240 permutations where Mr and Mrs Singh are next to each other. We need to consider the permutations where they are **not** next to each other.

> ⚠ It is always a good idea to look for links between parts of a question.

Practice questions 1.1

1. The letters of the word 'COUNTERS' are to be arranged.
   (a) In how many ways can this be done?
   (b) In how many ways can this be done if the 'word' begins with a C?
   (c) In how many ways can this be done if the O and the U are separated?
   (d) What is the probability that the arrangement contains the word 'COUNT'?

2. How many arrangements of the word 'PICTURE' have all the vowels together?

3. The letters of the word 'TABLE' are to be arranged.
   (a) How many different arrangements are possible?
   (b) If one of the arrangements is selected at random, what is the probability that the vowels are separated?

4. How many arrangements of the word 'INCLUDE' start and end with a vowel?

5. Six boys, Andrew, Brian, Colin, Daniel, Eddie and Fred, line up for a photo.
   (a) How many possible arrangements are there?
   (b) How many possible arrangements are there in which:
      (i)   Andrew is at one end of the line?
      (ii) Andrew is not at either end?
      (iii) Andrew is at the left end of the line or Fred is at the right end, or both?
   Brian, Colin and Daniel are brothers.
   (c) In a random arrangement of the six boys, what is the probability that:
      (i) all three brothers sit together?
      (ii) there are brothers on both ends of the line?

6. In a random arrangement of the digits 1, 2, 3, 4, 5, 6, 7, 8, 9, what is the probability that the odd numbers will all be separated?

1.2 CHOOSING FROM GROUPS WHEN ORDER DOES NOT MATTER

WORKED EXAMPLE 1.2

A team of 10 is chosen from a class of 14 girls and 12 boys.

(a) How many of the possible selections contain the same number of girls and boys?

(b) In how many ways can the team be selected if it must contain at least two boys?

(a) 5 girls can be chosen in $\binom{14}{5}$ ways.

5 boys can be chosen in $\binom{12}{5}$ ways.

So number of selections is $\binom{14}{5}\binom{12}{5} = 1585584$

> Apply the product principle as we are choosing 5 girls AND 5 boys.

(b) There are $\binom{12}{0}\binom{14}{10}$ ways of choosing 0 boys.

There are $\binom{12}{1}\binom{14}{9}$ ways of choosing 1 boy.

So the number of ways with at least 2 boys is

$$\binom{26}{10} - \left[\binom{12}{0}\binom{14}{10} + \binom{12}{1}\binom{14}{9}\right] = 5286710$$

> ⚠ The phrase 'at least' (or 'at most') is often an indicator that you should look at the opposite situation and subtract from the total.

> We are not interested in a selection with 0 boys (therefore 10 girls) or a selection with only 1 boy (therefore 9 girls). We count these and subtract from the total.

Practice questions 1.2

7. A game uses a pack of 20 cards. There are 14 different yellow cards and 6 different blue cards.

  (a) How many different sets of 4 cards can be dealt?

  (b) A player is dealt 4 cards. What is the probability that they are all blue?

  (c) How many ways are there of getting 2 yellow cards and 2 blue cards?

  (d) How many ways are there of getting at least 1 blue card?

8. A college offers 7 revision sessions for Mathematics and 5 revision sessions for Chemistry.

  (a) Leila wants to attend 5 revision sessions. How many different choices can she make?

  (b) Joel wants to attend 2 Mathematics sessions and 3 Chemistry sessions. In how many ways can he choose which sessions to attend?

  (c) Frank randomly selects 5 sessions. Find the probability that at least one of them is Mathematics.

1.3 CHOOSING FROM GROUPS WHEN ORDER DOES MATTER

WORKED EXAMPLE 1.3

Ten athletes compete in a race.

(a) In how many different ways can the first three places be filled?
(b) In how many different ways can the first three places be filled if Carl is one of them?

(a) The number of ways to select and place 3 athletes out of the 10 is $^{10}P_3 = 720$.

> The order of the placing in the race does matter, so use ^nP_r.

(b) There are 3 options for Carl's position.

Once his position is fixed, there are $^9P_2 = 72$ ways of placing 2 other athletes out of the remaining 9.

Therefore, there are $3 \times 72 = 216$ ways.

> Deal with the constraint first: there are a limited number of options for Carl's position.

Practice questions 1.3

9. Rachel has nine cards, each with a different number from 1–9 written on them. She selects six cards at random, to form a six-digit number. How many different six-digit numbers are possible?

10. A bag contains 26 tiles, each with a different letter.
    (a) Player 1 selects four tiles and places them in order. How many different 'words' can he get?
    (b) Player 2 selects another four tiles, one at a time, and places them directly after the first player's tiles. How many different eight-letter 'words' can they form in this way?

11. (a) A car registration number consists of two different digits chosen from 1–9 followed by three different letters. How many possible registration numbers are there?
    (b) How many possible registration numbers are there if the digits can be repeated (but the letters cannot)?

12. Ten athletes compete in a race. In how many different ways can the three medals be awarded if Sally wins either a gold or a silver?

13. Four letters are chosen from the word 'EQUATIONS' and arranged in order. How many of the possible arrangements contain at least one consonant?

1.4 SOLVING EQUATIONS WITH BINOMIAL COEFFICIENTS AND FACTORIALS

WORKED EXAMPLE 1.4

 Solve the equation $\binom{n}{3} = 220$.

$$\binom{n}{3} = 220$$

$$\Leftrightarrow \frac{n(n-1)(n-2)}{6} = 220$$

This is a cubic equation, which is not easy to solve by factorisation.

 Put equations of this form straight into your calculator. Avoid doing any manipulations as this may give rise to mistakes.

From a table on the GDC, $n = 12$.

As n is a whole number, it is easier to use a table rather than a graph. We need to extend the table until we find the answer.

Check your answer! $\binom{12}{3} = 220$, so you know your answer is correct.

Practice questions 1.4

 14. Solve the equation $\binom{n}{2} = 28$.

Remember that: $\binom{n}{1} = n$; $\binom{n}{2} = \frac{n(n-1)}{2}$; $\binom{n}{3} = \frac{n(n-1)(n-2)}{6}$

15. Ahmed has some marbles. He lists all the possible ways of selecting three marbles, and finds that there are 35 possibilities. How many marbles does Ahmed have?

 16. Solve the equation $(n+1)! = 110(n-1)!$

The link between one factorial and the next can be shown algebraically as: $(n+1)! = (n+1) \times n!$

17. Solve the equation $n! + (n-1)! = 24(n-2)!$

18. Solve the equation ${}^nP_4 = 12 \times {}^nP_3$.

Mixed practice 1

1. Five students are to be selected from a class of 12 to go on a Mathematics trip.

    (a) How many possible selections are there?

    (b) What is the probability that Jonny and Lin are both selected?

2. A car registration number consists of two different letters followed by six digits chosen from 1–9 (the digits can be repeated). How many different registration numbers are possible?

3. Solve the equation $\binom{n}{2} = 210$.

4. A football team consists of 1 goalkeeper, 4 defenders, 4 midfielders and 2 strikers. The coach needs to pick the team from a squad of 3 goalkeepers, 7 defenders, 9 midfielders and 3 strikers. In how many different ways can he pick the team?

5. How many different three-digit numbers can be formed from the digits 1–7:

    (a) if no digit can be repeated?

    (b) if repetitions are allowed?

6. Olivia has 5 green pens and 3 purple pens. She needs to select 4 pens to put in her bag.

    (a) How many possible selections include 2 green and 2 purple pens?

    (b) How many possible selections include at least 1 purple pen?

7. A bag contains six tiles with the letters A, E, U, D, G and Z. The tiles are selected at random and arranged to form a 'word'. What is the probability that this permutation starts and ends with a consonant?

8. Daniel and Theo each have n tiles with a different letter on each. Daniel picks three tiles and arranges them in a sequence (so ABC is a different sequence from ACB).

    (a) Write down an expression for the number of possible sequences Daniel can make.

    Daniel returns his tiles and then Theo selects three tiles without arranging them.

    (b) Given that Daniel can make 50 more sequences than Theo can make selections, find the value of n.

9. (a) Write down the number of possible permutations of the word 'COMPUTER'.

    (b) How many of the permutations have all the vowels together?

    (c) How many of the permutations end in TER?

    (d) How many of the permutations have the letters T, E, R next to each other?

10. A class contains 10 boys and 12 girls, all with different names.

    (a) Find an expression for the number of ways in which they could be arranged for a photo if:

        (i) it is in one long line of 22 people

        (ii) it is in two rows of 11 people.

    (b) The teacher wants to form a committee from the class which contains Max, Lizzy, Jessie and two other students. In how many ways can this be done?

    (c) Another group of students consists of 3 girls and 3 boys. They form a line for a photo. In how many ways can this be done if:

        (i) all the boys are kept together?

        (ii) all the boys are kept apart?

    (d) Another class of n students have a race. There are 1320 different ways of awarding medals for the top three places (assuming that there are no ties). Find n.

Going for the top 1

1. How many permutations of the word 'SELECTION' have all of the vowels separated?

2. A four-digit number is formed from the digits 1, 2, 3, 4 and 5.

    (a) How many such numbers can be formed if each digit can be used only once?

    (b) How many such numbers can be formed if each digit can be used more than once?

    (c) If each digit can be used only once, how many of the numbers are greater than 3000 and even?

3. How many distinct ways are there of arranging the letters AAABBBB?

4. (a) Show that the equation $\binom{n}{3} = \binom{n+1}{2} - 5$, can be written in the form $f(n) = 0$, where $f(x) = x^3 - 6x^2 - x + 30$.

    (b) Show that $(x + 2)$ is a factor of $f(x)$.

    (c) Hence find all the solutions of the equation $\binom{n}{3} = \binom{n+1}{2} - 5$.

2 EXPONENTS AND LOGARITHMS

WHAT YOU NEED TO KNOW

- The rules of exponents:
  - $a^m \times a^n = a^{m+n}$
  - $\dfrac{a^m}{a^n} = a^{m-n}$
  - $(a^m)^n = a^{mn}$
  - $a^{\frac{m}{n}} = \sqrt[n]{a^m}$
  - $a^{-n} = \dfrac{1}{a^n}$
  - $a^n \times b^n = (ab)^n$
  - $\dfrac{a^n}{b^n} = \left(\dfrac{a}{b}\right)^n$

- The relationship between exponents and logarithms:
  - $a^x = b \iff x = \log_a b$ where a is called the base of the logarithm
  - $\log_a a^x = x$
  - $a^{\log_a x} = x$

- The rules of logarithms:
  - $\log_a x + \log_a y = \log_a xy$
  - $\log_a x - \log_a y = \log_a\left(\dfrac{x}{y}\right)$
  - $k \log_a x = \log_a x^k$
  - $\log_a\left(\dfrac{1}{x}\right) = -\log_a x$
  - $\log_a 1 = 0$

- The change of base rule: $\log_b a = \dfrac{\log_c a}{\log_c b}$

- There are two common abbreviations for logarithms to particular bases:
  - $\log_{10} x$ is often written as $\log x$
  - $\log_e x$ is often written as $\ln x$

- The graphs of exponential and logarithmic functions:

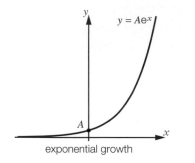

exponential growth

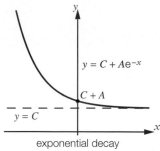

exponential decay

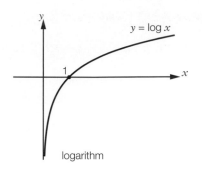

logarithm

> ### ⚠️ EXAM TIPS AND COMMON ERRORS
>
> - You must know what you *cannot* do with logarithms:
>
>   - $\log(x + y)$ cannot be simplified; it is **not** $\log x + \log y$
>
>   - $\log(e^x + e^y)$ cannot be simplified; it is **not** $x + y$
>
>   - $(\log x)^2$ is **not** $2\log x$, whereas $\log x^2 = 2\log x$
>
>   - $e^{2 + \log x} = e^2 e^{\log x} = e^2 x$ **not** $e^2 + x$

2.1 SOLVING EXPONENTIAL EQUATIONS

WORKED EXAMPLE 2.1

Solve the equation $4 \times 5^{x+1} = 3^x$, giving your answer in the form $\dfrac{\log a}{\log b}$.

$$\log(4 \times 5^{x+1}) = \log(3^x)$$
$$\Leftrightarrow \log 4 + \log(5^{x+1}) = \log(3^x)$$

> Since the unknown is in the power, we take logarithms of each side.
>
> We then use the rules of logarithms to simplify the expression. First use
>
> $\log(ab) = \log a + \log b$

> ⚠ A common mistake is to say that $\log(4 \times 5^{x+1}) = \log 4 \times \log(5^{x+1})$.

$$\Leftrightarrow \log 4 + (x+1)\log 5 = x \log 3$$

> We can now use $\log a^k = k \log a$ to get rid of the powers.

$$\Leftrightarrow \log 4 + x \log 5 + \log 5 = x \log 3$$
$$\Leftrightarrow x \log 3 - x \log 5 = \log 4 + \log 5$$
$$\Leftrightarrow x(\log 3 - \log 5) = \log 4 + \log 5$$

> Expand the brackets and collect the terms containing x on one side.

$$\Leftrightarrow x = \frac{\log 4 + \log 5}{\log 3 - \log 5}$$
$$\Leftrightarrow x = \frac{\log 20}{\log\left(\dfrac{3}{5}\right)}$$

> Use the rules of logarithms to write the solution in the correct form:
>
> $\log u + \log b = \log ab$
>
> $\log a - \log b - \log\left(\dfrac{a}{b}\right)$

Practice questions 2.1

1. Solve the equation $5^{3x+1} = 15$, giving your answer in the form $\dfrac{\log a}{\log b}$ where a and b are integers.

2. Solve the equation $3^{2x+1} = 4^{x-2}$, giving your answer in the form $\dfrac{\log p}{\log q}$ where p and q are rational numbers.

3. Solve the equation $3 \times 2^{x-3} = \dfrac{1}{5^{2x}}$, giving your answer in the form $\dfrac{\log p}{\log q}$ where p and q are rational numbers.

2.2 SOLVING DISGUISED QUADRATIC EQUATIONS

WORKED EXAMPLE 2.2

Find the exact solution of the equation $3^{2x+1} - 11 \times 3^x = 4$.

$$3^{2x+1} - 11 \times 3^x = 4$$
$$\Leftrightarrow 3 \times 3^{2x} - 11 \times 3^x = 4$$
$$\Leftrightarrow 3 \times (3^x)^2 - 11 \times 3^x = 4$$

We need to find a substitution to turn this into a quadratic equation.

First, express 3^{2x+1} in terms of 3^x:
$$3^{2x+1} = 3^{2x} \times 3^1 = 3 \times (3^x)^2$$

> ⚠ Look out for an a^{2x} term, which can be rewritten as $(a^x)^2$.

Let $y = 3^x$. Then

$$3y^2 - 11y - 4 = 0$$
$$\Leftrightarrow (3y + 1)(y - 4)$$
$$\Leftrightarrow y = -\frac{1}{3} \text{ or } y = 4$$

After substituting y for 3^x, this becomes a standard quadratic equation, which can be factorised and solved.

> ▶▶ Disguised quadratic equations may also be encountered when solving trigonometric equations, which is covered in Chapter 6.

$$\therefore 3^x = -\frac{1}{3} \text{ or } 3^x = 4$$

Remember that $y = 3^x$.

$3^x = -\frac{1}{3}$ is impossible since $3^x > 0$ for all x.

> ⚠ With disguised quadratic equations, often one of the solutions is impossible.

$$3^x = 4$$
$$\Leftrightarrow \log 3^x = \log 4$$
$$\Leftrightarrow x \log 3 = \log 4$$
$$\Leftrightarrow x = \frac{\log 4}{\log 3}$$

Since x is in the power, we take logarithms of both sides. We can then use $\log a^k = k \log a$ to get rid of the power.

Practice questions 2.2

4. Solve the equation $2^{2x} - 5 \times 2^x + 4 = 0$.

5. Find the exact solution of the equation $e^x - 6e^{-x} = 5$.

6. Solve the simultaneous equations $e^{x+y} = 6$ and $e^x + e^y = 5$.

2.3 LAWS OF LOGARITHMS

WORKED EXAMPLE 2.3

If $x = \log a$, $y = \log b$ and $z = \log c$, write $2x + y - 0.5z + 2$ as a single logarithm.

$2\log a + \log b - 0.5\log c + 2$

$-\log a^2 + \log b - \log c^{0.5} + 2$

> We need to rewrite the expression as a single logarithm. In order to apply the rules for combining logarithms, each log must have no coefficient in front of it. So we first need to use $k\log x = \log x^k$.

$= \log a^2 b - \log c^{0.5} + 2$

$= \log\left(\dfrac{a^2 b}{\sqrt{c}}\right) + 2$

> We can now use $\log x + \log y = \log(xy)$ and
> $\log x - \log y = \log\left(\dfrac{x}{y}\right)$.

$= \log\left(\dfrac{a^2 b}{\sqrt{c}}\right) + \log 100$

$= \log\left(\dfrac{100 a^2 b}{\sqrt{c}}\right)$

> We also need to write 2 as a logarithm so that it can then be combined with the first term. Since $10^2 = 100$, we can write 2 as $\log 100$.

 Remember that log on its own is taken to mean $\log_{10}$.

Practice questions 2.3

7. Given $x = \log a$, $y = \log b$ and $z = \log c$, write $3x - 2y + z$ as a single logarithm.

8. Given $a = \log x$, $b = \log y$ and $c = \log z$, find an expression in terms of a, b and c for $\log\left(\dfrac{10xy^2}{\sqrt{z}}\right)$

9. Given that $\log a + 1 = \log b^2$, express a in terms of b.

10. Given that $\ln y = 2 + 4\ln x$, express y in terms of x.

 11. Consider the simultaneous equations
    $e^{2x} + e^y = 800$
    $3\ln x + \ln y = 5$
    (a) For each equation, express y in terms of x.
    (b) Hence solve the simultaneous equations.

2.4 SOLVING EQUATIONS INVOLVING LOGARITHMS

WORKED EXAMPLE 2.4

 Solve the equation $4\log_4 x = 9\log_x 4$.

$$\log_x 4 = \frac{\log_4 4}{\log_4 x} = \frac{1}{\log_4 x}$$

Therefore

$$4\log_4 x = 9\log_x 4$$

$$\Leftrightarrow 4\log_4 x = 9 \times \frac{1}{\log_4 x}$$

> We want to have logarithms involving just one base so that we can apply the rules of logarithms. Here we use the change of base rule to turn logs with base x into logs with base 4. (Alternatively, we could have turned them all into base x instead.)

$$\Leftrightarrow 4\left(\log_4 x\right)^2 = 9$$

$$\Leftrightarrow \left(\log_4 x\right)^2 = \frac{9}{4}$$

> Multiply through by $\log_4 x$ to get the log terms together.

> ⚠ Make sure you use brackets to indicate that the whole of $\log_4 x$ is being squared, not just x; $(\log_4 x)^2$ is **not** $2\log_4 x$, but $\log_4 x^2$ would be.

$$\log_4 x = \frac{3}{2} \quad \text{or} \quad \log_4 x = -\frac{3}{2}$$

> Take the square root of both sides; don't forget the negative square root.

$$\text{So} \quad x = 4^{\frac{3}{2}} \quad \text{or} \quad x = 4^{-\frac{3}{2}}$$

$$= 8 \qquad\qquad = \frac{1}{8}$$

> Use $\log_a b = x \Leftrightarrow b = a^x$ to 'undo' the logs.

Practice questions 2.4

 12. Solve the equation $\log_4 x + \log_4 (x-6) = 2$.

 13. Solve the equation $2\log_2 x - \log_2 (x+1) = 3$, giving your answers in simplified surd form.

> ⚠ Make sure you check your answers by substituting them into the original equation.

 14. Solve the equation $25\log_2 x = \log_x 2$.

 15. Solve the equation $\log_4 (4-x) = \log_{16}(9x^2 - 10x + 1)$.

2.5 PROBLEMS INVOLVING EXPONENTIAL FUNCTIONS

WORKED EXAMPLE 2.5

When a cup of tea is made, its temperature is 85°C. After 3 minutes the tea has cooled to 60°C. Given that the temperature T (°C) of the cup of tea decays exponentially according to the function $T = A + Ce^{-0.2t}$, where t is the time measured in minutes, find:

(a) the values of A and C (correct to three significant figures)

(b) the time it takes for the tea to cool to 40°C.

(a) When $t = 0$: $85 = A + C$ $\cdots$ (1)

When $t = 3$: $60 = A + Ce^{-0.6}$ $\cdots$ (2)

> Substitute the given values for T (temperature) and t (time) into $T = A + Ce^{-0.2t}$, remembering that $e^0 = 1$.

$(1) - (2)$ gives $25 = (1 - e^{-0.6})$

So $C = \dfrac{25}{1 - e^{-0.6}} = 55.4 \, (3\,SF)$

Then, from (1),

$A = 85 - C = 85 - 55.4 = 29.6 \, (3\,SF)$

> Note that A is the long-term limit of the temperature, which can be interpreted as the temperature of the room.

(b) When $T = 40$:

$29.6 + 55.4e^{-0.2t} = 40$

> Now we can substitute for T, A and C.

$\Rightarrow e^{-0.2t} = \dfrac{40 - 29.6}{55.4}$

$\Rightarrow \ln(e^{-0.2t}) = \ln\left(\dfrac{40 - 29.6}{55.4}\right)$

> Since the unknown t is in the power, we take logarithms of both sides and then 'cancel' e and ln using $\log_a(a^x) = x$.

$\Rightarrow -0.2t = \ln\left(\dfrac{40 - 29.6}{55.4}\right)$

$\Rightarrow t = 8.36$ minutes

> Remember that ln means $\log_e$.

Practice questions 2.5

16. The amount of reactant, V (grams), in a chemical reaction decays exponentially according to the function $V = M + Ce^{-0.32t}$, where t is the time in seconds since the start of the reaction. Initially there was 4.5 g of reactant, and this had decayed to 2.6 g after 7 seconds.

(a) Find the value of C.

(b) Find the value that the amount of reactant approaches in the long term.

17. A population of bacteria grows according to the model $P = Ae^{kt}$, where P is the size of the population after t minutes. Given that after 2 minutes there are 200 bacteria and after 5 minutes there are 1500 bacteria, find the size of the population after 10 minutes.

Mixed practice 2

1. Solve the equation $3 \times 9^x - 10 \times 3^x + 3 = 0$.

2. Find the exact solution of the equation $2^{3x+1} = 5^{5-x}$.

3. Solve the simultaneous equations
   $$\ln x^2 + \ln y = 15$$
   $$\ln x + \ln y^3 = 10$$

4. Given that $y = \ln x - \ln(x + 2) + \ln(x^2 - 4)$, express x in terms of y.

5. The graph with equation $y = 4\ln(x - a)$ passes through the point $(5, \ln 16)$. Find the value of a.

6. (a) An economic model predicts that the demand, D, for a new product will grow according to the equation $D = A - Ce^{-0.2t}$, where t is the number of days since the product launch. After 10 days the demand is 15 000 and it is increasing at a rate of 325 per day.

   (i) Find the value of C.

   (ii) Find the initial demand for the product.

   (iii) Find the long-term demand predicted by this model.

   (b) An alternative model is proposed, in which the demand grows according to the formula $D = B\ln\left(\dfrac{t + 10}{5}\right)$. The initial demand is the same as that for the first model.

   (i) Find the value of B.

   (ii) What is the long-term prediction of this model?

   (c) After how many days will the demand predicted by the second model become larger than the demand predicted by the first model?

Going for the top 2

1. Find the exact solution of the equation $2^{3x-4} \times 3^{2x-5} = 36^{x-2}$, giving your answer in the form $\dfrac{\ln p}{\ln q}$ where p and q are integers.

2. Given that $\log_a b^2 = c^2$ and $\log_b a = c + 1$, express a in terms of b.

3. In a physics experiment, Maya measured how the force, F, exerted by a spring depends on its extension, x. She then plotted the values of $a = \ln F$ and $b = \ln x$ on a graph, with b on the horizontal axis and a on the vertical axis. The graph was a straight line, passing through the points $(2, 4.5)$ and $(4, 7.2)$. Find an expression for F in terms of x.

3 POLYNOMIALS

WHAT YOU NEED TO KNOW

- A polynomial is a sum of terms of the form ax^n where n is a positive integer or zero. The order (or degree) of a polynomial is defined by the highest value of n.

  - A polynomial of order 1 is called linear.

  - A polynomial of order 2 is called quadratic.

  - A polynomial of order 3 is called cubic.

- The quadratic equation $ax^2 + bx + c = 0$ has solutions given by the quadratic formula:

$$x = \frac{-b \pm \sqrt{b^2 - 4ac}}{2a}$$

  - The number of real solutions to a quadratic equation is determined by the discriminant, $\Delta = b^2 - 4ac$.

    - If $\Delta > 0$, there are two distinct solutions.

    - If $\Delta = 0$, there is one (repeated) solution.

    - If $\Delta < 0$, there are no real solutions.

- The graph of $y = ax^2 + bx + c$ has a line of symmetry at $x = -\dfrac{b}{2a}$.

- If $f(x)$ is a polynomial, the solutions to $f(x) = 0$ may also be called the roots or zeros of the polynomial. A polynomial of order n has at most n zeros (according to the Fundamental Theorem of Algebra).

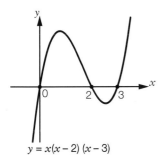

$y = x(x - 2)(x - 3)$

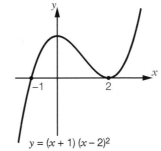

$y = (x + 1)(x - 2)^2$

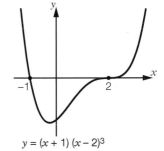

$y = (x + 1)(x - 2)^3$

If a polynomial has a single root, the graph will pass through the x-axis there.	If a polynomial has a (repeated) double root, the graph will touch the x-axis there.	If a polynomial has a (repeated) triple root, the graph will pass through the x-axis there in a point of inflexion.

- A polynomial $f(x)$ can be divided by a polynomial $g(x)$ if the order of $f(x)$ is greater than or equal to the order of $g(x)$:

$$\frac{f(x)}{g(x)} = Q(x) + \frac{r(x)}{g(x)}$$

  where $Q(x)$ is the quotient and has an order given by the difference of the orders of $f(x)$ and $g(x)$, and $r(x)$ is the remainder and has an order of one less than the order of $g(x)$.

  - The remainder theorem says that if $g(x) = x - a$, the remainder is a constant, r, such that $r = f(a)$.

  - The factor theorem says that if $f(a) = 0$, then $(x - a)$ is a factor of $f(x)$.

- For a polynomial equation $a_n x^n + a_{n-1} x^{n-1} + a_{n-2} x^{n-2} + \ldots + a_1 x + a_0 = 0$:

  - the sum of the roots is $-\dfrac{a_{n-1}}{a_n}$

  - the product of the roots is $(-1)^n \dfrac{a_0}{a_n}$

> The sum and product of roots are most often encountered for quadratics, so it is worth remembering those specific results particularly well. For the quadratic equation $ax^2 + bx + c = 0$ with roots p and q, $p + q = -\dfrac{b}{a}$ and $pq = \dfrac{c}{a}$.

- An expression of the form $(a + b)^n$ can be expanded quickly using the binomial theorem:

$$(a + b)^n = a^n + \binom{n}{1} a^{n-1}b + \ldots + \binom{n}{r} a^{n-r}b^r + \ldots + b^n$$

⚠ EXAM TIPS AND COMMON ERRORS

- Polynomials can be divided to find the quotient polynomial $Q(x)$ explicitly; however, where possible, use the remainder theorem, factor theorem or sum of the roots rather than going through the division process.

> ▶▶ Worked Example 3.3 looks at a case where it is necessary to find the quotient polynomial explicitly, but Worked Example 3.4 illustrates the use of the other methods.

- Questions involving the discriminant are often disguised. You may have to interpret them to realise that you need to find the *number* of solutions rather than the *actual* solutions.

- Look out for quadratic expressions in disguise. A substitution is often a good way of making the expression explicitly quadratic.

3.1 USING THE DISCRIMINANT

WORKED EXAMPLE 3.1

The line $y = kx - 1$ is tangent to the curve $y = x^2$. Find the possible values of k.

 These types of question can be done using calculus (by finding the equation of the tangent), but using the discriminant makes it much easier.

 Using calculus to find the equations of tangents (and normals) is covered in Chapter 9.

$y = kx - 1 \quad \cdots (1)$

$y = x^2 \qquad \cdots (2)$

Substituting (2) into (1):

$x^2 = kx - 1$

$\Rightarrow x^2 - kx + 1 = 0$

We use the fact that the tangent and the curve intersect at only one point to establish that there can only be one solution to their simultaneous equations.

Since there can only be one root, $b^2 - 4ac = 0$:

$(-k)^2 - 4 \times 1 \times 1 = 0$

$\Leftrightarrow k^2 = 4$

$\Leftrightarrow k = \pm 2$

For this quadratic to have only one solution, the discriminant must be zero.

 Do not forget the plus or minus symbol. The question asks for values rather than a value, indicating that there is more than one solution.

Practice questions 3.1

1. Find the set of values of k for which the equation $2x^2 - kx + (2k + 1) = 0$ has two distinct real solutions.

2. Find the values of k such that the quadratic expression $kx^2 + kx + 6$ is always positive.

 Questions involving discriminants often lead to solving quadratic inequalities, which is covered in Prior learning.

3. Given that the curve $y = 3x^2 + x - 2$ and the line $y = ax - 5$ do not intersect, find the range of possible values of a.

3.2 SKETCHING POLYNOMIAL FUNCTIONS

WORKED EXAMPLE 3.2

Find a polynomial of degree 3 whose graph is as shown below. Give your answer in the form $ax^3 + bx^2 + cx + d$.

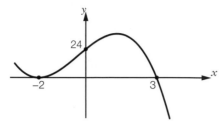

Double root at $x=-2 \Rightarrow (x+2)^2$ is a factor.

Single root at $x=3 \Rightarrow (x-3)$ is a factor.

Therefore, $f(x) = a(x+2)^2(x-3)$

> We start by looking at the nature of the roots and creating a factorised form of the polynomial.
> We need a constant a here, as we cannot just assume that the coefficient of x^3 is 1.

$f(0) = 24$, so

$a(2)^2(-3) = 24$

$\Rightarrow -12a = 24$

$\Rightarrow a = -2$

> We can find a by considering the y-intercept and substituting $x = 0$ and $f(x) = 24$.

So, $f(x) = -2(x+2)^2(x-3)$

$\quad = -2(x^2+4x+4)(x-3)$

$\quad = -2x^3 - 2x^2 + 16x + 24$

> Substitute $a = -2$ into the factorised form and then expand to find the equation in the form required.

Practice questions 3.2

4. Sketch the graph of $y = (x+3)^2(2-x)$, labelling clearly any axes intercepts. You do not need to find the coordinates of any stationary points.

5. Find, in expanded form, the equation of the cubic graph shown below.

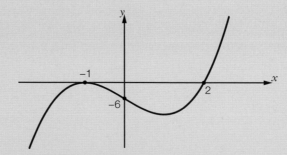

3.3 POLYNOMIAL DIVISION

WORKED EXAMPLE 3.3

 Find $\dfrac{3x^3 + 8x^2 - 5x - 11}{x + 2}$.

$$\frac{3x^3 + 8x^2 - 5x - 11}{x + 2} = ax^2 + bx + c + \frac{r}{x + 2}$$

We know that the answer will be of the form $Q(x) + \dfrac{r}{x + 2}$, where the order of $Q(x)$ will be the difference between the orders of the denominator and numerator of the fraction (hence a quadratic) and the remainder will be of order one less than the denominator (hence a constant).

$$\Rightarrow 3x^3 + 8x^2 - 5x - 11 = (ax^2 + bx + c)(x + 2) + r$$
$$= ax^3 + 2ax^2 + bx^2 + 2bx + cx + 2c + r$$
$$= ax^3 + (2a + b)x^2 + (2b + c)x + 2c + r$$

Multiply through by $(x + 2)$, expand the RHS and collect like terms.

Equating coefficients:

x^3: $3 = a$

x^2: $8 = 2a + b$ and so $b = 2$

x^1: $-5 = 2b + c$ and so $c = -9$

x^0: $-11 = 2c + r$ and so $r = 7$

We can now equate the coefficients of each power of x on both sides of the equation and solve successively for a, b, c and r.

So,

$$3x^3 + 8x^2 - 5x - 11 = (3x^2 + 2x - 9)(x + 2) + 7$$
$$\Rightarrow \frac{3x^3 + 8x^2 - 5x - 11}{x + 2} = 3x^2 + 2x - 9 + \frac{7}{x + 2}$$

Substitute these values and divide through by the original denominator $(x + 2)$ to get the answer in the required form.

Practice questions 3.3

 6. Find $\dfrac{2x^4 + 3x^3 + 2x - 15}{x^2 - 2x + 5}$.

 7. Given that $2x + 1$ is a factor of $f(x) = 6x^3 - 7x^2 - 29x - 12$, factorise $f(x)$ completely.

 8. $2x^2 + 5x - 12$ is a factor of $f(x) = 2x^3 + ax^2 - 22x + b$.
   (a) Find a and b.
   (b) Solve $f(x) = 0$.

3.4 FINDING THE COEFFICIENTS OF A POLYNOMIAL

WORKED EXAMPLE 3.4

The sum of the zeros of the polynomial $f(x) = 2x^3 + ax^2 + 7x + b$ is 10, and $f(x)$ leaves a remainder of 14 when divided by $(x + 2)$. Find the values of a and b.

The sum of the roots is given by $-\dfrac{a}{2}$.

So $-\dfrac{a}{2} = 10$

$\Rightarrow a = -20$

> Taking the first piece of information in the question, we can form a simple equation by using the formula for the sum of the roots of a polynomial:
> $$-\frac{a_{n-1}}{a_n} = -\frac{a_2}{a_3}$$

$(x + 2) = (x - (-2))$

By the remainder theorem, $f(-2) = 14$.

So,

$2 \times (-8) - 20 \times (4) + 7 \times (-2) + b = 14$

$\Rightarrow -110 + b = 14$

$\Rightarrow b = 124$

> Using the second piece of information, we can apply the remainder theorem.

Practice questions 3.4

9. The polynomial $f(x) = ax^3 + 10x^2 + 5x + b$ has three roots with a product of -6, and $f(x)$ has a factor of $(x + 1)$. Find the values of a and b.

10. The polynomial $p(x) = 2x^3 + ax^2 + bx + 3$ leaves a remainder of 5 when divided by $(x - 2)$ and a remainder of -1 when divided by $(x + 1)$. Find the values of a and b.

11. The sum of the roots of the polynomial $p(x) = x^3 + bx^2 - 5x + d$ is equal to twice the product of the roots. Given that one of the roots is $x = 1$, find the values of b and d.

12. Consider the polynomial $f(x) = ax^3 + bx^2 + cx + d$. The remainder when $f(x)$ is divided by $(x - 1)$ is 11, and the remainder when divided by $(x + 1)$ is 7.
    (a) Form an equation in b and d.
    (b) Given that the sum of the roots is -5 and the product is 8, find a, b, c and d.

3.5 LINKING EQUATIONS VIA THEIR ROOTS

WORKED EXAMPLE 3.5

The quadratic equation $ax^2 + bx + c = 0$ has roots α and β. Find a quadratic equation with roots $\dfrac{1}{\alpha}$ and $\dfrac{1}{\beta}$.

Using the sum and product of the roots of the original quadratic:

$$\alpha + \beta = -\frac{b}{a}$$

$$\alpha\beta = \frac{c}{a}$$

> We start by writing down a relationship between the roots of the original quadratic, α and β, and the coefficients a, b and c.

For a quadratic with roots $\dfrac{1}{\alpha}$ and $\dfrac{1}{\beta}$, the product of the roots is

$$\frac{1}{\alpha} \times \frac{1}{\beta} = \frac{1}{\alpha\beta} = 1 \div \left(\frac{c}{a}\right) = \frac{a}{c}$$

> Next, we relate the sum and product of roots of the new quadratic to the sum and product of roots of the original quadratic.

The sum of the roots is:

$$\frac{1}{\alpha} + \frac{1}{\beta} = \frac{\alpha + \beta}{\alpha\beta} = \left(-\frac{b}{a}\right) \div \left(\frac{c}{a}\right) = -\frac{b}{c}$$

A quadratic equation with roots $\dfrac{1}{\alpha}$ and $\dfrac{1}{\beta}$ is:

$$x^2 + \frac{b}{c}x + \frac{a}{c} = 0$$

> To keep the equation as simple as possible, we let the coefficient of x^2 equal 1. (We could also multiply our equation through by c to obtain another possible equation: $cx^2 + bx + a = 0$.)

Practice questions 3.5

13. Let α and β be the roots of the quadratic equation $x^2 + 5x + 3 = 0$. Find a quadratic equation with roots α^2 and β^2.

14. The quadratic equation $ax^2 + bx + c = 0$ has roots α and β. Find a quadratic equation with roots 2α and 2β.

15. The equation $ax^3 + bx^2 + cx + d = 0$ has solutions 1, p and q. The equation

$x^3 + \alpha x^2 + \beta x + \gamma = 0$ has solutions 1, $\dfrac{1}{p}$ and $\dfrac{1}{q}$. Show that $\gamma = \dfrac{a}{d}$, and find an expression

for α in terms of c and d, simplifying your answer.

3.6 APPLYING THE BINOMIAL THEOREM

WORKED EXAMPLE 3.6

Find the coefficient of x^4 in the expansion of $\left(x - \dfrac{5}{x}\right)^6$.

The general term in the expansion is $\dbinom{6}{r}x^{6-r}\left(-\dfrac{5}{x}\right)^r$

> Start with the form of a general term. We could also have chosen $\dbinom{6}{r}x^6\left(-\dfrac{5}{x}\right)^{6-r}$ but this is algebraically harder to work with.

$$= \binom{6}{r}x^{6-r} \times x^{-r} \times (-5)^r$$

$$= \binom{6}{r}x^{6-2r} \times (-5)^r$$

> Simplify using the rules of exponents.

> ⚠ Be careful with negative signs in the binomial expansion. Ensure they stay within brackets so that the power is applied to the negative sign.

Require that $6 - 2r = 4$

$\therefore 2r = 2$

and so $r = 1$

> We need the term in x^4, so equate that to the power of x in the general term.

The relevant term is therefore $\dbinom{6}{1}x^4(-5)^1 = -30x^4$

> Substitute $r = 1$ into $\dbinom{6}{r}x^{6-2r} \times (-5)^r$ to find the required term.

So the coefficient is -30.

> ⚠ Make sure you answer the question; you were asked to find the coefficient, not the whole term.

Practice questions 3.6

16. Find the constant term in the expansion of $\left(x^2 - \dfrac{3}{x}\right)^9$.

17. The third term in the binomial expansion of $(1 + px)^7$ is $84x^2$. Find:
   (a) the possible values of p
   (b) the fifth term in the expansion.

Mixed practice 3

1. Find the simplest polynomial which fits the graph below.

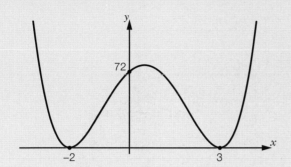

2. Find the term that is independent of x in the expansion of $\left(x^3 + \dfrac{3}{x} \right)^8$.

3. The cubic expression $x^3 + 10x^2 + cx + d$ has a factor of $(x+1)$ and leaves a remainder of 5 when divided by $(x-2)$. Find the values of c and d.

4. The curve $y = x^2 + kx + 2$ never touches the x-axis. Find the possible values of k.

5. The roots of the cubic equation $x^3 + bx^2 + cx + d$ form an arithmetic sequence. Show that the second term depends only on b.

6. Find the quadratic term in the expansion of $(2 + x)(3 - 2x)^5$.

7. The line $y = x + k$ is tangent to the curve $x^2 + y^2 = 9$. Find the possible values of k.

8. (a) Find the first four terms in ascending powers of x in the expansion of $(2 - x)^5$.

   (b) Hence find the value of 1.99^5 correct to 5 decimal places.

9. The quadratic equation $ax^2 + bx + c = 0$ has roots α and β. Find an equation with roots $\alpha + 2\beta$ and $2\alpha + \beta$.

10. The quartic equation $x^4 + bx^3 + cx^2 + dx + e = 0$ has repeated roots at $x = \alpha$ and $x = \beta$, where $\beta > \alpha$.

   (a) Show that $e \geq 0$.

   (b) Show that $\alpha^2 + \beta^2 = \dfrac{b^2}{4} - 2\sqrt{e}$.

   (c) Find an expression for $\beta - \alpha$.

11. Consider the function $f(x) = (1+x)^n$, where $n \in \mathbb{Z}^+$.

(a) Show that the sum of the roots (including complex roots) of the equation $(1+x)^n = k$ is independent of k, and that the product of the roots has modulus independent of n.

(b) If $k > 1$, sketch the graph of $y = f(x) - k$ when:

    (i) n is odd

    (ii) n is even.

(c) If the remainder when $f(x)$ is divided by $(x-1)$ is 16, find the value of n.

(d) If the coefficient of x^2 in $f(x)$ is 136, find the value of n.

(e) By substituting an appropriate value of x into $f(x)$, simplify an expression for
$$\binom{n}{0} + \binom{n}{1} + \binom{n}{2} + \ldots + \binom{n}{n}.$$

Going for the top 3

1. The remainder when the polynomial $f(x)$ is divided by $x^2 + 7x + 12$ is $(3x + 2)$. Find the remainder when $f(x)$ is divided by $(x + 4)$.

2. The coefficient of x^2 in the expansion of $(1+ax)^n$ is 54 and the coefficient of x is 12. Find the values of a and n.

3. Find two polynomials which fit the following graph and only have zeros as shown on the graph.

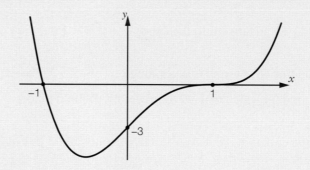

4. Show that the condition for the quartic equation $x^4 + bx^2 + c = 0$ to have four solutions is that $b^2 > 4c > 0$.

4 FUNCTIONS, GRAPHS AND EQUATIONS

WHAT YOU NEED TO KNOW

- A function is a rule where for every input there is only one output. Graphically, any vertical line will cross its graph no more than once.

  - For a one-to-one function, each output corresponds to only one input. For a many-to-one function, some outputs may come from more than one input.

  - The domain of a function is the set of allowed inputs. Typical reasons to restrict a domain include:

    - division by zero

    - square rooting of a negative number

    - taking the logarithm of a negative number or zero.

  - The range is the set of all possible outputs of a function. The easiest way of finding the range is to sketch the graph.

- Composing functions means applying one function to the result of another:

  - $fg(x)$ is the function f applied to the output of the function g. This can also be written as $f \circ g(x)$ or $f(g(x))$.

- An inverse function, $f^{-1}(x)$, is a function which undoes the effect of another function.

  - $ff^{-1}(x) = f^{-1}f(x) = x$

  - To find $f^{-1}(x)$, write $y = f(x)$, rearrange to get x in terms of y, and then replace each y with an x.

  - Only one-to-one functions have inverse functions. It may be necessary to restrict the domain of a function to make it one-to-one before finding the inverse.

  - Inverse functions have certain properties:

    - The graph of $y = f^{-1}(x)$ is the reflection of the graph $y = f(x)$ in the line $y = x$.

    - The domain of $f^{-1}(x)$ is the same as the range of $f(x)$. The range of $f^{-1}(x)$ is the same as the domain of $f(x)$.

  - If a function is the same as its inverse, it is called a self-inverse function.

- The rational function $f(x) = \dfrac{ax+b}{cx+d}$ has a graph called a hyperbola.

  - The x-intercept is at $x = -\dfrac{b}{a}$
  - The y-intercept is at $y = \dfrac{b}{d}$

  - The vertical asymptote is $x = -\dfrac{d}{c}$
  - The horizontal asymptote is $y = \dfrac{a}{c}$

- A change to a function results in a change to the graph of the function.

Transformation of $y = f(x)$	Transformation of the graph
$y = f(x) + c$	Translation $\begin{pmatrix} 0 \\ c \end{pmatrix}$
$y = f(x + d)$	Translation $\begin{pmatrix} -d \\ 0 \end{pmatrix}$
$y = pf(x)$	Vertical stretch of factor p, away from the x-axis for $p > 0$
$y = f(qx)$	Horizontal stretch of factor $\dfrac{1}{q}$, towards the y-axis for $q > 0$
$y = -f(x)$	Reflection in the x-axis.
$y = f(-x)$	Reflection in the y-axis.
$y = \lvert f(x) \rvert$	The part of the graph which is below the x-axis is reflected in the x-axis.
$y = f(\lvert x \rvert)$	The part of the graph which is to the left of the y-axis is replaced by the reflection in the y-axis of the part of the graph which is to the right of the y-axis.

- To sketch a reciprocal function, $y = \dfrac{1}{f(x)}$, consider points on the graph of $y = f(x)$ and connect this information together:

$y = f(x)$	$y = \dfrac{1}{f(x)}$
Large and positive	Small and positive
1	1
Small and positive	Large and positive
0	Vertical asymptote
Small and negative	Large and negative
−1	−1
Large and negative	Small and negative
Vertical asymptote	0
Maximum point	Minimum point
Minimum point	Maximum point

To sketch a reciprocal function, ask yourself questions such as: What happens when x is large and negative? What happens when x is large and positive? What happens when $y = f(x)$ has a root? What happens when $y = f(x)$ has a vertical asymptote? What happens when $y = f(x)$ has a turning point? Put this information together to make a rough sketch.

- If $f(x)$ is an odd function:

  - $f(-x) = -f(x)$

  - The graph of $y = f(x)$ has rotational symmetry of order 2 about the origin.

- If $f(x)$ is an even function:
  - $f(-x) = f(x)$
  - The graph of $y = f(x)$ has reflectional symmetry in the y-axis.
- To solve inequalities, sketch the graphs of the functions and identify the regions where one graph is above the other.
- To solve a system of linear equations, use pairs of equations to eliminate one variable at a time.
  - If the result is $x = a$, the equations have a unique solution.

     When there is a unique solution, you can find it using the simultaneous equation solver on your GDC.

  - If the result is $0 = 0$, the equations have an infinite number of solutions. By setting $x = \lambda$, the equation of the line of solutions can be found.
  - If the result is $0 =$ some other number, the equations have no solution.

   Solving a system of equations by elimination is used when looking at the intersections of lines and planes in Chapter 7.

⚠ EXAM TIPS AND COMMON ERRORS

- The range of a function is the same as the domain of the inverse function, which is sometimes a useful way of finding or checking the range.

- When solving equations or inequalities involving the modulus function, always sketch the graphs first, even if the question does not ask you to do so.

4.1 DOMAIN AND RANGE

WORKED EXAMPLE 4.1

If $f(x) = \dfrac{1}{\ln x}$:

(a) find the largest possible domain of $f(x)$

(b) find the range of $f(x)$ if the domain is $x \geq e$.

(a) $x > 0$ as this is the domain of $\ln x$.

But also require $\ln x \neq 0$ to avoid division by zero, so $x \neq 1$.

Hence the domain is $x > 0, x \neq 1$.

 The two restrictions relevant here are logs having to take a positive argument and not dividing by zero.

(b)

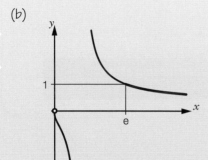

The range is $0 < y \leq 1$.

 Always sketch the graph when finding the range.

Use the graph to state what y values can occur.

It is not obvious from the GDC that the x-axis is an asymptote here. You need to know that $\ln x$ slowly gets larger and larger as x gets larger, which means that $\dfrac{1}{\ln x}$ slowly tends to the x-axis.

Practice questions 4.1

 1. Find the largest possible domain of the function $f(x) = \dfrac{1}{\sqrt{9 - x^2}}$.

 2. Find the domain of the function $f(x) = \dfrac{1}{1-x} - \dfrac{1}{1+x}$.

 If a question asks for 'the domain' of a function, you should give **the largest possible real domain**.

3. Find in terms of a the range of the function $y = x^2 - 6ax + a^2$.

4.2 INVERSE AND COMPOSITE FUNCTIONS

WORKED EXAMPLE 4.2

If $f(x) = \dfrac{1}{\sqrt{x}+1}$, $x \geq 0$ and $g(x) = 3x - 1$, solve the equation $gf^{-1}(x) = 11$.

$$y = \frac{1}{\sqrt{x}+1} \Rightarrow \sqrt{x}+1 = \frac{1}{y}$$

$$\Rightarrow \sqrt{x} = \frac{1}{y}-1$$

$$\Rightarrow x = \left(\frac{1}{y}-1\right)^2$$

> We first need to find $f^{-1}(x)$.
> Set $y = f(x)$, rearrange to make x the subject, and then replace each y with an x.

Therefore $f^{-1}(x) = \left(\dfrac{1}{x}-1\right)^2$

$$gf^{-1}(x) = g\left(\left(\frac{1}{x}-1\right)^2\right) = 3\left(\frac{1}{x}-1\right)^2 - 1$$

> Compose the two functions by replacing each x in $g(x)$ with $\left(\dfrac{1}{x}-1\right)^2$.

$$3\left(\frac{1}{x}-1\right)^2 - 1 = 11$$

$$\Leftrightarrow \left(\frac{1}{x}-1\right)^2 = 4$$

$$\Leftrightarrow \frac{1}{x}-1 = \pm 2$$

So $x = \dfrac{1}{3}$ or $x = -1$

> It is easier to take the square root of both sides rather than multiply out the brackets here, but remember the + and − signs when doing so.

Practice questions 4.2

4. If $f(x) = e^{ax+b}$, find $f^{-1}(x)$.

5. If $f(x) = \dfrac{x}{1-\sqrt{x}}$, $x \geq 0$ and $g(x) = 3x+1$, solve the equation $f^{-1}g(x) = \dfrac{9}{16}$.

Hint: do not attempt to find $f^{-1}(x)$.

6. A function is defined in the following table:

x	1	2	3	4	5	6	7	8	9
$f(x)$	7	1	6	4	2	4	9	8	3

(a) Explain whether this function is one-to-one or many-to-one.

(b) Find $f \circ f(3)$.

(c) Find $f^{-1}(9)$.

4.3 TRANSFORMATIONS OF GRAPHS

WORKED EXAMPLE 4.3

If $f(x) = x^3 + \sin x$:

(a) Find the resulting function when the graph of $f(x)$ is transformed by applying a translation with vector $\begin{pmatrix} 3 \\ 6 \end{pmatrix}$ followed by a vertical stretch with scale factor 2 away from the x-axis.

(b) Describe the transformation which transforms the graph of $y = f(x)$ to the graph of $g(x) = 8x^3 + \sin(2x)$.

(c) Is $f(x)$ an even function, an odd function or neither? Justify your answer.

(a) Translation with vector $\begin{pmatrix} 3 \\ 6 \end{pmatrix}$:

$$f(x-3)+6 = (x-3)^3 + \sin(x-3) + 6$$

> Relate each transformation to function notation: $f(x-3)$ translates the graph 3 units to the right; $f(x)+6$ translates the graph 6 units up.

Then, applying a vertical stretch with scale factor 2:

$$2(f(x-3)+6) = 2((x-3)^3 + \sin(x-3) + 6)$$

> $2f(x)$ stretches the graph vertically with scale factor 2.

> You don't need to simplify your final expression unless a particular form is specified.

(b) $8x^3 + \sin(2x) = (2x)^3 + \sin(2x) = f(2x)$

This is a horizontal stretch away from the y-axis with scale factor $\dfrac{1}{2}$.

> Write $g(x)$ in terms of $f(x)$ and relate this form to a transformation.

(c) $f(-x) = (-x)^3 + \sin(-x)$

$\qquad\quad = -x^3 - \sin x$

and $-f(x) = -x^3 - \sin x$

As $f(-x) = -f(x)$, $f(x)$ is an odd function.

> Compare $f(-x)$ with $f(x)$.
> Since x^3 and $\sin x$ are both odd functions, it is likely that $f(x)$ is also odd, so we check whether $-f(x)$ and $f(-x)$ are the same.

Practice questions 4.3

7. Sketch the graph of $y = |\sin 2x|$ for $0 \le x \le \pi$.

8. Describe two transformations which transform the graph of $y = x^2$ to the graph of:

(a) $y = 3(x - 2)^2$

(b) $y = |x^2 - 2|$

9. The diagram shows the graph of $y = f(x)$.

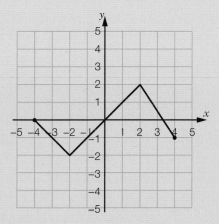

On separate diagrams sketch the following graphs, labelling appropriately.

(a) $y = 3f(2x)$

(b) $y = |f(x)|$

(c) $y = f(|x|)$

10. The graph of $y = 2x^3 - 5x$ is translated 3 units in the positive vertical direction and 2 units to the left, and is then reflected in the x-axis. Find the equation of the resulting graph in the form $y = ax^3 + bx^2 + cx + d$.

11. Below is the graph of $y = a\cos(bx + c)$.

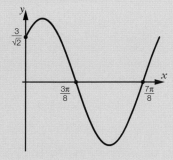

Find the values of a, b and c.

4.4 RECIPROCAL FUNCTIONS AND TRANSFORMATIONS

WORKED EXAMPLE 4.4

(a) Sketch the graph of $y = \dfrac{x+1}{2-x}$, labelling all the axis intercepts and asymptotes.

(b) The graph of $y = f(x)$ is shown below. Sketch the graph of $y = \dfrac{1}{f(x)}$, labelling all the axis intercepts, asymptotes and stationary points.

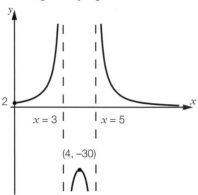

(a) When $y = 0$, $x = -1$; when $x = 0$, $y = \dfrac{1}{2}$.

Asymptotes: vertical $x = 2$, horizontal $y = -1$.

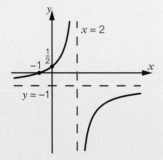

> This is a rational function of the form
> $f(x) = \dfrac{ax+b}{cx+d}$, so the graph is a hyperbola.
>
> We can find the x- and y-intercepts by substituting $y = 0$ and $x = 0$, respectively.
>
> The vertical asymptote occurs when the denominator is zero and the horizontal asymptote is at $y = \dfrac{a}{c}$.

(b) y-intercept: $y = \dfrac{1}{2}$

x-intercepts: $x = 3, 5$

Minimum point: $\left(4, -\dfrac{1}{30}\right)$.

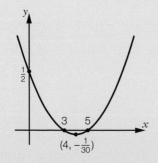

> We can find the y-intercept of $\dfrac{1}{f(x)}$ by taking the reciprocal of the y-intercept of $f(x)$, and the x-intercepts will occur where $f(x)$ has vertical asymptotes.
>
> $\dfrac{1}{f(x)}$ will have a minimum at $x = 4$ where $f(x)$ has a maximum.
>
> We can complete the sketch by noting that as $f(x)$ becomes very small, $\dfrac{1}{f(x)}$ becomes very large.

Practice questions 4.4

12. Sketch the graph of $y = \dfrac{2x-a}{x+b}$ where a and b are positive constants. State the equations of all the asymptotes and the coordinates of axis intercepts.

13. (a) Find the coordinates of the zeros and the vertex of the function $f(x) = x^2 - 4x - 5$.

(b) Sketch the graph of $y = \dfrac{1}{x^2 - 4x - 5}$, showing all the asymptotes, axis intercepts and the coordinates of any stationary points.

14. If $f(x) = \dfrac{3x-1}{2x+3}$:

(a) find an expression for $f^{-1}(x)$

(b) state the domain and range of
    (i) $f(x)$ (ii) $f^{-1}(x)$

15. The diagram shows the graph of $y = f(x)$.

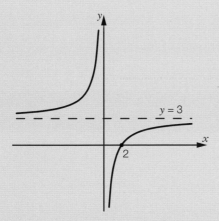

On separate diagrams sketch the graphs of:

(a) $y = \dfrac{1}{f(x)}$

(b) $y = |f(x)|$

(c) $y = f^{-1}(x)$

4.5 SOLVING INEQUALITIES

WORKED EXAMPLE 4.5

 Solve the inequality $|2x| > 3 - x$.

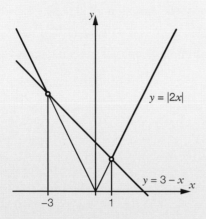

Intersections: $x = 1$ and $x = -3$

So $x < -3$ or $x > 1$.

> ⚠ Always sketch the graph when solving inequalities.

> ○— Highlight the part of the graph of $y = |2x|$ which is above the graph of $y = 3 - x$.

> ○— Find the intersection points.

> ○— Read the answers off the graph.

Practice questions 4.5

 16. Solve the inequality $x^3 > 4x$.

> When using a calculator there is no need to rearrange the inequality; just plot the two sides.

 17. Solve the inequality $|x - 2| \leq x^2 - 4$.

 18. (a) Factorise $x^3 - 5x^2 + 6x$.

(b) Sketch the graph of $y = x^3 - 5x^2 + 6x$.

(c) Hence solve the inequality $x^3 + 6x < 5x^2$.

 19. (a) Sketch the graph of $y = |x + 4|$.

(b) Hence, or otherwise, solve the inequality $|x + 4| > 6 - x$.

20. (a) On the same axes, sketch the graphs of $y = 2|x| - 5$ and $y = |x - 2|$.

(b) Solve the inequality $2|x| - 5 > |x - 2|$.

4.6 SYSTEMS OF LINEAR EQUATIONS

WORKED EXAMPLE 4.6

Find the value of a for which the following system of equations has infinitely many solutions, and in this case find the Cartesian equation of the line of solutions in the form $\dfrac{x-a_1}{d_1} = \dfrac{y-a_2}{d_2} = \dfrac{z-a_3}{d_3}$.

$$\begin{cases} x+y+z=1 \\ x+2y+3z=5 \\ x+3y+5z=a \end{cases}$$

$$(2)-(1) \begin{cases} x+y+z=1 & \cdots(1) \\ y+2z=4 & \cdots(4) \\ 2y+4z=a-1 & \cdots(5) \end{cases}$$

Labelling the original equations (1), (2) and (3), we aim to eliminate x and y from (3). First, eliminate x from (2) and (3) by subtracting (1) from each of them.

$$(5)-2\times(4) \begin{cases} x+y+z=1 & \cdots(1) \\ y+2z=4 & \cdots(4) \\ 0=a-9 & \cdots(6) \end{cases}$$

Now we can eliminate y from (5) by multiplying (4) by 2 and subtracting.

The system only has solutions when $a=9$.

For any solutions to exist, the RHS of (6) must be 0 (to be consistent with the LHS).

Let $z=\lambda$. Then

$(4) \Rightarrow y=4-2z=4-2\lambda$

$(1) \Rightarrow x=1-y-z=1-(4-2\lambda)-\lambda=\lambda-3$

There are now only two equations with three unknowns, so we need to express x and y in terms of z.

Making λ the subject of each of these:

$\lambda=x+3$

$\lambda=\dfrac{4-y}{2}$

$\lambda=z$

$\therefore x+3=\dfrac{4-y}{2}=z$

To give the Cartesian equation of the line, we need to make λ the subject of the equations for x, y and z and then equate these three expressions.

 This solution can be interpreted as the equation of the line of intersection of three planes. See Chapter 7.

Practice questions 4.6

21. For each of the following, find the values of a for which the system has a unique solution. Where possible, find the solution in terms of a. For the values of a for which there are infinitely many solutions, find the general solution of the system.

(a) $\begin{cases} x+y+z=8 \\ 3x+y-z=18 \\ 2x+y-z=4+2a \end{cases}$

(b) $\begin{cases} 2x+y+z=3 \\ x+y+3z=10 \\ x+y+az=10 \end{cases}$

Mixed practice 4

1. Explain why an even function cannot have an inverse function.

2. (a) Sketch the graph of $y = x^2 - x - 6$.

   (b) Hence state the domain of the function $f(x) = \ln(x^2 - x - 6)$.

3. Find the values of k for which the following system of equations has infinitely many solutions:

$$\begin{cases} x - 2y + z = 2 \\ x + y - 3z = k \\ 2x - y - 2z = k^2 \end{cases}$$

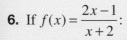

4. Sketch the graph of $y = 5 - 2|x + 3|$, giving the coordinates of any intersection points with the axes and the coordinates of the minimum or maximum point.

5. Find, in terms of a, the domain of the function $f(x) = \sqrt{x^2 - a^2}$.

6. If $f(x) = \dfrac{2x - 1}{x + 2}$:

   (a) Sketch the graph of $y = f(x)$.

   (b) Find an expression for $f^{-1}(x)$ and state its range.

   (c) Find the domain of the function $g(x) = f^{-1}(2 - x)$.

   (d) Solve the equation $f(x) = g(x)$.

7. (a) Sketch the graph of $y = 2\sin\left(x - \dfrac{\pi}{3}\right)$ for $x \in [0, 2\pi]$, including the coordinates of all the axis intercepts and maximum and minimum points.

   (b) On the same axes, sketch the graph of $y = \dfrac{1}{2}\csc\left(x - \dfrac{\pi}{3}\right)$ for $x \in [0, 2\pi]$.

8. (a) On the same axes, sketch the graphs of:

   (i) $y = |3x - 7|$

   (ii) $y = |x^2 - x - 12|$

   (b) Solve the inequality $|x^2 - x - 12| < |3x - 7|$.

9. Consider a function, f, defined by $f(x) = \dfrac{ax - a^2 + 1}{x - a}$.

   (a) Show that $f(x) = p + \dfrac{q}{x - a}$ where p and q are constants to be determined in terms of a.

   (b) Hence give two transformations which change the graph of $y = \dfrac{1}{x}$ into the graph of $y = f(x)$.

   (c) Sketch the graph of $y = f(x)$, labelling all asymptotes and points of intersection with the axes.

   (d) Sketch on a separate diagram the graph of $y = \left| f\left(|x|\right) \right|$.

   (e) Find and simplify $f \circ f(x)$.

   (f) Find $f^{-1}(x)$.

   (g) What property of the graph of $y = f(x)$ does your answer to (f) demonstrate?

Going for the top 4

1. (a) Rearrange the equation $y = \dfrac{x^2 - 3x + 3}{x - 2}$ to find an expression for x in terms of y.

   (b) Hence, or otherwise, find an expression for the range of $f(x) = \dfrac{x^2 - 3x + 3}{x - 2}$.

2. (a) On the same axes, sketch the graphs of $y = \ln x$ and $y = 2\ln(x - 2)$.

   (b) Hence solve the inequality $\ln x \geq 2\ln(x - 2)$.

3. Consider the system of equations

$$\begin{cases} 3x + 2y - z = 4 \\ 2x - 4y + 3z = 1 \\ x + y + az = k \end{cases}$$

Give the condition(s) for which this system has:

   (a) a unique solution

   (b) infinitely many solutions

   (c) no solutions.

5 SEQUENCES AND SERIES

WHAT YOU NEED TO KNOW

- The notation for sequences and series:
    - u_n represents the nth term of the sequence u.
    - S_n denotes the sum of the first n terms of the sequence.
    - $\displaystyle\sum_{r=k}^{n} u_r$ denotes the sum of the kth term to the nth term, so $\displaystyle S_n = \sum_{r=1}^{n} u_r$.
- Sequences can be described in two ways:
    - using recursive definitions to define how u_{n+1} depends on u_n
    - using deductive rules (the nth term formula) to define how u_n depends on n.
- An arithmetic sequence has a constant difference, d, between terms: $u_{n+1} = u_n + d$
    - $u_n = u_1 + (n-1)d$
    - $S_n = \dfrac{n}{2}(2u_1 + (n-1)d) = \dfrac{n}{2}(u_1 + u_n)$
- A geometric sequence has a constant ratio, r, between terms: $u_{n+1} = ru_n$
    - $u_n = u_1 r^{n-1}$
    - $S_n = \dfrac{u_1(r^n - 1)}{r - 1} = \dfrac{u_1(1 - r^n)}{1 - r}, \; r \neq 1$
    - When $|r| < 1$, S_n approaches a limit as n increases, called the sum to infinity: $S_\infty = \dfrac{u_1}{1-r}$

⚠ EXAM TIPS AND COMMON ERRORS

- Many questions on sequences and series involve forming and then solving simultaneous equations.
- For questions on geometric sequences, you may need to use logarithms or rules of exponents.
- You may need to use the list feature on your calculator to solve problems involving sequences.
- You only ever need to use the first sum formula for geometric sequences.
- Geometric sequences are often used to solve problems involving percentage increase or decrease, such as investments and mortgages.

5.1 ARITHMETIC SEQUENCES AND SERIES

WORKED EXAMPLE 5.1

The third term of an arithmetic sequence is 15 and the sixth term is 27.

(a) Find the tenth term.

(b) Find the sum of the first ten terms.

(c) The sum of the first n terms is 5250. Find the value of n.

> ⚠️ You will often have to find a term of a sequence and a sum of a sequence in different parts of the same question. Make sure you are clear which you are being asked for.

(a) $u_3 = u_1 + 2d = 15$ $\quad \cdots$ (1)

$u_6 = u_1 + 5d = 27$ $\quad \cdots$ (2)

(2) − (1): $3d = 12 \Rightarrow d = 4$ and so $u_1 = 7$

Hence, $u_{10} = u_1 + 9d = 7 + 9 \times 4 = 43$

> We can form two equations from the given information about the third and sixth terms.
> It is then clear that we need to solve these simultaneously for u_1 and d.

(b) $S_{10} = \dfrac{10}{2}(u_1 + u_{10})$

$= 5(7 + 43)$

$= 250$

> There are two possible formulae for the sum of an arithmetic sequence. Since we know the first and last terms (from part (a)), we use $S_n = \dfrac{n}{2}(u_1 + u_n)$.

(c) $5250 = \dfrac{n}{2}(2u_1 + (n-1)d)$

$= \dfrac{n}{2}(14 + 4(n-1))$

> Again we need a formula for the sum, but this time the other formula is the one to use as n is the only unknown here. Form an equation and solve it using a GDC.

The solutions (from GDC) are $n = 50$ or -52.5; but n must be a positive integer, so $n = 50$.

Practice questions 5.1

1. The fifth term of an arithmetic sequence is 64 and the eighth term is 46.

  (a) Find the thirtieth term.

  (b) Find the sum of the first twelve terms.

2. The first four terms of an arithmetic sequence are 16, 15.5, 14, 13.5.

  (a) Find the twentieth term.

  (b) Which term is equal to zero?

  (c) The sum of the first n terms is 246. Find the possible values of n.

5.2 GEOMETRIC SEQUENCES AND SERIES

WORKED EXAMPLE 5.2

The second term of a geometric sequence is −5 and the sum to infinity is 12.
Find the common ratio and the first term.

$u_2 = u_1 r = -5 \quad \cdots (1)$

$S_\infty = \dfrac{u_1}{1-r} = 12 \quad \cdots (2)$

From (2): $u_1 = 12(1-r)$

Substituting into (1): $12r(1-r) = -5$

$\therefore r = -0.316$ or $r = 1.32$ (from GDC)

Since the sum to infinity exists, $|r| < 1$ and
so $r = -0.316$.

Hence $u_1 = 12(1-(-0.316)) = 15.8$

> We can form two equations from the given information about the second term and sum to infinity.
>
> It is then clear that we need to solve these simultaneously for u_1 and r.

 There is no need to rearrange the final equation as it can be solved using a GDC.

 The condition that $|r| < 1$ should be remembered as part of the formula for S_∞.

Practice questions 5.2

3. The fourth term of a geometric sequence is −16 and the sum to infinity is 32.
   Show that there is only one possible value of the common ratio and find this value.

4. The fifth term of a geometric series is 12 and the seventh term is 3.
   Find the two possible values of the sum to infinity of the series.

5. The sum of the first three terms of a geometric sequence is 38 and the sum of the first four terms is 65. Find the first term and the common ratio, $r > 1$.

6. The fifth term of a geometric sequence is 128 and the sixth term is 512.
   (a) Find the common ratio and the first term.
   (b) Which term has a value of 32 768?
   (c) How many terms are needed before the sum of all the terms in the sequence exceeds 100 000?

7. The first three terms of a geometric sequence are $2x + 4$, $x + 5$, $x + 1$, where x is a real number.
   (a) Find the two possible values of x.
   (b) Given that it exists, find the sum to infinity of the series.

5.3 APPLICATIONS

WORKED EXAMPLE 5.3

Daniel invests $500 at the beginning of each year in a scheme that earns interest at a rate of 4% per annum, paid at the end of the year.

Show that the first year, n, in which the scheme is worth more than $26\,000$ satisfies $n > \dfrac{\ln k}{\ln 1.04}$ where k is a constant to be found. Hence determine n.

Amount in the scheme at the end of the first year:
500×1.04

> Generate the first and second terms of the sequence to establish a pattern.

Amount at the end of the second year:
$(500 + 500 \times 1.04) \times 1.04$
$= 500 \times 1.04 + 500 \times 1.04^2$

> ⚠ With more complicated questions of this type, it is always a good idea to write down the first few terms to see whether you have an arithmetic or geometric series, and to understand exactly how the series is being formed.

So, amount at the end of the nth year:
$500 \times 1.04 + 500 \times 1.04^2 + \ldots + 500 \times 1.04^n$

> This is a geometric series with $u_1 = 500 \times 1.04$ and $r = 1.04$.

$S_n = \dfrac{500 \times 1.04\,(1.04^n - 1)}{1.04 - 1}$
$\quad = 13\,000\,(1.04^n - 1)$

> We can use the formula for the sum of the first n terms of a geometric sequence to form an inequality, which we solve to find n.

So, for the amount to exceed $\$26\,000$:

$13\,000\,(1.04^n - 1) > 26\,000$
$\Rightarrow 1.04^n - 1 > 2$
$\Rightarrow 1.04^n > 3$

$\Rightarrow \ln\left(1.04^n\right) > \ln 3$
$\Rightarrow n \ln 1.04 > \ln 3$

> The unknown n is in the power, so use logarithms to solve the inequality.

$\Rightarrow n > \dfrac{\ln 3}{\ln 1.04} = 28.01\,(2\,\text{DP})$

> ◀ Logarithms are covered in Chapter 2.

Therefore, $k = 3$ and $n = 29$.

Practice questions 5.3

8. A starting salary for a teacher is \$25 000 and there is an annual increase of 3%.

    (a) How much will the teacher earn in their tenth year?

    (b) How much will the teacher earn in total during a 35-year teaching career?

    (c) Find the first year in which the teacher earns more than \$35 000.

    (d) How many years would the teacher have to work in order to earn a total of \$1 million?

9. Beth repays a loan of \$10 500 over a period of n months. She repays \$50 in the first month, \$55 in the second, and so on, with the monthly repayments continuing to increase by \$5 each month.

    (a) How much will Beth repay in the 28th month?

    (b) Show that $n^2 + 19n - 4200 = 0$.

    (c) Hence find the number of months taken to repay the loan in full.

10. A ball is dropped from a height of 3 m. Each time it hits the ground it bounces up to 90% of its previous height.

    (a) How high does it bounce on the fifth bounce?

    (b) On which bounce does the ball first reach a maximum height of less than 1 m?

    (c) Assuming the ball keeps bouncing until it rests, find the total distance travelled by the ball.

11. Theo has a mortgage of \$127 000 which is to be repaid in annual instalments of \$7000. Once the annual payment has been made, 3.5% interest is added to the remaining balance at the beginning of the next year.

    (a) Show that at the end of the third year the amount owing is given by

$$127000 \times 1.035^2 - 7000(1 + 1.035 + 1.035^2)$$

    (b) By forming a similar expression for the amount owing after n years, show that

$$n > \frac{\ln k}{\ln 1.035} + 1$$

    where k is a constant to be found.

    (c) Hence find the number of years it will take Theo to pay off his mortgage.

Mixed practice 5

1. The fourth term of an arithmetic sequence is 17. The sum of the first twenty terms is 990. Find the first term, a, and the common difference, d, of the sequence.

2. The fourth, tenth and thirteenth terms of a geometric sequence form an arithmetic sequence. Given that the geometric sequence has a sum to infinity, find its common ratio correct to three significant figures.

3. Evaluate $\displaystyle\sum_{r=1}^{12} 4r + \left(\frac{1}{3}\right)^r$ correct to four significant figures.

4. Find an expression for the sum of the first 20 terms of the series

   $$\ln x + \ln x^4 + \ln x^7 + \ln x^{10} + \dots$$

   giving your answer as a single logarithm.

5. A rope of length 300 m is cut into several pieces, whose lengths form an arithmetic sequence with common difference d. If the shortest piece is 1 m long and the longest piece is 19 m, find d.

6. Aaron and Blake each open a savings account. Aaron deposits $100 in the first month and then increases his deposits by $10 each month. Blake deposits $50 in the first month and then increases his deposits by 5% each month. After how many months will Blake have more money in his account than Aaron?

Going for the top 5

1. (a) (i) Prove that the sum of the first n terms of a geometric sequence with first term a and common ratio r is given by:

   $$S_n = \frac{a(r^n - 1)}{r - 1}$$

   (ii) Hence establish the formula for the sum to infinity, clearly justifying any conditions imposed on the common ratio r.

   (b) Show that in a geometric sequence with common ratio r, the ratio of the sum of the first n terms to the sum of the next n terms is $1 : r^n$.

   (c) In a geometric sequence, the sum of the seventh term and four times the fifth term equals the eighth term.

   (i) Find the ratio of the sum of the first 10 terms to the sum of the next 10 terms.

   (ii) Does the sequence have a sum to infinity? Explain your answer.

2. Find the sum of all integers between 1 and 1000 which are not divisible by 7.

6 TRIGONOMETRY

WHAT YOU NEED TO KNOW

- The graphs of trigonometric functions:

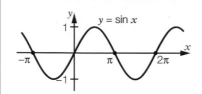 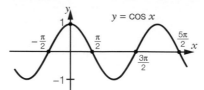 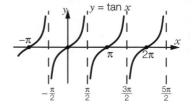

- The graphs of reciprocal trigonometric functions:

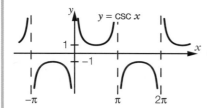 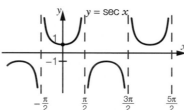 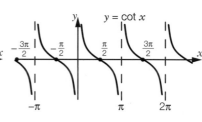

- The graphs of inverse trigonometric functions:

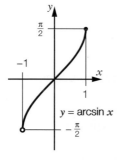 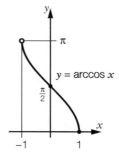 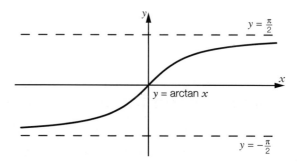

- The following exact values:

	0	$\dfrac{\pi}{6}$	$\dfrac{\pi}{4}$	$\dfrac{\pi}{3}$	$\dfrac{\pi}{2}$
sin	0	$\dfrac{1}{2}$	$\dfrac{\sqrt{2}}{2}$	$\dfrac{\sqrt{3}}{2}$	1
cos	1	$\dfrac{\sqrt{3}}{2}$	$\dfrac{\sqrt{2}}{2}$	$\dfrac{1}{2}$	0
tan	0	$\dfrac{1}{\sqrt{3}}$	1	$\sqrt{3}$	

- Trigonometric functions are related through:
  - Identities:
    $$\tan\theta = \frac{\sin\theta}{\cos\theta} \qquad \sec\theta = \frac{1}{\cos\theta} \qquad \mathrm{cosec}\,\theta = \frac{1}{\sin\theta}$$

    $$\cot\theta = \frac{1}{\tan\theta} = \frac{\cos\theta}{\sin\theta}$$
  - Pythagorean identities:
    - $\cos^2\theta + \sin^2\theta = 1$
    - $1 + \tan^2\theta = \sec^2\theta$
    - $1 + \cot^2\theta = \csc^2\theta$
  - Double angle identities:
    - $\sin 2\theta = 2\sin\theta\cos\theta$
    - $\cos 2\theta = \cos^2\theta - \sin^2\theta = 2\cos^2\theta - 1 = 1 - 2\sin^2\theta$
    - $\tan 2\theta = \dfrac{2\tan\theta}{1 - \tan^2\theta}$
  - Compound angle identities:
    - $\sin(A \pm B) = \sin A\cos B \pm \cos A\sin B$
    - $\cos(A \pm B) = \cos A\cos B \mp \sin A\sin B$
    - $\tan(A \pm B) = \dfrac{\tan A \pm \tan B}{1 \mp \tan A\tan B}$
- To prove trigonometric identities, start with one side of the identity (often the left-hand side) and transform this until it equals the other side.
- When solving trigonometric equations of the form $\sin A = k$, $\cos A = k$ or $\tan A = k$:
  - Draw a graph to see how many solutions there are.
  - Use $\sin^{-1}$, $\cos^{-1}$ or $\tan^{-1}$ to find one possible value of A: A_0.
  - Find the second solution, A_1, by using the symmetry of the graph:
    - For $\sin A = k$, $A_1 = \pi - A_0$
    - For $\cos A = k$, $A_1 = 2\pi - A_0$
    - For $\tan A = k$, $A_1 = A_0 + \pi$
  - Find all the solutions in the required interval for A by adding multiples of 2π.
- With more complicated equations, it may be necessary to first use one or more of the identities to manipulate the equation into a form that can be solved.

> ⚠ A common type of equation that you should look out for is a 'disguised quadratic' arising from the use of one of the Pythagorean identities or the $\cos 2x$ formulae.

- A function $a\sin x \pm b\cos x$ can be written in the form $R\sin(x \pm \alpha)$ or $R\cos(x \pm \alpha)$ using the relevant compound angle identity.

- The sine and cosine rules are used to find the sides and angles of any triangle:

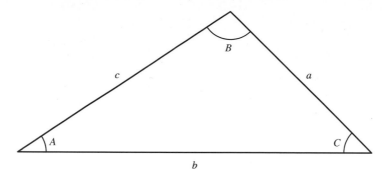

- Sine rule: $\dfrac{a}{\sin A} = \dfrac{b}{\sin B} = \dfrac{c}{\sin C}$

- Cosine rule: $c^2 = a^2 + b^2 - 2ab\cos C$, or $\cos C = \dfrac{a^2 + b^2 - c^2}{2ab}$

- The sine rule is only used when a side and its opposite angle are given.

- The area of a triangle can be found using $\text{Area} = \dfrac{1}{2}ab\sin C$.

- In a circle of radius r with an angle of θ radians subtended at the centre:
  - the length of the arc AB: $l = r\theta$
  - the area of the sector AOB: $A = \dfrac{1}{2}r^2\theta$

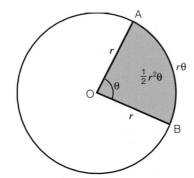

6.1 TRANSFORMATIONS OF TRIGONOMETRIC GRAPHS

WORKED EXAMPLE 6.1

The graph shown has equation $y = c - a\sin\left(\dfrac{x}{b}\right)$.
Find the values of a, b and c.

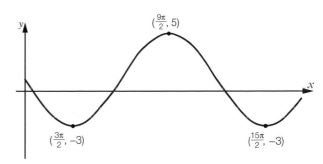

$$y_{\max} - y_{\min} = 5 - (-3) = 8$$

$$\therefore a = \frac{8}{2} = 4$$

a has the effect of stretching the sine curve vertically. The distance between the maximum and minimum values of the original sine curve is 2. The minus sign in front of *a* causes a vertical reflection; it does not affect the amplitude.

◀◀ **Transforming graphs is covered in Chapter 4.**

$$\text{period} = \frac{15\pi}{2} - \frac{3\pi}{2} = 6\pi$$

$$\therefore b = \frac{6\pi}{2\pi} = 3$$

Dividing *x* by *b* stretches the sine curve horizontally by a factor of *b*. The period of the original sine curve is 2π.

$$c = 1$$

c causes a vertical translation. After multiplication by $-a = -4$, the minimum and maximum values would be -4 and 4 respectively, but here they are -3 and 5.

Practice questions 6.1

1. The graph shown has equation $y = a\sin\left(bx - \dfrac{\pi}{6}\right)$.
Find the values of a and b.

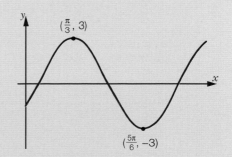

2. Find the range of the function $f(x) = \dfrac{2}{5 + 2\sin x}$.

3. Find the smallest positive value of x for which $\dfrac{1}{3 - \sin\left(x - \dfrac{\pi}{4}\right)}$ takes its maximum value.

6.2 PROVING TRIGONOMETRIC IDENTITIES

WORKED EXAMPLE 6.2

Show that $\dfrac{\cos x}{1-\sin x} + \dfrac{\cos x}{1+\sin x} = 2\sec x$ for $x \neq k\pi$.

$\text{LHS} = \dfrac{\cos x}{1-\sin x} + \dfrac{\cos x}{1+\sin x}$

> We will start from the left-hand side (LHS) and transform it until we get the right-hand side (RHS).

$= \dfrac{\cos x(1+\sin x)}{(1-\sin x)(1+\sin x)} + \dfrac{\cos x(1-\sin x)}{(1+\sin x)(1-\sin x)}$

$= \dfrac{\cos x + \cos x \sin x}{1-\sin^2 x} + \dfrac{\cos x - \cos x \sin x}{1-\sin^2 x}$

> To combine these fractions, create a common denominator of $1-\sin^2 x$.

$= \dfrac{2\cos x}{1-\sin^2 x}$

$= \dfrac{2\cos x}{\cos^2 x} \quad (\text{as } \sin^2 x = 1 - \cos^2 x)$

> We can then use the identity $\sin^2 x + \cos^2 x = 1$ on the denominator.

$= \dfrac{2}{\cos x}$

$= 2\sec x = \text{RHS}$

 It is not always obvious how to get from one side to the other. If you're not sure, transform each side separately and meet in the middle.

Practice questions 6.2

4. Show that $\dfrac{\cos 4x}{\cos 2x + \sin 2x} = \cos 2x - \sin 2x$.

5. Show that $\sec^2 x(\cot^2 x - \cos^2 x) = \cot^2 x$.

6. Prove that $\dfrac{\cos 2x + 1}{\cos^2 x} + \dfrac{1 - \cos 2x}{\sin^2 x} = 4$.

7. Show that $\dfrac{\csc x - \sin x}{\cos x} - \dfrac{\sec x - \cos x}{\sin x} = 2\cot 2x$.

8. Prove that $\dfrac{\sin 2x + \sin x}{1 + \cos 2x + \cos x} = \tan x$.

9. Show that $\csc x - \sin x = \cot x \cos x$.

6.3 USING IDENTITIES TO FIND EXACT VALUES OF TRIGONOMETRIC FUNCTIONS

WORKED EXAMPLE 6.3

 Given that $\cos A = \dfrac{1}{3}$ and $A \in \left[0, \dfrac{\pi}{2}\right]$, find the exact values of:

(a) $\csc A$

(b) $\sin 2A$

(a) $\sin^2 A = 1 - \cos^2 A$

$\qquad = 1 - \dfrac{1}{9} = \dfrac{8}{9}$

$\therefore \sin A = \pm\sqrt{\dfrac{8}{9}} = \pm\dfrac{2\sqrt{2}}{3}$

> $\csc A = \dfrac{1}{\sin A}$, so we need to find $\sin A$ from the given value of $\cos A$. To do this we can use the identity $\sin^2 A + \cos^2 A = 1$.

> **Remember the $\pm$ when you take the square root.**

For $A \in \left[0, \dfrac{\pi}{2}\right]$, $\sin A \ge 0$

$\therefore \sin A = \dfrac{2\sqrt{2}}{3}$

$\Rightarrow \csc A = \dfrac{1}{\sin A} = \dfrac{3}{2\sqrt{2}}$

> We now have to choose either the positive or negative value, so consider the sine function in the given interval $0 \le A \le \dfrac{\pi}{2}$.

(b) $\sin 2A = 2 \sin A \cos A$

$\qquad = 2\left(\dfrac{2\sqrt{2}}{3}\right)\left(\dfrac{1}{3}\right)$

$\qquad = \dfrac{4\sqrt{2}}{9}$

> As we need $\sin 2A$, the only option is to use the sine double angle identity.
> Substitute the values for $\sin A$ and $\cos A$.

Practice questions 6.3

 10. Given that $\cos 2\theta = \dfrac{2}{3}$ and $\theta \in \left[\dfrac{\pi}{2}, \pi\right]$, find the exact value of $\cos\theta$.

 11. Given that $\cos\theta = \dfrac{3}{4}$ and $\theta \in \left[\dfrac{3\pi}{2}, 2\pi\right]$, find the exact value of $\sin\theta$.

 12. Given that $\tan A = 2$ and $A \in \left[0, \dfrac{\pi}{2}\right]$, find the exact value of $\sin A$.

6.4 SOLVING TRIGONOMETRIC EQUATIONS

WORKED EXAMPLE 6.4

 Solve the equation $\csc 3x = 2$ for $x \in \left[0, \dfrac{\pi}{2}\right]$.

$$\csc 3x = 2 \Leftrightarrow \sin 3x = \frac{1}{2}$$

$$\sin^{-1}\left(\frac{1}{2}\right) = \frac{\pi}{6}$$

 First, convert the original equation into sine form so that we can use $\sin^{-1}$ to find the first value of $3x$.

⚠️ Always start by converting equations involving sec, csc or cot into a form containing cos, sin or tan only.

$$x \in \left[0, \frac{\pi}{2}\right] \Rightarrow 3x \in \left[0, \frac{3\pi}{2}\right]$$

Find the range of possible values for $3x$.

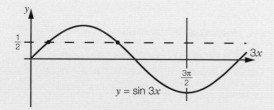

Draw the graph to see how many solutions there are in the required interval. Here only two are needed.

$$3x = \frac{\pi}{6} \text{ or } \pi - \frac{\pi}{6} = \frac{5\pi}{6}$$

$$\therefore x = \frac{\pi}{18} \text{ or } \frac{5\pi}{18}$$

 For the sine function, the second value will always be $\pi -$ (first value).
Finally, divide by 3 to find x.

⚠️ It is a common error to divide by 3 first and then find the second value. Always find all the possible values in the interval first and then make x the subject at the end.

Practice questions 6.4

 13. Solve the equation $\sec 2x = \sqrt{2}$ for $x \in [0, \pi]$.

14. Solve the equation $\tan 3x = \sqrt{3}$ for $x \in [-\pi, \pi]$.

 15. Solve the equation $\sin\left(3x + \dfrac{\pi}{4}\right) = \dfrac{\sqrt{3}}{2}$ for $x \in [-\pi, \pi]$.

16. Solve the equation $3\csc^2 2x = 4$ for $0 \le x \le 2\pi$.

6.5 USING IDENTITIES TO SOLVE TRIGONOMETRIC EQUATIONS

WORKED EXAMPLE 6.5

Solve the equation $3\sin^2 x + 1 = 4\cos x$ for $x \in [-\pi, \pi]$.

$$3\sin^2 x + 1 = 4\cos x$$
$$\Leftrightarrow 3(1 - \cos^2 x) + 1 = 4\cos x$$
$$\Leftrightarrow 3 - 3\cos^2 x + 1 = 4\cos x$$

Using the identity $\sin^2 x + \cos^2 x = 1$, we can replace the $\sin^2$ term and thereby form an equation that contains only one type of trigonometric function (cos).

> ⚠ If possible, use an identity to ensure that there is only one type of trigonometric function in the equation.

$$\Leftrightarrow 3\cos^2 x + 4\cos x - 4 = 0$$
$$\Leftrightarrow (3\cos x - 2)(\cos x + 2) = 0$$
$$\Leftrightarrow \cos x = \frac{2}{3} \text{ or } \cos x = -2$$
$$\therefore \cos x = \frac{2}{3} \quad (\text{as } -1 \le \cos x \le 1)$$

This now becomes a standard quadratic equation, which can be factorised and solved.

◀ Disguised quadratics are also encountered in Chapter 2 when solving exponential equations.

$$\cos^{-1}\left(\frac{2}{3}\right) = 0.841 \ (3\,\text{SF})$$

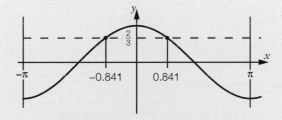

Draw the graph to see how many solutions there are in the required interval. Here only two are needed.

$2\pi - 0.841 = 5.44$ is not in the interval

$5.44 - 2\pi$ is in the interval

$\therefore x = \pm 0.841$

For the cosine function, the second value will always be 2π – (first value), but here that is not in the required interval. Therefore, subtract 2π from this value to get the second answer.

Practice questions 6.5

17. Solve the equation $3\csc^2 \theta + 5\cot \theta = 5$ for $\theta \in [-\pi, \pi]$.

18. Solve the equation $\cos 2x - 2 = 5\cos x$ for $x \in [0, 2\pi]$.

19. Solve the equation $\cot x = 2\cos x$ for $-\pi < x < \pi$.

20. Find the values of $\theta \in [0, \pi]$ for which $\tan^2 2\theta - 4\sec 2\theta + 5 = 0$.

6.6 FUNCTIONS OF THE FORM $a\sin x + b\cos x$

WORKED EXAMPLE 6.6

Express $f(x) = 2\cos x - 5\sin x$ in the form $R\cos(x + \alpha)$ where $R > 0$ and $\alpha \in \left[0, \dfrac{\pi}{2}\right]$.

$$R\cos(x + \alpha) = R(\cos x \cos \alpha - \sin x \sin \alpha)$$
$$= R\cos\alpha\cos x - R\sin\alpha\sin x$$

First expand $R\cos(x + \alpha)$ using the compound angle identity.

Comparing with $2\cos x - 5\sin x$ gives:

$R\cos\alpha = 2 \quad \cdots (1)$

$R\sin\alpha = 5 \quad \cdots (2)$

Equate the coefficients of $\cos x$ and $\sin x$ to get equations for $R\cos\alpha$ and $R\sin\alpha$.

$(1)^2 + (2)^2$:

$R^2\cos^2\alpha + R^2\sin^2\alpha = 2^2 + 5^2$

$\Rightarrow R^2(\cos^2\alpha + \sin^2\alpha) = 2^2 + 5^2$

$\Rightarrow R^2 = 29$

$\therefore R = \sqrt{29}$

To solve these simultaneous equations, eliminate α by squaring and adding and then applying the identity $\cos^2\alpha + \sin^2\alpha = 1$.

$(2) \div (1)$:

$\dfrac{R\sin\alpha}{R\cos\alpha} = \dfrac{5}{2}$

$\Leftrightarrow \tan\alpha = \dfrac{5}{2}$

To eliminate R, use $\tan\alpha = \dfrac{\sin\alpha}{\cos\alpha}$.

$\therefore \alpha = \tan^{-1}\left(\dfrac{5}{2}\right) = 1.19 \text{ (3 SF)}$

$\therefore 2\cos x - 5\sin x = \sqrt{29}\cos(x + 1.19)$

Write the expression in the required form.

Practice questions 6.6

21. Find the exact values for $R > 0$ and $\theta \in \left[0, \dfrac{\pi}{2}\right]$ such that $\sqrt{3}\sin x + \cos x = R\sin(x + \theta)$.

Hence find the minimum value of $\dfrac{2}{3 + \sqrt{3}\sin x + \cos x}$.

 These question types will always tell you which form to use: $R\sin(x \pm \alpha)$ or $R\cos(x \pm \alpha)$.

22. Show that $5\cos x + 3\sin x$ can be written in the form $R\cos(x - \alpha)$. Hence find the coordinates of the maximum point on the graph of $y = 5\cos x + 3\sin x$ for $x \in [0, 2\pi]$.

6.7 GEOMETRY OF TRIANGLES AND CIRCLES

WORKED EXAMPLE 6.7

The diagram shows a circle with centre C and radius 12 cm. Points P and Q are on the circumference on the circle and $P\hat{C}Q = 0.72$ radians.

(a) Find the length of the chord PQ.

(b) Find the area of the shaded region.

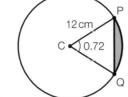

(a) Using the cosine rule in triangle PCQ:

$$PQ^2 = 12^2 + 12^2 - 2 \times 12 \times 12 \cos 0.72$$

$$= 71.5$$

$$\therefore PQ = 8.45 \text{ cm}$$

 CP = CQ = 12 since CP and CQ are both radii. As we don't have an angle and its opposite side, we need to use the cosine rule.

🖩 Make sure your calculator is in radian mode.

(b) Area of sector PCQ:

$$\frac{1}{2}r^2\theta = \frac{1}{2} \times 12^2 \times 0.72 = 51.84$$

Area of triangle PCQ:

$$\frac{1}{2}ab\sin C = \frac{1}{2}(12)(12)\sin 0.72 = 47.5$$

We can find the area of the shaded region by subtracting the area of the triangle from the area of the sector.

Shaded area = $51.84 - 47.5 = 4.36 \text{ cm}^2$

Practice questions 6.7

23. A sector of a circle with angle 0.65 radians has area 14.8 cm². Find the radius of the circle.

24. The diagram shows a rectangle and a sector of a circle. Find the perimeter.

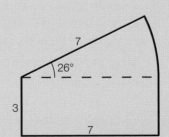

25. A vertical cliff BT, of height 50 m, stands on horizontal ground. The angle of depression of the top of a lighthouse, L, from the top of the cliff is 20°. The angle of elevation of L from the bottom of the cliff is 15°. Find the height of the lighthouse.

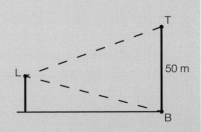

 The angle of elevation is the angle above the horizontal. The angle of depression is the angle below the horizontal.

Mixed practice 6

1. The area of the triangle shown in the diagram is $12\,\text{cm}^2$. Find the value of x.

2. The triangle shown in the diagram has angles θ and 2θ. Find the value of θ in degrees.

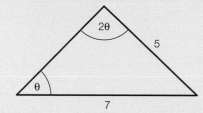

3. The area of the shaded region is $6.2\,\text{cm}^2$.
   (a) Show that $\theta - \sin\theta = 0.496$.
   (b) Find the value of θ in radians.

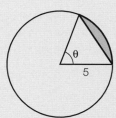

4. In the diagram, O is the centre of the circle and PT is the tangent to the circle at T. The radius of the circle is $7\,\text{cm}$ and the distance PT is $12\,\text{cm}$.
   (a) Find the area of triangle OPT.
   (b) Find the size of $\text{P}\hat{\text{O}}\text{T}$.
   (c) Find the area of the shaded region.

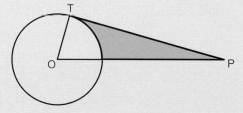

5. Two observers, positioned on horizontal ground at A and B, are trying to measure the height of a vertical tree, GT. The distance AB is $20\,\text{m}$, $\text{G}\hat{\text{A}}\text{B} = 65°$ and $\text{G}\hat{\text{B}}\text{A} = 80°$. From A, the angle of elevation of the top of the tree is $18°$.
   (a) Find the distance of A from the bottom of the tree.
   (b) Find the height of the tree.

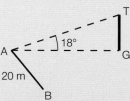

6. (a) Given that $\cot x + \tan x = 4$ and $x \in \left[0, \dfrac{\pi}{4}\right]$, find the exact value of $\tan x$.

   (b) (i) Show that $\cot x + \tan x = 2\csc 2x$.
       (ii) Hence solve the equation $\cot x + \tan x = 4$ for $x \in [0, \pi]$.

   (c) Find the exact value of $\tan\left(\dfrac{\pi}{12}\right)$.

7. Solve the equation $3\sin 2\theta = \tan 2\theta$ for $\theta \in \left[-\dfrac{\pi}{2}, \dfrac{\pi}{2}\right]$.

8. (a) The function f is defined by $f(x) = 3x^2 - 2x + 5$ for $-1 \le x \le 1$. Find the coordinates of the vertex of the graph of $y = f(x)$.

   (b) The function g is defined by $g(\theta) = 3\cos 2\theta - 4\cos \theta + 13$ for $0 \le \theta \le 2\pi$.

       (i) Show that $g(\theta) = 6\cos^2 \theta - 4\cos \theta + 10$.

       (ii) Hence find the minimum value of $g(\theta)$.

9. In the diagram, AC is the diameter of the semicircle, BD is perpendicular to AC, AB = 2 and BC = 1, and $B\hat{A}D = C\hat{A}E = \theta$. Let $R = AD - CE$.

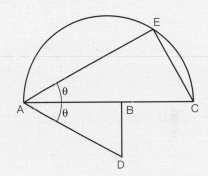

   (a) Find an expression for R in terms of θ.

   (b) Show that R has a stationary value when $2\sin \theta = 3\cos^3 \theta$.

   (c) Assuming that this stationary value is a minimum, find the smallest possible value of AD − CE.

Going for the top 6

1. Let $y = \cos x$.

   (a) Write $\cos 2x$ in terms of y.

   (b) Show that $\arccos(2y^2 - 1) = 2\arccos y$.

   (c) Evaluate $\arcsin y + \arccos y$.

2. The figure shown consists of three squares. Let $A\hat{D}B = \alpha$ and $A\hat{D}C = \beta$. Use a compound angle formula to find the sum $\alpha + \beta$.

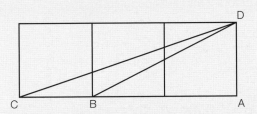

3. (a) Show that $\cos[(A - B)x] - \cos[(A + B)x] = 2\sin Ax \sin Bx$.

   (b) Hence show that $\displaystyle\sum_{r=1}^{n} \sin x \sin(2r - 1)x = \dfrac{1 - \cos 2nx}{2}$.

   (c) Solve the equation $\sin^2 x + \sin x \sin 3x = \dfrac{1}{4}$ if $0 < x < \pi$.

   (d) Evaluate $\sin \dfrac{\pi}{5} + \sin \dfrac{3\pi}{5} + \sin \dfrac{5\pi}{5} + \sin \dfrac{7\pi}{5} + \sin \dfrac{9\pi}{5}$.

7 VECTORS

WHAT YOU NEED TO KNOW

- A vector can represent the position of a point relative to the origin (position vector) or the displacement from one point to another.
  - The components of a position vector are the coordinates of the point.
  - If points A and B have position vectors a and b, the displacement vector $\overrightarrow{AB} = b - a$.
  - The position vector of the midpoint of [AB] is $\frac{1}{2}(a + b)$.
- A vector (in 3-dimensional space) can be represented by its components: $v = \begin{pmatrix} v_1 \\ v_2 \\ v_3 \end{pmatrix} = v_1 i + v_2 j + v_3 k$
  - The magnitude of v is $|v| = \sqrt{v_1^2 + v_2^2 + v_3^2}$.
  - The unit vector in the same direction as v is $\hat{v} = \frac{1}{|v|}v$.
  - The distance between two points A and B, with position vectors a and b, is $AB = |b - a|$.
- The scalar product (or dot product) can be used to calculate the angle between two vectors:

  $\cos\theta = \dfrac{v \cdot w}{|v||w|}$ where $v \cdot w = v_1 w_1 + v_2 w_2 + v_3 w_3$

  - If vectors a and b are perpendicular, $a \cdot b = 0$.
  - If vectors a and b are parallel, $a \cdot b = |a||b|$; in particular, $a \cdot a = |a|^2$.
  - The scalar product has many properties similar to those of multiplication:
    - $a \cdot b = b \cdot a$
    - $(ka) \cdot b = k(a \cdot b)$
    - $a \cdot (b + c) = a \cdot b + a \cdot c$
- The vector product (or cross product) of vectors v and w is denoted by $v \times w$:

  $v \times w = \begin{pmatrix} v_2 w_3 - v_3 w_2 \\ v_3 w_1 - v_1 w_3 \\ v_1 w_2 - v_2 w_1 \end{pmatrix}$

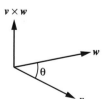

  - The magnitude of the vector product is:

    $|v \times w| = |v||w|\sin\theta$
  - The vector product can be used to find the area of some geometrical figures:
    - Area of parallelogram $= |v \times w|$
    - Area of triangle $= \frac{1}{2}|v \times w|$

    where v and w form two adjacent sides of the shape.

- If vectors a and b are perpendicular, $|a \times b| = |a||b|$.

- If vectors a and b are parallel, $a \times b = 0$; in particular, $a \times a = 0$.

- The vector product has many properties similar to those of multiplication:

  - $a \times b = -b \times a$

  - $(ka) \times b = k(a \times b)$

  - $a \times (b + c) = a \times b + a \times c$

- A straight line can be described by:

  - a Cartesian equation $\dfrac{x - a_1}{d_1} = \dfrac{y - a_2}{d_2} = \dfrac{z - a_3}{d_3}$

  - a vector equation $r = a + \lambda d$, where:

    - $d = \begin{pmatrix} d_1 \\ d_2 \\ d_3 \end{pmatrix}$ is the direction vector of the line

    - $A(a_1, a_2, a_3)$ is one point on the line.

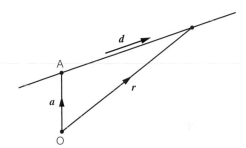

- A plane can be described by:

  - a Cartesian equation $n_1 x + n_2 y + n_3 z = a \cdot n$ (which can also be written in scalar product form $r \cdot n = a \cdot n$)

  - a vector equation $r = a + \lambda d_1 + \mu d_2$, where:

    - d_1 and d_2 are direction vectors of two lines in the plane

    - $n = \begin{pmatrix} n_1 \\ n_2 \\ n_3 \end{pmatrix}$ is the normal vector of the plane: $n = d_1 \times d_2$

    - $A(a_1, a_2, a_3)$ is one point in the plane.

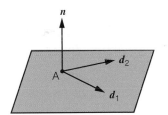

- To find the intersection:

  - of two lines, set the two position vectors equal to each other and use two of the equations to find the unknown parameters (checking that the parameter values satisfy the third equation)

  - between a line and a plane, substitute x, y and z from the equation of the line into the Cartesian equation of the plane, and solve to find the parameter

  - of two or three planes, solve the system of equations given by the Cartesian equations of the planes.

- To find the angle between two lines, two planes, or a line and a plane, identify two direction vectors which make the required angle, and then use $\cos \theta = \dfrac{v \cdot w}{|v||w|}$.

- The shortest distance between:

  - a point and a line occurs when the connecting vector is perpendicular to the direction vector of the line

  - a point and a plane occurs along a normal vector to the plane

  - two lines occurs when the connecting vector is perpendicular to the direction vectors of both lines.

  Although not required by the syllabus, the following formulae may be useful for finding shortest distances.

  - The shortest distance between the line $r = a + \lambda d$ and the point with position vector b is $\dfrac{|(a - b) \times d|}{|d|}$.

  - The shortest distance between the lines $r = a_1 + \lambda d_1$ and $r = a_2 + \lambda d_2$ is $\dfrac{|(a_2 - a_1) \cdot n|}{|n|}$, where $n = d_1 \times d_2$.

- An object starting at the point with position vector a and moving with (constant) velocity vector v moves along a path given by $r = a + tv$, where t is the time after the start of the motion.

 EXAM TIPS AND COMMON ERRORS

- Use a vector diagram to show all the given information and add to it as you work through a question.

- To *show* that two vectors are perpendicular, use $a \cdot b = 0$. To *find* a vector perpendicular to two given vectors, use $a \times b$.

- Be careful with the vector product: $a \times b = -b \times a$. (Note the negative sign; it **is not** true that $a \times b = b \times a$.)

- In long questions, it may be possible to answer a later part without having done all the previous parts.

- Be clear on the difference between the coordinates of a point, (a_1, a_2, a_3), and the position vector of the point, $\begin{pmatrix} a_1 \\ a_2 \\ a_3 \end{pmatrix}$.

7.1 PROVING GEOMETRICAL PROPERTIES USING VECTORS

WORKED EXAMPLE 7.1

ABCD is a square. Points M, N, P and Q lie on the sides [AB], [BC], [CD] and [DA] so that
$AM:MB = BN:NC = CP:PD = DQ:QA = 2:1$. Let $\overrightarrow{AB} = \boldsymbol{b}$ and $\overrightarrow{AD} = \boldsymbol{d}$.

Prove that [QN] and [MP] are perpendicular.

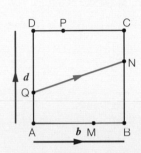

> ⚠ Always draw a diagram for questions involving geometrical figures.

$$\overrightarrow{QN} = \overrightarrow{QD} + \overrightarrow{DC} + \overrightarrow{CN}$$

$$= \frac{2}{3}\boldsymbol{d} + \boldsymbol{b} + \frac{1}{3}(-\boldsymbol{d})$$

$$= \boldsymbol{b} + \frac{1}{3}\boldsymbol{d}$$

> We need an expression for $\overrightarrow{QN}$ in terms of $\boldsymbol{b}$ and $\boldsymbol{d}$. Note that a ratio of $2:1$ means $\frac{2}{3}$ and $\frac{1}{3}$, respectively, of the total length, and that moving backwards along a vector (in this case $\boldsymbol{d}$) means a negative sign.

$$\overrightarrow{MP} = \overrightarrow{MB} + \overrightarrow{BC} + \overrightarrow{CP}$$

$$= \frac{1}{3}\boldsymbol{b} + \boldsymbol{d} + \frac{2}{3}(-\boldsymbol{b}) = -\frac{1}{3}\boldsymbol{b} + \boldsymbol{d}$$

> Similarly, we find an expression for $\overrightarrow{MP}$ in terms of $\boldsymbol{b}$ and $\boldsymbol{d}$.

$$\overrightarrow{MP} \cdot \overrightarrow{QN} = \left(-\frac{1}{3}\boldsymbol{b} + \boldsymbol{d}\right) \cdot \left(\boldsymbol{b} + \frac{1}{3}\boldsymbol{d}\right)$$

> To prove that $\overrightarrow{MP}$ and $\overrightarrow{QN}$ are perpendicular, we need to show that $\overrightarrow{MP} \cdot \overrightarrow{QN} = 0$.

$$= -\frac{1}{3}\boldsymbol{b} \cdot \boldsymbol{b} + \boldsymbol{d} \cdot \boldsymbol{b} - \frac{1}{9}\boldsymbol{b} \cdot \boldsymbol{d} + \frac{1}{3}\boldsymbol{d} \cdot \boldsymbol{d}$$

> The brackets can be expanded with the scalar product just as with normal multiplication.

$$= -\frac{1}{3}|\boldsymbol{b}|^2 + \boldsymbol{b} \cdot \boldsymbol{d} - \frac{1}{9}\boldsymbol{b} \cdot \boldsymbol{d} + \frac{1}{3}|\boldsymbol{d}|^2$$

> Use the facts that $\boldsymbol{b} \cdot \boldsymbol{d} = \boldsymbol{d} \cdot \boldsymbol{b}$ and $\boldsymbol{b} \cdot \boldsymbol{b} = |\boldsymbol{b}|^2$.

$$= \frac{8}{9}\boldsymbol{b} \cdot \boldsymbol{d} = 0$$

Hence [QN] and [MP] are perpendicular.

> Since the sides of a square have equal length and are perpendicular, $|\boldsymbol{b}| = |\boldsymbol{d}|$ and $\boldsymbol{b} \cdot \boldsymbol{d} = 0$.

Practice questions 7.1

1. Points A, B, C and D have position vectors $\boldsymbol{a}, \boldsymbol{b}, \boldsymbol{c}$ and $\boldsymbol{d}$, respectively. M is the midpoint of [AB] and N is the midpoint of [BC].

(a) Express $\overrightarrow{MN}$ in terms of $\boldsymbol{a}, \boldsymbol{b}$ and $\boldsymbol{c}$.

P is the midpoint of [CD] and Q is the midpoint of [DA].

(b) By finding an expression for $\overrightarrow{QP}$ in terms of $\boldsymbol{a}, \boldsymbol{c}$ and $\boldsymbol{d}$, show that MNPQ is a parallelogram.

7.2 APPLICATIONS OF THE VECTOR PRODUCT

WORKED EXAMPLE 7.2

Points A, B and C have coordinates $(-3, 1, 5)$, $(1, 1, 2)$ and $(1, -2, 7)$, respectively.

(a) Find a vector perpendicular to both (AB) and (AC).

(b) Find the area of the triangle ABC.

> ⚠️ Remember that (AB) represents the line through A and B (infinite), while [AB] is the line segment (finite) and AB means the length of [AB].

(a)
$$\overrightarrow{AB} \times \overrightarrow{AC} = \begin{pmatrix} 4 \\ 0 \\ -3 \end{pmatrix} \times \begin{pmatrix} 4 \\ -3 \\ 2 \end{pmatrix}$$

$$= \begin{pmatrix} 0-9 \\ -12-8 \\ -12-0 \end{pmatrix} = \begin{pmatrix} -9 \\ -20 \\ -12 \end{pmatrix}$$

> The vector product of two vectors is perpendicular to both of them, and we calculate this using the formula $\boldsymbol{a} \times \boldsymbol{b} = \begin{pmatrix} a_2b_3 - a_3b_2 \\ a_3b_1 - a_1b_3 \\ a_1b_2 - a_2b_1 \end{pmatrix}$.

(b) Area $= \dfrac{1}{2}\left|\overrightarrow{AB} \times \overrightarrow{AC}\right|$

$$= \dfrac{1}{2}\sqrt{(-9)^2 + (-20)^2 + (-12)^2} = 12.5$$

> We can find the area of a triangle with sides $\boldsymbol{a}$ and $\boldsymbol{b}$ using the formula $\dfrac{1}{2}|\boldsymbol{a} \times \boldsymbol{b}|$, but note that we have to use the actual vectors $\overrightarrow{AB}$ and $\overrightarrow{AC}$ rather than any other parallel vectors (that is, we must not 'simplify' either vector by dividing through by a common factor).

Practice questions 7.2

2. Three points A, B and C are such that $\overrightarrow{AB} = 3\boldsymbol{i} - \boldsymbol{j} + 5\boldsymbol{k}$ and $\overrightarrow{AC} = -\boldsymbol{i} + 3\boldsymbol{j} + \boldsymbol{k}$.
   (a) Calculate $\overrightarrow{AB} \times \overrightarrow{AC}$.
   (b) Find the area of the triangle ABC.

3. Let $\boldsymbol{p} = \boldsymbol{i} + \boldsymbol{j} + 3\boldsymbol{k}$ and $\boldsymbol{q} = \boldsymbol{i} - 3\boldsymbol{k}$.
   (a) Calculate $\boldsymbol{p} \times \boldsymbol{q}$.
   (b) Find a unit vector perpendicular to both $\boldsymbol{p}$ and $\boldsymbol{q}$.

7.3 EQUATION OF A LINE AND THE INTERSECTION OF LINES

WORKED EXAMPLE 7.3

(a) Find a vector equation of the line l_1 passing through points A(2, 1, 3) and B(−1, 1, 2).

(b) Show that l_1 does not intersect the line with equation $\dfrac{x-1}{2} = y+1 = \dfrac{z}{3}$.

(a) $r = a + \lambda d$

$$d = \overrightarrow{AB} = b - a = \begin{pmatrix} -1 \\ 1 \\ 2 \end{pmatrix} - \begin{pmatrix} 2 \\ 1 \\ 3 \end{pmatrix} = \begin{pmatrix} -3 \\ 0 \\ -1 \end{pmatrix}$$

> We need the position vector of one point on the line and the direction vector of the line: a is the position vector of point A on the line, and $\overrightarrow{AB}$ is a vector in the direction of the line.

So a vector equation is $r = \begin{pmatrix} 2 \\ 1 \\ 3 \end{pmatrix} + \lambda \begin{pmatrix} -3 \\ 0 \\ -1 \end{pmatrix}$

> ⚠ We could also have used b as the point on the line and/or taken $\overrightarrow{BA}$ to be our d.

(b) For l_1: $r = \begin{pmatrix} x \\ y \\ z \end{pmatrix} = \begin{pmatrix} 2-3\lambda \\ 1 \\ 3-\lambda \end{pmatrix}$

$\therefore x = 2-3\lambda,\ y = 1,\ z = 3-\lambda$

> By letting $r = \begin{pmatrix} x \\ y \\ z \end{pmatrix}$ in the equation for l_1 and combining the two vectors on the RHS into one, we can get expressions for x, y and z.

Substitute into the equation of l_2:

$$\frac{(2-3\lambda)-1}{2} = (1)+1 = \frac{(3-\lambda)}{3}$$

> If l_1 and l_2 intersect, there must be a solution for λ when the equations of the two lines are solved simultaneously.

$$\therefore \begin{cases} \dfrac{1-3\lambda}{2} = 2 \Rightarrow \lambda = -1 \\[2mm] 2 = \dfrac{3-\lambda}{3} \Rightarrow \lambda = -3 \end{cases}$$

> We can split the equation for l_2 into two separate equations.
>
> Because these two equations do not have a common solution for λ, the lines do not intersect.

λ value not consistent, so the lines do not intersect.

Practice questions 7.3

4. (a) Find a vector equation of the line passing through the points A(−3, 1, 2) and B(−3, 3, 7).

   (b) Find the coordinates of the point where this line meets the line with equation
   $$\frac{x-1}{-2} = \frac{y+1}{3} = \frac{z+2}{7}.$$

5. Determine whether the lines $r = \begin{pmatrix} 2 \\ 3 \\ 8 \end{pmatrix} + s \begin{pmatrix} 1 \\ 4 \\ 0 \end{pmatrix}$ and $r = \begin{pmatrix} 5 \\ 1 \\ 3 \end{pmatrix} + t \begin{pmatrix} -1 \\ 10 \\ 2 \end{pmatrix}$ intersect. If they do, find the point of intersection.

7.4 EQUATION OF A PLANE

WORKED EXAMPLE 7.4

Find the Cartesian equation of the plane containing the point A(3, 1, 4) and the line with equation
$$r = \begin{pmatrix} 1 \\ 1 \\ 2 \end{pmatrix} + t \begin{pmatrix} -1 \\ 1 \\ 0 \end{pmatrix}.$$

$$d_1 = \begin{pmatrix} -1 \\ 1 \\ 0 \end{pmatrix}$$

$$d_2 = \begin{pmatrix} 3 \\ 1 \\ 4 \end{pmatrix} - \begin{pmatrix} 1 \\ 1 \\ 2 \end{pmatrix} = \begin{pmatrix} 2 \\ 0 \\ 2 \end{pmatrix}$$

$$\therefore n = d_1 \times d_2 = \begin{pmatrix} -1 \\ 1 \\ 0 \end{pmatrix} \times \begin{pmatrix} 2 \\ 0 \\ 2 \end{pmatrix} = \begin{pmatrix} 2 \\ 2 \\ -2 \end{pmatrix}$$

We need a normal vector to the plane; this will be perpendicular to two vectors that lie in the plane. One such vector is the direction vector of the line and the other can be found by noting that (1, 1, 2) from the equation of the line (as well as point A) lies in the plane.

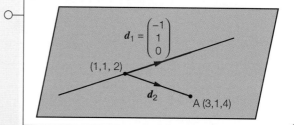

$$r \cdot n = a \cdot n$$

$$\begin{pmatrix} x \\ y \\ z \end{pmatrix} \cdot \begin{pmatrix} 2 \\ 2 \\ -2 \end{pmatrix} = \begin{pmatrix} 3 \\ 1 \\ 4 \end{pmatrix} \cdot \begin{pmatrix} 2 \\ 2 \\ -2 \end{pmatrix}$$

For the point in the plane, we can use A.

To get the Cartesian equation, write r as $\begin{pmatrix} x \\ y \\ z \end{pmatrix}$.

$$\Leftrightarrow 2x + 2y - 2z = 6 + 2 - 8$$
$$\Leftrightarrow 2x + 2y - 2z = 0$$
$$\Leftrightarrow x + y - z = 0$$

Practice questions 7.4

6. Find the Cartesian equation of the plane containing the line with equation $r = \begin{pmatrix} 2 \\ 1 \\ 1 \end{pmatrix} + t \begin{pmatrix} -1 \\ 1 \\ 2 \end{pmatrix}$ and the point (4, 1, 2).

7. Find the Cartesian equation of the plane containing the points A(−1, 1, 2), B(3, 2, 1) and C(0, 0, 5).

8. (a) Find the coordinates of the point of intersection of the lines with equations
   $r = (2i + j + 7k) + \lambda(-i + 2j + 3k)$ and $r = (2i + 2j + k) + \mu(-2i + 3j + 12k)$.
   (b) Find the Cartesian equation of the plane containing the two lines.

7.5 INTERSECTIONS INVOLVING PLANES

WORKED EXAMPLE 7.5

 Find a vector equation of the line of intersection of the planes $2x - y + z = 3$ and $x - y - 2z = 7$.

$\begin{cases} 2x - y + z = 3 & \cdots (1) \\ x - y - 2z = 7 & \cdots (2) \end{cases}$

$(1) - 2 \times (2) \begin{cases} 2x - y + z = 3 & \cdots (1) \\ y + 5z = -11 & \cdots (3) \end{cases}$

> The points on the line of intersection satisfy both equations, so we need to solve the pair of equations using elimination.
> We start by eliminating x.

◀◀ Systems of equations are covered in Chapter 4.

Let $z = t$.

From (3): $y = -11 - 5t$. Substitute into (1):

$x = \dfrac{3 + y - z}{2}$

$= \dfrac{3 + (-11 - 5t) - t}{2}$

$= \dfrac{-8 - 6t}{2}$

$= -4 - 3t$

> Since there are three unknowns but only two equations, we cannot find a unique solution; however, we can express both x and y in terms of z.

$\therefore \begin{pmatrix} x \\ y \\ z \end{pmatrix} = \begin{pmatrix} -4 - 3t \\ -11 - 5t \\ 0 + 1t \end{pmatrix}$

> Let (x, y, z) be the coordinates of any point on the line of intersection. To find the vector equation of the line, write the coordinates as a position vector.

$\Rightarrow r = \begin{pmatrix} -4 \\ -11 \\ 0 \end{pmatrix} + t \begin{pmatrix} -3 \\ -5 \\ 1 \end{pmatrix}$

> Finally, write the equation of the line in the form $r = a + td$.

Practice questions 7.5

9. Find a vector equation of the line of intersection of the planes with equations $3x - y + z = 16$ and $x - 2y + 2z = 12$.

10. Find the coordinates of the point where the line with equation $r = (5i + j + 2k) + \lambda(i - 3j + k)$ meets the plane with equation $x + 2y + z = 11$.

11. Find the coordinates of the point of intersection of the planes $\Pi_1: x + y - 3z = -9$, $\Pi_2: 3x + y = 2$ and $\Pi_3: x + y + z = 3$.

7.6 ANGLES BETWEEN LINES AND PLANES

WORKED EXAMPLE 7.6

Find the angle between the line with equation $r = (-i + 2j + 3k) + \lambda(2i + j - 2k)$ and the plane with equation $2x + 3y - 7z = 5$.

A normal to the plane $2x + 3y - 7z = 5$ is $n = \begin{pmatrix} 2 \\ 3 \\ -7 \end{pmatrix}$

> Since the Cartesian equation of a plane is derived from the vector equation $r \cdot n = a \cdot n$ with $r = \begin{pmatrix} x \\ y \\ z \end{pmatrix}$, we can see that $n = \begin{pmatrix} 2 \\ 3 \\ -7 \end{pmatrix}$.

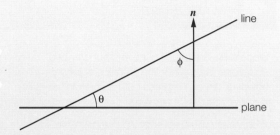

> A diagram clarifies the relationship between the normal, the line and the angle (θ) between the line and the plane.

$$\cos\phi = \frac{d \cdot n}{|d||n|}$$

> We cannot find θ directly, but we can find the angle ϕ between the line and the normal by using the scalar product formula.

$$= \frac{\begin{pmatrix} 2 \\ 1 \\ -2 \end{pmatrix} \cdot \begin{pmatrix} 2 \\ 3 \\ -7 \end{pmatrix}}{\sqrt{2^2 + 1^2 + (-2)^2}\sqrt{2^2 + 3^2 + (-7)^2}}$$

 ! When finding the angle between two lines, always use the direction vectors of the lines in the scalar product formula.

$$= \frac{21}{\sqrt{9}\sqrt{62}}$$

$$\therefore \phi = 27.3°$$

So, $\theta = 90° - \phi = 62.7°$

> Now we can find the required angle θ.

Practice questions 7.6

12. Find the angle between the lines $r = (i + 2k) + \lambda(3i + 4j + 12k)$ and $r = -2j + \mu(2i + 2j + k)$.

13. Find the acute angle that the line with equation $r = 4j + \lambda(2i - j + 5k)$ makes with the y-axis.

14. Find the acute angle between the line $\dfrac{x+6}{-2} = \dfrac{y-2}{3} = \dfrac{z+4}{-6}$ and the plane $2x - 6y + 5z = 63$.

15. (a) Write down a normal to each of the planes $\Pi_1: x - 2y - 5z = 7$ and $\Pi_2: 3x - 7y - z = 4$.
   (b) Hence find the angle between the planes Π_1 and Π_2.

7.7 DISTANCES FROM LINES AND PLANES

WORKED EXAMPLE 7.7

Find the shortest distance between the lines $r = i + 2k + \lambda(i - j + k)$ and $r = 11j + \mu(2i - k)$.

Consider a general point P on the line l_1 and a general point Q on the line l_2. Then

$$p = \begin{pmatrix} 1+\lambda \\ -\lambda \\ 2+\lambda \end{pmatrix} \quad \text{and} \quad q = \begin{pmatrix} 2\mu \\ 11 \\ -\mu \end{pmatrix}$$

> The position vector of any point on a line is given by the equation of that line.

$$\overrightarrow{QP} = p - q = \begin{pmatrix} 1+\lambda \\ -\lambda \\ 2+\lambda \end{pmatrix} - \begin{pmatrix} 2\mu \\ 11 \\ -\mu \end{pmatrix} = \begin{pmatrix} 1+\lambda-2\mu \\ -\lambda-11 \\ 2+\lambda+\mu \end{pmatrix}$$

> We can now find a general vector, $\overrightarrow{QP}$, connecting the two lines.

$$\begin{pmatrix} 1+\lambda-2\mu \\ -\lambda-11 \\ 2+\lambda+\mu \end{pmatrix} \cdot \begin{pmatrix} 1 \\ -1 \\ 1 \end{pmatrix} = 0 \quad \text{and} \quad \begin{pmatrix} 1+\lambda-2\mu \\ -\lambda-11 \\ 2+\lambda+\mu \end{pmatrix} \cdot \begin{pmatrix} 2 \\ 0 \\ -1 \end{pmatrix} = 0$$

> This connecting vector will be shortest when it is perpendicular to the direction vectors of both lines.

 In any question involving the shortest distance, a perpendicular vector is always needed.

$$\Leftrightarrow \begin{cases} (1+\lambda-2\mu)+(\lambda+11)+(2+\lambda+\mu)=0 \\ (2+2\lambda-4\mu)+0-(2+\lambda+\mu)=0 \end{cases}$$

> Use a GDC to solve the simultaneous equations.

$$\Leftrightarrow \lambda=-5, \mu=-1$$

$$\therefore \overrightarrow{QP} = \begin{pmatrix} 1-5+2 \\ 5-11 \\ 2-5-1 \end{pmatrix} = \begin{pmatrix} -2 \\ -6 \\ -4 \end{pmatrix}$$

> Substitute back to find $\overrightarrow{QP}$.

$$d = |\overrightarrow{QP}| = \sqrt{(-2)^2 + (-6)^2 + (-4)^2} = 2\sqrt{14} \approx 7.48$$

> The distance is the length of $\overrightarrow{QP}$.

Practice questions 7.7

16. Find the perpendicular distance from A(1, 1, 2) to the line $r = (i - 2j + 3k) + t(i + 2k)$.

17. The point M has position vector $2i - 3j + k$ and the plane Π has equation $3x - y + z = 17$.
    (a) Write down the equation of the line through M which is perpendicular to Π.
    (b) Hence find the distance from the point M to the plane Π.

18. Find the shortest distance between the lines $r = (i - k) + \lambda(i + j + k)$ and $\dfrac{x-2}{3} = \dfrac{y+1}{4} = \dfrac{z-3}{5}$.

7.8 APPLYING VECTORS TO MOTION

WORKED EXAMPLE 7.8

An aircraft taking off from $0i + 10j + 0k$ km moves with velocity $150i + 150j + 40k$ km h^{-1}, where the vector i represents East, j represents North and k represents vertically up.

(a) If t is the time in hours, write down a vector equation for the motion of the aircraft.

(b) Find the speed of the aircraft.

(c) Find the angle of elevation of the aircraft.

(a) $r = \begin{pmatrix} 0 \\ 10 \\ 0 \end{pmatrix} + t \begin{pmatrix} 150 \\ 150 \\ 40 \end{pmatrix}$

> We can use the standard form $r = a + tv$ to describe the path of the aircraft.

> ⚠ You can use either i, j, k notation or column vector notation, whichever you are more comfortable with, but do not forget that an equation needs '$r =$'.

(b) Speed $= \sqrt{150^2 + 150^2 + 40^2} \approx 216$ km h^{-1}

> Speed is the modulus of the velocity vector.

(c) The resultant speed of the components in the easterly and northerly directions is:
$\sqrt{150^2 + 150^2} \approx 212$ km h^{-1}

So the angle of elevation θ satisfies

$\tan\theta = \dfrac{40}{212}$

$\therefore \theta \approx 10.7°$

> The velocity is made up of a component 'along the ground' (the resultant of the i and j components) and a vertical (k) component.

> ⚠ Even though 212 km h^{-1} is written in the working, the calculation should be done using the full accuracy stored in the calculator.

Practice questions 7.8

19. The path of a flying bird is modelled by $r = 4ti + 6tj + (12 - t)k$ metres where t is in seconds.

    (a) Find the speed of the bird.

    (b) Find the angle of depression of its flight.

    (c) How far has the bird travelled when it lands on the ground?

20. A ship starts at $0i + 0j$ km and moves with velocity $20i + 5j$ km h^{-1}. A second ship starts at $7i + 12j$ km and moves with velocity $-19i - 8j$ km h^{-1}. Show that the ships have the same speed but do not collide.

Mixed practice 7

1. Let $a = \begin{pmatrix} 3 \\ -1 \\ 2 \end{pmatrix}$, $b = \begin{pmatrix} 1 \\ 1 \\ p \end{pmatrix}$ and $c = \begin{pmatrix} 2 \\ 22 \\ 8 \end{pmatrix}$.

    (a) Find $a \times b$.

    (b) Find the value of p such that $a \times b$ is parallel to c.

2. Point A has position vector $3i + 2j - k$. Point D lies on the line with equation $r = (i - j + 5k) + \lambda(-i + j - 2k)$. Find the value of λ such that (AD) is parallel to the x-axis.

3. Two vectors are given by $a = \begin{pmatrix} \sin\theta \\ \cos\theta \end{pmatrix}$ and $b = \begin{pmatrix} \cos\theta \\ \sin 2\theta \end{pmatrix}$, where $\theta \in [0, 2\pi]$. Find all possible values of θ for which a and b are perpendicular.

4. Three points have coordinates A(3, 1, 1), B(4, 1, 3) and C(3, $q + 1$, $q +1$), where $q > 0$.

    (a) Find a vector perpendicular to both $\overrightarrow{AB}$ and $\overrightarrow{AC}$.

    (b) Given that the area of the triangle ABC is $6\sqrt{2}$, find the value of q.

    (c) Find the Cartesian equation of the plane containing the points A, B and C.

5. (a) Find a vector equation of the line l passing through the points P(3, −1, 2) and Q(−1, 1, 7).

    (b) The point M has position vector $3i - 4j + k$. Find the acute angle between (PM) and l.

    (c) Hence find the shortest distance from M to the line l.

6. Three points have coordinates A(3, 0, 2), B(−1, 4, 1) and C(−4, 1, 3). Find the coordinates of point D such that ABCD is a parallelogram.

7. The tetrahedron MABC has vertices with coordinates A(1, −1, 3), B(2, 1, 2), C(0, 1, 5) and M(9, 2, 5).

    (a) (i) Calculate $\overrightarrow{AB} \times \overrightarrow{AC}$.

    (ii) Find the Cartesian equation of the plane ABC.

    (b) (i) Write down the equation of the line through M which is perpendicular to the plane ABC.

    (ii) Find the coordinates of the foot of the perpendicular from M to the plane ABC.

    (iii) Hence find the volume of the tetrahedron.

    (c) Calculate the angle between the edge [MB] and the base ABC.

8. The angle between vectors $p = i + 2j + 2k$ and $q = xi + xj + 2k$ is 60°.

    (a) Find constants a, b and c such that $ax^2 + bx + c = 0$.

    (b) Hence find the angle between the vector q and the z-axis.

9. PQRS is a rhombus with $\overrightarrow{PQ} = \boldsymbol{a}$ and $\overrightarrow{QR} = \boldsymbol{b}$. The midpoints of the sides [PQ], [QR], [RS] and [SP] are A, B, C and D, respectively.

   (a) Express $\overrightarrow{AB}$ and $\overrightarrow{BC}$ in terms of $\boldsymbol{a}$ and $\boldsymbol{b}$.

   (b) (i) Explain why $\boldsymbol{a} \cdot \boldsymbol{a} = \boldsymbol{b} \cdot \boldsymbol{b}$.

       (ii) Show that [AB] and [BC] are perpendicular.

   (c) What type of quadrilateral is ABCD?

10. Three points have coordinates A(4, 1, 2), B(1, 5, 1) and C(λ, λ, 3).

   (a) Find the value of λ for which the triangle ABC has a right angle at B.

   (b) For this value of λ, find the coordinates of point D on the side [AC] such that AD = 2DC.

11. Find the angle between the two planes with equations $2x + 3y - 4z = 5$ and $6x - 2y - 3z = 4$.

12. (a) Show that the point A with coordinates $(-1, 5, 3)$ does not lie on the line l with equation
$$r = \begin{pmatrix} -2 \\ 3 \\ 1 \end{pmatrix} + \lambda \begin{pmatrix} 1 \\ 2 \\ -1 \end{pmatrix}.$$

   (b) Find the coordinates of the point B on l such that [AB] is perpendicular to l.

13. (a) Find the coordinates of the point Q where the line l_1, with equation $r = \begin{pmatrix} 1 \\ -1 \\ 3 \end{pmatrix} + t \begin{pmatrix} 1 \\ 1 \\ 3 \end{pmatrix}$, meets the plane with equation $x - 3y + z = 17$.

   (b) Write down the equation of the line l_2 through Q which is parallel to the line with equation $\dfrac{x+1}{3} = \dfrac{2-y}{7} = \dfrac{z}{3}$.

   (c) Find the angle between l_1 and l_2.

14. The line l_1 has vector equation $r = \lambda \begin{pmatrix} 3 \\ 5 \\ 1 \end{pmatrix}$ and the line l_2 has vector equation $r = \begin{pmatrix} 9 \\ 15 \\ 3 \end{pmatrix} + \mu \begin{pmatrix} 2 \\ 0 \\ -1 \end{pmatrix}$.

   (a) Show that the two lines meet and find the point of intersection.

   (b) Find the angle between the two lines.

   Two flies are flying in an empty room. One fly starts in a corner at position (0, 0, 0) and every second flies 3 cm in the x direction, 5 cm in the y direction and 1 cm up in the vertical z direction.

   (c) Find the speed of this fly.

   The second fly starts at the point (9, 15, 3) cm and each second travels 2 cm in the x direction and 1 cm down in the vertical z direction.

   (d) Show that the two flies do not meet.

   (e) Find the distance between the flies when they are at the same height.

   (f) Find the minimum distance between the two flies.

Going for the top 7

1. Two unit vectors $\boldsymbol{a}$ and $\boldsymbol{b}$ are given such that $|\boldsymbol{a}+2\boldsymbol{b}| = |\boldsymbol{b}-2\boldsymbol{a}|$.

   (a) Find the value of $\boldsymbol{a} \cdot \boldsymbol{b}$.

   (b) Hence find the angle between $\boldsymbol{a}$ and $\boldsymbol{b}$.

2. Two lines have vector equations $l_1 : \boldsymbol{r} = \begin{pmatrix} 1 \\ 3 \\ 1 \end{pmatrix} + \lambda \begin{pmatrix} 1 \\ -1 \\ 2 \end{pmatrix}$ and $l_2 : \boldsymbol{r} = \begin{pmatrix} 5 \\ -1 \\ -6 \end{pmatrix} + \mu \begin{pmatrix} 1 \\ 1 \\ 3 \end{pmatrix}$.

   Points A on l_1 and B on l_2 are such that (AB) is perpendicular to both lines.

   (a) Show that $\mu_A - \lambda_B = 1$.

   (b) Find another linear equation connecting λ_B and μ_A.

   (c) Hence find the shortest distance between the two lines.

3. Three planes have equations: $\Pi_1 : x - 2y + z = 0$, $\Pi_2 : 3x - z = 4$ and $\Pi_3 : x + y - z = k$.

   (a) Show that for all values of k, the planes do not intersect at a unique point.

   (b) Find the value of k for which the intersection of the three planes is a line, and find the vector equation of this line.

4. Two planes have equations $\Pi_1 : x - 2y + 3z = 7$ and $\Pi_2 : x - 2y + 3z = -21$. By finding the shortest distance between each plane and the origin, determine the distance between Π_1 and Π_2.

8 COMPLEX NUMBERS

WHAT YOU NEED TO KNOW

- A complex number, z, is a number that can be written in the form $z = a + b\mathrm{i}$ (Cartesian form), where a and b are real numbers and $\mathrm{i}^2 = -1$:

    - a is the real part of z, written as $\mathrm{Re}(z)$.

    - b is the imaginary part of z, written as $\mathrm{Im}(z)$.

    - The complex conjugate of z, written as z^*, is $a - b\mathrm{i}$.

- If two complex numbers are equal, their real parts are the same and their imaginary parts are the same.

- Complex numbers can be represented on an Argand diagram with the real part on the x-axis and the imaginary part on the y-axis.

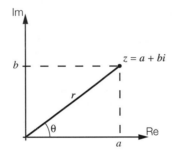

- The distance of the complex number from the origin is called the modulus of z, written as $|z|$ or r. There are two important formulae for $|z|$:

    - $|z| = \sqrt{a^2 + b^2}$

    - $|z|^2 = zz^*$

- The anticlockwise angle the complex number makes with the positive real axis is called the argument of z, written as $\arg z$ or θ:

    - $\tan\theta = \dfrac{b}{a}$

- From this information, a complex number can also be described in polar form:

    - $z = r(\cos\theta + \mathrm{i}\sin\theta) = r\operatorname{cis}\theta = r\mathrm{e}^{\mathrm{i}\theta}$

- Arithmetic with complex numbers depends upon the operation and the form used.

  - In Cartesian form:

    - Addition, subtraction and multiplication are done in the same way as for normal numbers.

    - To divide two complex numbers, multiply the top and bottom of the fraction by the complex conjugate of the denominator: $\dfrac{z}{w} = \dfrac{zw^*}{ww^*} = \dfrac{1}{|w|^2} zw^*$.

  - In polar form:

    - Add complex numbers on an Argand diagram like vectors.

    - To multiply two complex numbers, multiply their moduli and add their arguments:

      $|zw| = |z||w| \qquad \arg(zw) = \arg z + \arg w$

    - To divide two numbers, divide their moduli and subtract their arguments:

      $\left|\dfrac{z}{w}\right| = \dfrac{|z|}{|w|} \qquad \arg\left(\dfrac{z}{w}\right) = \arg z - \arg w$

- De Moivre's theorem is a way of raising a complex number to a power:

  $$\left[r(\cos\theta + \mathrm{i}\sin\theta)\right]^n = r^n(\cos n\theta + \mathrm{i}\sin n\theta) = r^n \mathrm{e}^{\mathrm{i}n\theta} = r^n \operatorname{cis} n\theta$$

  ▶▶ You need to be able to prove De Moivre's theorem using the principle of mathematical induction. Mathematical induction is covered in Chapter 12, and a proof of this result is given as a worked solution to Mixed practice question 9 in that chapter.

- To solve equations:

  - If the equation involves complex conjugates, substitute in $z = a + b\mathrm{i}$ and $z^* = a - b\mathrm{i}$ and equate the real and imaginary parts on each side of the equation.

  - If the equation involves moduli, substitute in $z = a + b\mathrm{i}$ and use $|w|^2 = \left[\operatorname{Re}(w)\right]^2 + \left[\operatorname{Im}(w)\right]^2$.

    - It may be necessary to square both sides of the equation first or use $|z|^2 = zz^*$.

- A polynomial (with real coefficients) has roots that either are real or come in complex conjugate pairs – that is, if w is a root then so is w^*.

  - This means that the polynomial has a factor $(z - w)(z - w^*)$.

  - A useful shortcut is that if $w = a + b\mathrm{i}$, then $(z - w)(z - w^*) = z^2 - 2az + (a^2 + b^2)$.

- To express multiple angles of trigonometric functions (for example, $\sin n\theta$) in terms of powers of those functions, use De Moivre's theorem, $\cos n\theta + \mathrm{i}\sin n\theta = (\cos\theta + \mathrm{i}\sin\theta)^n$:

  - Expand the right-hand side using the binomial expansion.

  - Equate the real parts to get an expression for $\cos n\theta$, and equate the imaginary parts to get an expression for $\sin n\theta$.

- To express powers of trigonometric functions (for example, $\sin^n\theta$) in terms of functions of multiple angles, there are two groups of identities that can be used:

    - $\sin\theta = \dfrac{e^{i\theta} - e^{-i\theta}}{2i}$ and $\cos\theta = \dfrac{e^{i\theta} + e^{-i\theta}}{2}$

    - $z^n + \dfrac{1}{z^n} = 2\cos n\theta$ and $z^n - \dfrac{1}{z^n} = 2i\sin n\theta$ (proved using De Moivre's theorem)

- To solve equations of the form $z^n = w$:

    - Write w in polar form.

    - Let $z = r\operatorname{cis}\theta$ and apply De Moivre's theorem to get $z^n = r^n\operatorname{cis}n\theta$.

    - Find r and all possible values of θ.

        - Since $\operatorname{cis}(\theta) = \operatorname{cis}(\theta + 2\pi) = \operatorname{cis}(\theta + 4\pi) = \ldots$, there are n possible values of θ and the equation will have n solutions which form a regular polygon with vertices on a circle.

    - A special case is the solutions of the equation $z^n = 1$, called the roots of unity. They are $1, \operatorname{cis}\left(\dfrac{2\pi}{n}\right), \operatorname{cis}\left(\dfrac{4\pi}{n}\right), \ldots, \operatorname{cis}\left(\dfrac{2(n-1)\pi}{n}\right)$. They can also be written as $1, \omega, \omega^2, \ldots, \omega^{n-1}$, where $\omega = \operatorname{cis}\left(\dfrac{2\pi}{n}\right)$, and they lie on the unit circle.

 EXAM TIPS AND COMMON ERRORS

- Remember that the imaginary part is itself real; so $\operatorname{Im}(z) = b$ not bi.

- The fact that $\tan(\arg z) = \dfrac{y}{x}$ does not mean that $\arg z = \arctan\left(\dfrac{y}{x}\right)$. It could also be $\arctan\left(\dfrac{y}{x}\right) + \pi$. To distinguish between these cases, you need to think about which quadrant of the Argand diagram the complex number is in. It is always a good idea to sketch the diagram.

- Most graphical calculators can do complex arithmetic. You must be able to work quickly and accurately both with and without a calculator.

8.1 SOLVING EQUATIONS INVOLVING COMPLEX NUMBERS

WORKED EXAMPLE 8.1

(a) Solve the equation $z + 3i = 2z^* + 4$.

(b) If $|w - 1| = |w|$, find $\text{Re}(w)$.

(a) Let $z = a + bi$. Then

$$a + bi + 3i - 2(a - bi) + 4$$

$$a + (bi + 3)i = 2a + 4 - 2bi$$

> Since both z and z^* appear in the equation, we will write z in Cartesian form. (This is often, though not always, the best approach.)

Real parts: $a = 2a + 4$

Imaginary parts: $b + 3 = -2b$

> Equate the real and imaginary parts.

$$\therefore a = -4, b = -1$$

So $z = -4 - i$

(b) Let $w = a + bi$. Then

$$|(a + bi) - 1| = |a + bi|$$

$$\Rightarrow |(a - 1) + bi|^2 = |a + bi|^2$$

> Since we need to find the real part of w, it seems sensible to use Cartesian form.

 In general it is more helpful to consider $|z|^2$ rather than $|z|$.

$$\Rightarrow (a - 1)^2 + b^2 = a^2 + b^2$$

$$\Rightarrow a^2 - 2a + 1 = a^2$$

> We can now use modulus² = (Re)² + (Im)².

$$\Rightarrow a = \frac{1}{2} \text{ i.e. } \text{Re}(w) = \frac{1}{2}$$

 Be careful not to include i in the imaginary part.

Practice questions 8.1

1. Solve the equation $4z^* + 3iz = 7i$, where z is a complex number.

2. Solve the equation $(5i - 2)z = 8 + 9i$.

3. Given that $|z + i| = |z|$, find the imaginary part of z.

4. (a) Given that $|z + i| = |z - 3|$ where $z = a + bi$, show that $3a + b = 4$.
   (b) Given also that $|z| = \sqrt{2}$, find the possible values of z.

5. Solve the equation $3z^2 + (2 + 3i)z + (5i - 5) = 0$, giving your answers in the form $a + bi$.

6. (a) By writing $z = a + bi$, show that $zz^* = |z|^2$.

   (b) Given that $|z| = 5$, solve the equation $z^* + \dfrac{60i}{z} = 13$.

8.2 EVALUATING EXPRESSIONS INVOLVING COMPLEX NUMBERS

WORKED EXAMPLE 8.2

If $z = 1 + i$ and $w = 1 + \sqrt{3}i$, find $\left(\dfrac{z^*}{w}\right)^6$ in Cartesian form.

 With this type of question, the key is deciding whether to use Cartesian or polar form. In general, polar form works better with division and powers.

$|z| = \sqrt{1+1} = \sqrt{2}$, $\arg(z) = \tan^{-1}\left(\dfrac{1}{1}\right) = \dfrac{\pi}{4}$

> Raising a complex number to a large power is easier to do in polar form, so we start by finding the modulus and argument of z and w.

$|w| = \sqrt{1+3} = 2$, $\arg(w) = \tan^{-1}\left(\dfrac{\sqrt{3}}{1}\right) = \dfrac{\pi}{3}$

> If the complex number is not in the first quadrant, always sketch the Argand diagram to find the argument.

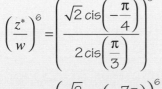

$\left(\dfrac{z^*}{w}\right)^6 = \left(\dfrac{\sqrt{2}\,\text{cis}\left(-\dfrac{\pi}{4}\right)}{2\,\text{cis}\left(\dfrac{\pi}{3}\right)}\right)^6$

> Remember that if $z = \text{cis}\,\theta$ then $z^* = \text{cis}(-\theta)$.

$= \left(\dfrac{\sqrt{2}}{2}\,\text{cis}\left(-\dfrac{7\pi}{12}\right)\right)^6$

> To divide complex numbers in polar form, we subtract their arguments: $-\dfrac{\pi}{4} - \dfrac{\pi}{3} = -\dfrac{7\pi}{12}$.

$= \left(\dfrac{\sqrt{2}}{2}\right)^6 \text{cis}\left(6\left(-\dfrac{7\pi}{12}\right)\right)$

$= \dfrac{1}{8}\,\text{cis}\left(-\dfrac{7\pi}{2}\right)$

> Use De Moivre's theorem.

$= \dfrac{1}{8}\,\text{cis}\left(\dfrac{\pi}{2}\right) = \dfrac{1}{8}i$

> Unless stated otherwise, the argument should be between $-\pi$ and π, so we add 2π.

Practice questions 8.2

7. Let $z_1 = 2\left(\cos\dfrac{\pi}{3} + i\sin\dfrac{\pi}{3}\right)$ and $z_2 = \cos\dfrac{\pi}{6} + i\sin\dfrac{\pi}{6}$. Write $\dfrac{z_1^3 z_2}{z_1^*}$ in the form $r(\cos\theta + i\sin\theta)$, giving θ in terms of π.

8. Let $z_1 = 1 - i$ and $z_2 = -1 + i\sqrt{3}$.
   (a) Write z_1 and z_2 in the form $re^{i\theta}$.
   (b) Hence find $\dfrac{z_1^2}{z_2^3}$ in Cartesian form.

8.3 FINDING SOLUTIONS TO POLYNOMIAL EQUATIONS

WORKED EXAMPLE 8.3

$1 + i$ is a root of the cubic equation $z^3 + az^2 + bz + 16$, where a and b are real numbers.

(a) Find the other two roots.

(b) Hence find the coefficients a and b.

(a) Since $1 + i$ is a root, so is $1 - i$.

> The roots come in complex conjugate pairs.

Let the third root be w.

The product of the roots is $(-1)^3 \times \dfrac{16}{1} = -16$.

> Since we know two of the roots, we can use the product of the roots to find the third one.

So, $(1+i)(1-i)w = -16$

$\Leftrightarrow (1^2 + 1^2)w = -16$

$\Leftrightarrow w = -8$

> ◀ The sum and product of the roots of a polynomial are covered in Chapter 3.

Hence the remaining roots are $1 - i$ and -8.

(b) The cubic has factors

$(z-(1+i))$, $(z-(1-i))$ and $(z+8)$.

> With roots z_1, z_2 and z_3, a cubic will have factors $(z - z_1)$, $(z - z_2)$ and $(z - z_3)$.

$\therefore z^3 + az^2 + bz + 16 = (z-(1+i))(z-(1-i))(z+8)$

$= [z^2 - (1-i)z - (1+i)z + (1+i)(1-i)](z+8)$

$= (z^2 - 2z + 2)(z+8)$

$= z^3 + 6z^2 - 14z + 16$

> Expand the factors, dealing with the two complex factors first.

Therefore, $a = 6$ and $b = -14$.

Practice questions 8.3

9. Given that $z = 3i$ is one root of the equation $z^3 + 2z^2 + 9z + 18 = 0$, find the remaining roots.

10. The cubic equation $z^3 + az^2 + bz + c = 0$ has real coefficients, and two of its roots are $z = -4$ and $z = 1 + 2i$. Find the values of a, b and c.

11. Let $f(z) = z^4 - 6z^3 + 14z^2 - 24z + 40$.

(a) Show that $f(2i) = 0$.

(b) Hence find the remaining solutions of the equation $f(z) = 0$.

8.4 FINDING MULTIPLE ANGLE FORMULAE FOR TRIGONOMETRIC FUNCTIONS

WORKED EXAMPLE 8.4

Derive a formula for $\cos 4\theta$ in terms of $\cos\theta$.

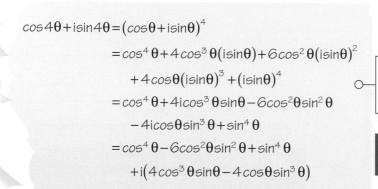

$$\cos 4\theta + i\sin 4\theta = (\cos\theta + i\sin\theta)^4$$
$$= \cos^4\theta + 4\cos^3\theta(i\sin\theta) + 6\cos^2\theta(i\sin\theta)^2$$
$$+ 4\cos\theta(i\sin\theta)^3 + (i\sin\theta)^4$$
$$= \cos^4\theta + 4i\cos^3\theta\sin\theta - 6\cos^2\theta\sin^2\theta$$
$$- 4i\cos\theta\sin^3\theta + \sin^4\theta$$
$$= \cos^4\theta - 6\cos^2\theta\sin^2\theta + \sin^4\theta$$
$$+ i(4\cos^3\theta\sin\theta - 4\cos\theta\sin^3\theta)$$

We will find $\cos 4\theta$ as the real part of $(\cos\theta + i\sin\theta)^4$.

◀◀ The binomial expansion is covered in Chapter 3.

Real parts:
$$\cos 4\theta = \cos^4\theta - 6\cos^2\theta\sin^2\theta + \sin^4\theta$$

Equate the real parts.

$$= \cos^4\theta - 6\cos^2\theta(1 - \cos^2\theta) + (1 - \cos^2\theta)^2$$
$$= \cos^4\theta - 6\cos^2\theta + 6\cos^4\theta + 1 - 2\cos^2\theta + \cos^4\theta$$
$$= 8\cos^4\theta - 8\cos^2\theta + 1$$

Use $\sin^2\theta = 1 - \cos^2\theta$ to write any parts of the expression involving $\sin\theta$ in terms of only $\cos\theta$.

Hence $\cos 4\theta = 8\cos^4\theta - 8\cos^2\theta + 1$.

Practice questions 8.4

12. Find an expression for $\sin 4\theta$ in terms of $\sin\theta$ and $\cos\theta$.

13. (a) Expand and simplify $(\cos\theta + i\sin\theta)^5$.
   (b) Hence find an expression for:
     (i) $\sin 5\theta$ in terms of $\sin\theta$
     (ii) $\cos 5\theta$ in terms of $\cos\theta$.

14. (a) By considering the real and imaginary parts of $(\cos\theta + i\sin\theta)^3$, find expressions for $\sin 3\theta$ and $\cos 3\theta$ in terms of $\sin\theta$ and $\cos\theta$.
   (b) Hence show that $\tan 3\theta = \dfrac{3\tan\theta - \tan^3\theta}{1 - 3\tan^2\theta}$.

8.5 FINDING FORMULAE FOR POWERS OF TRIGONOMETRIC FUNCTIONS

WORKED EXAMPLE 8.5

(a) Show that $\sin\theta = \dfrac{e^{i\theta} - e^{-i\theta}}{2i}$.

(b) Hence express $\sin^3\theta$ in terms of $\sin\theta$ and $\sin 3\theta$.

(a) $\cos\theta + i\sin\theta = e^{i\theta} \qquad \cdots (1)$

$\therefore \cos(-\theta) + i\sin(-\theta) = e^{i(-\theta)}$

i.e. $\cos\theta - i\sin\theta = e^{-i\theta} \qquad \cdots (2)$

> We can relate $\sin\theta$ (and $\cos\theta$) to $e^{i\theta}$.

> ⚠ Remember that $\cos(-\theta) = \cos\theta$ and $\sin(-\theta) = -\sin\theta$.

$(1)-(2) \Rightarrow (\cos\theta + i\sin\theta) - (\cos\theta - i\sin\theta) = e^{i\theta} - e^{-i\theta}$

$\Leftrightarrow 2i\sin\theta = e^{i\theta} - e^{-i\theta}$

$\Leftrightarrow \sin\theta = \dfrac{e^{i\theta} - e^{-i\theta}}{2i}$

> Eliminate $\cos\theta$ from equations (1) and (2).

(b) $\sin^3\theta = \left(\dfrac{e^{i\theta} - e^{-i\theta}}{2i}\right)^3$

> Use the identity shown in part (a).

$= \dfrac{e^{3i\theta} - 3e^{2i\theta}e^{-i\theta} + 3e^{i\theta}e^{-2i\theta} - e^{-3i\theta}}{-8i}$

> Expand using the binomial expansion.

$= \dfrac{e^{3i\theta} - 3e^{i\theta} + 3e^{-i\theta} - e^{-3i\theta}}{-8i}$

> ⚠ This question can also be done by expanding $\left(\dfrac{z - z^{-1}}{2i}\right)^3$ and then using $z^3 + z^{-3} = 2i\sin 3\theta$.

$= \dfrac{-\left(e^{3i\theta} - e^{-3i\theta}\right)}{4(2i)} + \dfrac{3\left(e^{i\theta} - e^{-i\theta}\right)}{4(2i)}$

$= -\dfrac{1}{4}\sin 3\theta + \dfrac{3}{4}\sin\theta$

> Group the terms to get expressions for $\sin\theta$ and $\sin 3\theta$.

Practice questions 8.5

15. Find an expression for $\cos^3\theta$ in terms of $\cos\theta$ and $\cos 3\theta$.

16. (a) Let $z = \cos\theta + i\sin\theta$. Show that $z^n + z^{-n} = 2\cos n\theta$.

(b) By expanding $(z - z^{-1})^4$ show that $\sin^4\theta = \dfrac{1}{8}\cos 4\theta - \dfrac{1}{2}\cos 2\theta + \dfrac{3}{8}$.

17. (a) Show that $\cos^5\theta = \dfrac{1}{16}(\cos 5\theta + A\cos 3\theta + B\cos\theta)$, where A and B are constants to be found.

(b) Hence find $\displaystyle\int \cos^5\theta \, d\theta$.

8.6 FINDING ROOTS OF COMPLEX NUMBERS

WORKED EXAMPLE 8.6

Solve the equation $z^5 = 16 + 16\sqrt{3}\,i$.

$$\left|16 + 16\sqrt{3}\,i\right| = \sqrt{256 + 768} = 32$$

$$\tan\theta = \frac{16\sqrt{3}}{16} = \sqrt{3} \quad \therefore \arg\left(16 + 16\sqrt{3}\,i\right) = \frac{\pi}{3}$$

> Identify the modulus and argument of the RHS so that the complex number can be written in polar form.

$$\text{Hence } 16 + 16\sqrt{3}\,i = 32\,\text{cis}\left(\frac{\pi}{3}\right)$$

Let $z = r\,\text{cis}\,\theta$. Then:

$$\left(r\,\text{cis}\,\theta\right)^5 = 32\,\text{cis}\left(\frac{\pi}{3}\right)$$

> Write z as $r\,\text{cis}\,\theta$ and use De Moivre's theorem.

$$\Leftrightarrow r^5\text{cis}(5\theta) = 32\,\text{cis}\left(\frac{\pi}{3}\right) \quad \text{(by De Moivre)}$$

> When solving any equation of the form $z^n = w$, always express z and w in polar form and then use De Moivre's theorem.

$$\therefore r^5 = 32 \Rightarrow r = \sqrt[5]{32} = 2$$

$$\text{cis}(5\theta) = \text{cis}\left(\frac{\pi}{3}\right)$$

$$\Rightarrow 5\theta = \frac{\pi}{3}, \frac{7\pi}{3}, \frac{13\pi}{3}, \frac{19\pi}{3}, \frac{25\pi}{3}$$

$$\therefore \theta = \frac{\pi}{15}, \frac{7\pi}{15}, \frac{13\pi}{15}, \frac{19\pi}{15}, \frac{25\pi}{15}$$

> $\text{cis}(\theta) = \text{cis}(\theta + 2\pi) = \text{cis}(\theta + 4\pi) = \ldots$ so values of 5θ are found by adding multiples of 2π to the original value. (Note that adding 2π to the final value, $\frac{25\pi}{3}$, would give $\theta = \frac{31\pi}{15} > 2\pi$, so there are no further unique values for θ in the interval $[0, 2\pi]$.)

Therefore, the solutions are $z = 2\,\text{cis}\left(\frac{\pi}{15}\right), 2\,\text{cis}\left(\frac{7\pi}{15}\right),$

$2\,\text{cis}\left(\frac{13\pi}{15}\right), 2\,\text{cis}\left(\frac{19\pi}{15}\right), 2\,\text{cis}\left(\frac{25\pi}{15}\right)$

> We expect 5 solutions to a polynomial equation of degree 5.

Practice questions 8.6

18. (a) Find the modulus and the argument of $4 - 4\sqrt{3}\,i$.

    (b) Hence solve the equation $z^3 = 4 - 4\sqrt{3}\,i$, giving your answers in polar form.

19. Find all the complex solutions of the equation $z^4 = 16$, giving your answers in Cartesian form. Show your solutions on an Argand diagram.

20. Solve the equation $z^6 + i = 0$.

Mixed practice 8

1. Let $z = 2\left(\cos\dfrac{2\pi}{3} + i\sin\dfrac{2\pi}{3}\right)$.

   (a) Write z^2, z^3 and z^4 in polar form.

   (b) Represent z, z^2, z^3 and z^4 on the same Argand diagram.

2. Express $z = 2i + \dfrac{1}{\sqrt{2} - i}$ in the form $a + bi$.

3. If z and w are complex numbers, solve the simultaneous equations

   $2iz + 5w = 6i$

   $3z + iw = 2 + 3i$

4. (a) Find the modulus and argument of $\sqrt{3} - i$.

   (b) Hence find the exact value of $\dfrac{1}{\left(\sqrt{3} - i\right)^9}$.

5. Given that $z = 5e^{i\pi/4}$ and $w = 2e^{i\pi/6}$, find the exact values of the modulus and argument of $\dfrac{z^3}{w^2}$.

6. $f(z) = z^4 + az^3 + bz^2 + cz + d$ where a, b, c and d are real numbers. Given that two of the roots of the equation $f(z) = 0$ are $1 + 2i$ and $3 - i$, write $f(z)$ as a product of two real quadratic factors.

7. Let 1, ω, ω^2, ω^3 and ω^4 be the roots of the equation $z^5 = 1$.

   (a) By expanding $(1 - \omega)(1 + \omega + \omega^2 + \omega^3 + \omega^4)$, show that $1 + \omega + \omega^2 + \omega^3 + \omega^4 = 0$.

   (b) Write ω in the form $\cos\theta + i\sin\theta$.

   (c) Hence find the value of $\cos\dfrac{2\pi}{5} + \cos\dfrac{4\pi}{5} + \cos\dfrac{6\pi}{5} + \cos\dfrac{8\pi}{5}$.

8. Let $z = \cos\theta + i\sin\theta$.

   (a) Show that $z^n - \dfrac{1}{z^n} = 2i\sin n\theta$.

   (b) By considering the binomial expansion of $\left(z - \dfrac{1}{z}\right)^5$ find the constants A and B such that $32\sin^5\theta = 2\sin 5\theta + A\sin 3\theta + B\sin\theta$.

   (c) Find the exact value of $\displaystyle\int_0^{\pi/3} 32\sin^5\theta \, d\theta$.

9. (a) (i) If $z = \dfrac{1}{2}\cos\theta + \dfrac{i}{2}\sin\theta$, show that $|z| < 1$.

(ii) Find an expression for $1 + \dfrac{1}{2}e^{i\theta} + \dfrac{1}{4}e^{2i\theta} + \dfrac{1}{8}e^{3i\theta} + \dots.$

(iii) Hence show that $\dfrac{1}{2}\sin\theta + \dfrac{1}{4}\sin 2\theta + \dfrac{1}{8}\sin 3\theta + \dots = \dfrac{2\sin\theta}{5 - 4\cos\theta}.$

(b) (i) If $z = \cos\theta + i\sin\theta$, show that $\dfrac{1}{z} = \cos\theta - i\sin\theta$.

(ii) Show that $\cos n\theta = \dfrac{1}{2}\left(z^n + \dfrac{1}{z^n}\right)$.

(iii) Hence solve $z^4 - 3z^3 + 4z^2 - 3z + 1 = 0$.

Going for the top 8

1. Two roots of the quintic equation $z^5 - 7z^4 + pz^3 + qz^2 + rz - 150 = 0$ (where p, q and r are real numbers) are 3 and $1 + 2i$.

(a) Write down a third root of the equation.

(b) One of the remaining two roots is $a + bi$. Show that $a^2 + b^2 = 10$.

(c) Find the values of a and b.

(d) Hence find the values of p, q and r.

2. Let $w = \dfrac{2}{z - i}$.

(a) Express z in terms of w.

(b) If $|z| = 1$, show that $\text{Im}(w) = 1$.

3. (a) Show that $\dfrac{e^{i\theta} + e^{-i\theta}}{2} = \cos\theta$.

(b) Find the value of $\cos(3i)$.

(c) Find the exact value of $\cos(\pi + 3i)$.

4. (a) If z is a complex number such that $z^2 + z = k$, where k is real, show that either z is real or $\text{Re}(z) = -\dfrac{1}{2}$.

(b) If z is not real, find the set of possible values for k.

5. Show that i^i is real.

9 DIFFERENTIATION

WHAT YOU NEED TO KNOW

- The derivative can be interpreted as the rate of change of one quantity as another changes, or as the gradient of a tangent to a graph.

- The notation for the derivative of $y = f(x)$ with respect to x is $\dfrac{dy}{dx}$ or $f'(x)$.

  - Differentiating again gives the second derivative, $\dfrac{d^2y}{dx^2}$ or $f''(x)$, which can be interpreted as the rate of change (or gradient) of $f'(x)$.

- Differentiation from first principles involves looking at the limit of the gradient of a chord. The formula is:

$$f'(x) = \lim_{h \to 0}\left(\frac{f(x+h) - f(x)}{h}\right)$$

- The basic rules of differentiation:

  - If $f(x) = x^n$ then $f'(x) = nx^{n-1}$.

  - $\left[kf(x)\right]' = kf'(x)$ for any constant k.

  - $\left[f(x) + g(x)\right]' = f'(x) + g'(x)$

- These derivatives are given in the Formula booklet:

$f(x)$	$f'(x)$	$f(x)$	$f'(x)$
$\sin x$	$\cos x$	$\arcsin x$	$\dfrac{1}{\sqrt{1-x^2}}$
$\cos x$	$-\sin x$	$\arccos x$	$-\dfrac{1}{\sqrt{1-x^2}}$
$\tan x$	$\sec^2 x$	$\arctan x$	$\dfrac{1}{1+x^2}$
$\sec x$	$\sec x \tan x$	e^x	e^x
$\csc x$	$-\csc x \cot x$	$\ln x$	$\dfrac{1}{x}$
$\cot x$	$-\csc^2 x$	a^x	$a^x(\ln a)$
		$\log_a x$	$\dfrac{1}{x \ln a}$

- The following derivatives of common functions composed with linear expressions are very useful. (They are not in the Formula booklet but follow from those that are when the chain rule is applied.)

$f(x)$	$f'(x)$
$(ax+b)^n$	$an(ax+b)^{n-1}$
e^{ax+b}	ae^{ax+b}
$\ln(ax+b)$	$\dfrac{a}{ax+b}$
$\sin(ax+b)$	$a\cos(ax+b)$
$\cos(ax+b)$	$-a\sin(ax+b)$
$\tan(ax+b)$	$a\sec^2(ax+b)$

- Further rules of differentiation:

  - The chain rule is used to differentiate composite functions:

    $$y = g(u), \text{ where } u = f(x) \implies \frac{dy}{dx} = \frac{dy}{du} \times \frac{du}{dx}$$

  - The product rule is used to differentiate two functions multiplied together:

    $$y = uv \implies \frac{dy}{dx} = u\frac{dv}{dx} + v\frac{du}{dx}$$

  - The quotient rule is used to differentiate one function divided by another:

    $$y = \frac{u}{v} \implies \frac{dy}{dx} = \frac{v\dfrac{du}{dx} - u\dfrac{dv}{dx}}{v^2}$$

- When a function is not written in the form $y = f(x)$, implicit differentiation is used. Differentiate each term separately, using the chain rule on all terms involving y:

$$\frac{d}{dx}[f(y)] = \frac{d}{dy}[f(y)] \times \frac{dy}{dx}$$

- The equation of a tangent at the point (x_1, y_1) is given by $y - y_1 = m(x - x_1)$ where $m = f'(x_1)$. The equation of the normal at the same point is given by $y - y_1 = m(x - x_1)$ where $m = -\dfrac{1}{f'(x_1)}$.

- If a function is increasing, $f'(x) > 0$; if a function is decreasing, $f'(x) < 0$. If the graph is concave up, $f''(x) > 0$; if the graph is concave down, $f''(x) < 0$.

- Stationary points of a function are points where the gradient is zero, i.e. $f'(x) = 0$. The second derivative can be used to determine the nature of a stationary point.

  - At a local maximum, $f''(x) \leq 0$.

- At a local minimum, $f''(x) \geq 0$.
- At a point of inflexion, $f''(x) = 0$ but $f'''(x) \neq 0$; there is a change in concavity of the curve.

- Optimisation problems involve setting up an expression and then finding the maximum or minimum value by differentiating or using a GDC.
  - If there is a constraint, it will be necessary to set up a second expression from this information and then substitute it into the expression to be optimised, thereby eliminating the second variable.
  - The optimal solution may occur at an end point of the domain as well as at a stationary point.

- The rate of change of a quantity often means the derivative with respect to time. Rates of change of more than two variables can be related using the chain rule:

$$\frac{dy}{dt} = \frac{dy}{dx} \times \frac{dx}{dt}$$

- Differentiate with respect to time to change an expression for displacement (s) into an expression for velocity (v) and then into one for acceleration (a):
  - $v = \dfrac{ds}{dt}$
  - $a = \dfrac{dv}{dt}$ $\left(\text{If velocity depends on displacement, } a = v\dfrac{dv}{ds}. \right)$

EXAM TIPS AND COMMON ERRORS

- Be careful when the variable is in the power. If you differentiate e^x with respect to x the answer is e^x **not** xe^{x-1}.
- Always use the product rule to differentiate a product. You cannot simply differentiate each element separately and multiply the answers together; the derivative of $x^2 \sin x$ is **not** $2x \cos x$.
- Make sure you are clear whether you have a product (such as $e^x \sin x$) or a composite function (such as $e^{\sin x}$) to differentiate. The latter is differentiated using the chain rule.
- It is sometimes easier to differentiate a quotient by turning it into a product (i.e. writing it as the numerator multiplied by the denominator raised to a negative power) and then differentiating using the product rule.
- Do not confuse the rules for differentiation and integration. Always check the sign when integrating or differentiating trigonometric functions, and carefully consider whether you should be multiplying or dividing by the coefficient of x.
- When differentiating trigonometric functions you **must** work in radians.

9.1 DIFFERENTIATION FROM FIRST PRINCIPLES

WORKED EXAMPLE 9.1

Use differentiation from first principles to prove that the derivative of x^3 is $3x^2$.

$$f'(x) = \lim_{h \to 0}\left(\frac{f(x+h) - f(x)}{h}\right)$$

$$= \lim_{h \to 0}\left(\frac{(x+h)^3 - x^3}{h}\right)$$

We start with the definition of the derivative at the point x (i.e. the formula for differentiation from first principles).

$$= \lim_{h \to 0}\left(\frac{x^3 + 3x^2h + 3xh^2 + h^3 - x^3}{h}\right)$$

$$= \lim_{h \to 0}\left(\frac{3x^2h + 3xh^2 + h^3}{h}\right)$$

We do not want to let the denominator tend to zero straight away, so first manipulate the numerator to get a factor of h that we can cancel with the h in the denominator.

$$= \lim_{h \to 0}\left(3x^2 + 3xh + h^2\right)$$

Divide top and bottom by h.

$$= 3x^2$$

Once there is no h in the denominator we can let $h \to 0$.

Practice questions 9.1

1. Prove from first principles that the derivative of x^4 is $4x^3$.

2. Prove from first principles that $\dfrac{d}{dx}(x^2 - 5x + 2) = 2x - 5$.

3. If $y = \dfrac{1}{x^2}$, use differentiation from first principles to show that $\dfrac{dy}{dx} = \dfrac{-2}{x^3}$.

4. (a) Show that $\sqrt{a} - \sqrt{b} = \dfrac{a-b}{\sqrt{a} + \sqrt{b}}$.

   (b) Show that $\dfrac{1}{\sqrt{x+h}} - \dfrac{1}{\sqrt{x}} = -\dfrac{h}{x\sqrt{x+h} + (x+h)\sqrt{x}}$.

   (c) Prove from first principles that the derivative of $\dfrac{1}{\sqrt{x}}$ is $-\dfrac{1}{2x\sqrt{x}}$.

9.2 THE PRODUCT, QUOTIENT AND CHAIN RULES

WORKED EXAMPLE 9.2

Differentiate $y = x e^{\sin x}$.

Let $u = x$. Then $\dfrac{du}{dx} = 1$

Let $v = e^{\sin x}$

 This is a product so we need to use the product rule. It doesn't matter which function is $u(x)$ and which is $v(x)$.

For $\dfrac{dv}{dx}$, let $w = \sin x$. Then $v = e^w$,

 $v(x)$ is a composite function, so use the chain rule.

$\dfrac{dw}{dx} = \cos x$ and $\dfrac{dv}{dw} = e^w$

⚠ You do not have to set out your working in this much detail; from $v = e^{\sin x}$ you can proceed straight to $\dfrac{dv}{dx} = e^{\sin x} \cos x$.

Therefore

$\dfrac{dv}{dx} = \dfrac{dv}{dw} \times \dfrac{dw}{dx}$

$= e^w \cos x$

$= e^{\sin x} \cos x$

So $\dfrac{dy}{dx} = u\dfrac{dv}{dx} + v\dfrac{du}{dx} = x \cos x \, e^{\sin x} + e^{\sin x}$

Now apply the product rule.

⚠ There is no need to simplify (or factorise) your answer, unless you are asked to do so.

Practice questions 9.2

5. Differentiate $y = e^{x^2} + \dfrac{\sin 3x}{2x}$.

6. Find the values of x for which the function $f(x) = \ln\left(\dfrac{2}{x^2 - 12}\right)$ has a gradient of 2.

7. Given that $f(x) = \dfrac{x^2 - 1}{x^2 + 2}$, find $f''(x)$ in the form $\dfrac{a - bx^2}{\left(x^2 + 2\right)^3}$.

8. (a) Show that $\dfrac{d}{dx}(\sec x) = \sec x \tan x$.

   (b) Given that $f(x) = \ln(\sec x + \tan x)$, show that $f'(x) = \sec x$.

   (c) Hence evaluate $\displaystyle\int_0^{\frac{\pi}{6}} \sec x \, dx$, giving your answer in the form $k \ln 3$.

9.3 TANGENTS AND NORMALS

WORKED EXAMPLE 9.3

Find the coordinates of the point where the normal to the curve $y = x^2$ at $x = a$ meets the curve again.

$\dfrac{dy}{dx} = 2x$

At $x = a$, $\dfrac{dy}{dx} = 2a$, i.e. gradient of tangent is $2a$

Therefore gradient of normal is $m = -\dfrac{1}{2a}$

> The normal is perpendicular to the tangent, so we need the gradient of the tangent first.

Equation of normal: $y - a^2 = -\dfrac{1}{2a}(x - a)$

> The normal is a straight line, so its equation is of the form $y - y_1 = m(x - x_1)$.

Intersection with $y = x^2$:

$$x^2 - a^2 = -\dfrac{1}{2a}(x - a)$$

> We need to find the point of intersection with $y = x^2$, so substitute $y = x^2$ into the equation of the normal.

$$\Rightarrow (x - a)(x + a) = -\dfrac{1}{2a}(x - a)$$

> Factorise the left-hand side (LHS) so that we have a common factor on both sides.

$$\Rightarrow (x - a)\left(x + a + \dfrac{1}{2a}\right) = 0$$

So $x = a$ or $x = -a - \dfrac{1}{2a}$ ($x = a$ was given)

> Move everything to the LHS and factorise. Do not divide by $(x - a)$ as this could result in the loss of a solution. Instead, we find all possible solutions and then reject any that are not relevant.

When $x = -a - \dfrac{1}{2a}$, $y = \left(-a - \dfrac{1}{2a}\right)^2$

> We can now find y by substituting into $y = x^2$.

So the coordinates of the point are

$$\left(-a - \dfrac{1}{2a}, \left(-a - \dfrac{1}{2a}\right)^2\right)$$

> ⚠ If asked to find the coordinates of a point, make sure you find both x- and y-coordinates.

Practice questions 9.3

9. Find the equation of the normal to the curve $y = e^{-3x^2}$ at the point where $x = 2$.

10. A tangent to the curve $y = \tan x$ for $-\dfrac{\pi}{2} < x < \dfrac{\pi}{2}$ is drawn at the point where $x = \dfrac{\pi}{4}$.

Find the x-coordinate of the point where this tangent intersects the curve again.

9.4 IMPLICIT DIFFERENTIATION

WORKED EXAMPLE 9.4

Find the gradient of the curve $y^2 + \sin(xy) + x^3 = 4$ at the point $(0, 2)$.

$$\frac{d}{dx}(y^2) + \frac{d}{dx}(\sin(xy)) + \frac{d}{dx}(x^3) = \frac{d}{dx}(4)$$

> We need to differentiate each term (on both sides) with respect to x.

$$\frac{d}{dx}(y^2) = 2y\frac{dy}{dx}$$

> Use the chain rule on all terms containing y.

$$\frac{d}{dx}(\sin(xy)) = \cos(xy) \times \left(x\frac{dy}{dx} + 1 \times y \right)$$

> For the $\sin(xy)$ term we will need to apply the product rule to xy (as well as the chain rule initially).

$$\therefore 2y\frac{dy}{dx} + \cos(xy)\left(x\frac{dy}{dx} + y \right) + 3x^2 = 0$$

> Now put everything together.

At the point with $x = 0$ and $y = 2$:

$$4\frac{dy}{dx} + \cos 0 \times \left(0\frac{dy}{dx} + 2 \right) + 3 \times 0 = 0$$

$$\Rightarrow 4\frac{dy}{dx} + 2 = 0$$

$$\Rightarrow \frac{dy}{dx} = -\frac{1}{2}$$

 If you are asked for the gradient at a particular point, you can substitute the given values into the differentiated equation without rearranging it.

Practice questions 9.4

11. Find the gradient of the normal to $y^2 + 3xy - 10x^2 = 0$ where $x = 1$, $y > 0$.

12. Find the coordinates of all the points on the curve $x^2 + y^2 - 3y = 10$ where $\dfrac{dy}{dx} = 0$.

13. Given that $\dfrac{x+1}{y-3} = 2xy^2$, find an expression for $\dfrac{dy}{dx}$.

14. The inverse function of $f(x) = \csc x$ is $f^{-1}(x) = \text{arccsc } x$.

    (a) Given that $y = \text{arccsc } x$, find $\dfrac{dx}{dy}$ in terms of y.

    (b) Hence express the derivative of $\text{arccsc } x$ in terms of x.

9.5 STATIONARY POINTS

WORKED EXAMPLE 9.5

 Find and classify the stationary points on the curve $y = 2x^3 - 9x^2 + 12x + 5$.

$\dfrac{dy}{dx} = 6x^2 - 18x + 12$

> At stationary points the first derivative is zero, so we need to find $\dfrac{dy}{dx}$ and then solve the equation $\dfrac{dy}{dx} = 0$.

For stationary points, $\dfrac{dy}{dx} = 0$:

$6x^2 - 18x + 12 = 0$

$\Leftrightarrow x^2 - 3x + 2 = 0$

$\Leftrightarrow (x - 1)(x - 2) = 0$

$\Leftrightarrow x = 1$ or $x = 2$

When $x = 1, y = 2 - 9 + 12 + 5 = 10$

When $x = 1, y = 2(2)^3 - 9(2)^2 + 12(2) + 5 = 9$

So stationary points are $(1, 10)$ and $(2, 9)$

> Find the y-coordinates and give the full coordinates of the stationary points.

$\dfrac{d^2 y}{dx^2} = 12x - 18$

> We can use the second derivative to determine the nature of the stationary points.

> ⚠ Make sure you differentiate the original expression for $\dfrac{dy}{dx}$ and not a manipulated version (such as $x^2 - 3x + 2$ here).

At $x = 1, \dfrac{d^2 y}{dx^2} = 12 - 18 = -6 < 0$

$\therefore (1, 10)$ is a local maximum.

At $x = 2, \dfrac{d^2 y}{dx^2} = 12(2) - 18 = 6 > 0$

$\therefore (2, 9)$ is a local minimum.

> Apply the second derivative test by substituting the x values into $\dfrac{d^2 y}{dx^2}$.

Practice questions 9.5

 15. Find and classify the stationary points on the curve $y = x^3 - 3x + 8$.

 16. Find and classify the stationary points on the curve $y = x\sin x + \cos x$ for $0 < x < 2\pi$.

 17. Find the maximum value of $y = \ln(x - \sin^2 x)$ for $0 < x \leq 2\pi$.

9.6 OPTIMISATION WITH CONSTRAINTS

WORKED EXAMPLE 9.6

 What is the area of the largest rectangle that can just fit under the curve $y = \sin x$, $0 \le x \le \pi$, if one side of the rectangle lies on the x-axis?

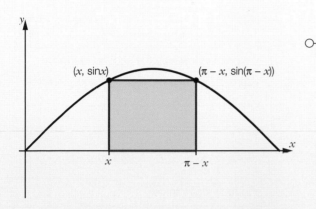

> We start by defining the variables, taking the bottom left corner of the rectangle as the point $(x, 0)$. Everything else then follows from the symmetry of the sine curve.

> ⚠ With harder optimisation problems a major difficulty can be defining the variables, as there may be more than one choice. In an unfamiliar situation, it is often a good idea to sketch a diagram to help.

Width of rectangle $= (\pi - x) - x = \pi - 2x$

So area $= (\pi - 2x)\sin x$

> Find an expression for the quantity that needs to be optimised, in this case area.

Using a GDC for the graph of area against x:

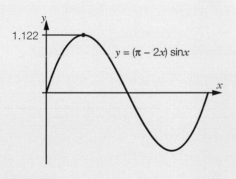

> Since this is a calculator question, we do not need to differentiate; but we do need to sketch the graph to justify that we have found a maximum (rather than any other stationary point) and that the maximum is not at an end point.

Therefore, the maximum area is 1.122 (4 SF).

Practice questions 9.6

18. An open cylindrical can has radius r and height h. The height and the radius can both change, but the volume remains fixed at $64\pi \, \text{cm}^2$. Find the minimum surface area of the can (including the base) and justify that the value you have found is a minimum.

19. Find the smallest surface area of a cone (including base) with volume $100 \, \text{cm}^3$.

20. If the surface area is fixed, prove that the largest volume of a square-based cuboid is attained when it is a cube.

9.7 POINTS OF INFLEXION

WORKED EXAMPLE 9.7

The curve $y = x^3 - 6x^2 + 5x + 2$ has a point of inflexion. Find its coordinates.

$$\frac{dy}{dx} = 3x^2 - 12x + 5$$

$$\Rightarrow \frac{d^2y}{dx^2} = 6x - 12$$

At a point of inflexion, $\frac{d^2y}{dx^2} = 0$:

$6x - 12 = 0$

$\Leftrightarrow x = 2$

At a point of inflexion the second derivative is zero, so we need to find $\frac{d^2y}{dx^2}$ and solve the equation $\frac{d^2y}{dx^2} = 0$.

When $x = 2$:

$y = (2)^3 - 6(2)^2 + 5(2) + 2 = -4$

So the point of inflexion is at $(2, -4)$.

Find the y-coordinate.

 If a question states that a curve has a point of inflexion and there is only one solution to $\frac{d^2y}{dx^2} = 0$, you can assume that you have found the point of inflexion; there is no need to check that $\frac{d^3y}{dx^3} \neq 0$.

Practice questions 9.7

21. Find the coordinates of the point of inflexion on the curve $y = x^3 - 12x^2 + 7$.

22. The graph of $y = 4x^3 - ax^2 + b$ has a point of inflexion at $(-1, 4)$. Find the values of a and b.

23. A curve has equation $y = (x^2 - a)e^x$.
    (a) Find the range of values of a for which the curve has at least one point of inflexion.
    (b) Given that one of the points of inflexion is a stationary point, find the value of a.
    (c) For this value of a, sketch the graph of $y = (x^2 - a)e^x$.

9.8 INTERPRETING GRAPHS

WORKED EXAMPLE 9.8

The graph shows $y = f'(x)$.

On the graph:

(a) Mark points corresponding to a local maximum of $f(x)$ with an A.

(b) Mark points corresponding to a local minimum of $f(x)$ with a B.

(c) Mark points corresponding to a point of inflexion of $f(x)$ with a C.

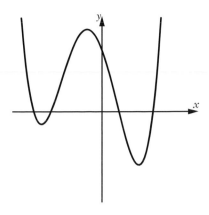

Local maximum points occur where the graph crosses the x-axis with a negative gradient.

> A local maximum has $f'(x) = 0$ and $f''(x) < 0$, i.e. the gradient of the graph of $y = f'(x)$ is negative.

⚠ Be clear whether you are considering the graph of $y = f(x)$, $y = f'(x)$ or $y = f''(x)$.

Local minimum points occur where the graph crosses the x-axis with a positive gradient.

> A local minimum has $f'(x) = 0$ and $f''(x) > 0$, i.e. the gradient of the graph of $y = f'(x)$ is positive.

Points of inflexion occur at stationary points on the graph.

> At a point of inflexion $f''(x) = 0$, i.e. the gradient of the graph of $y = f'(x)$ is zero (and the gradient is either positive on both sides of that point or negative on both sides).

Therefore:

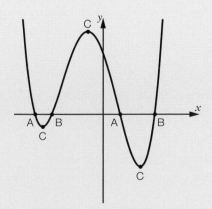

Practice questions 9.8

24. The graph shows $y = f'(x)$.

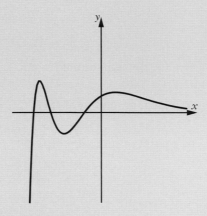

On the graph:

(a) Mark points corresponding to a local maximum of $f(x)$ with an A.

(b) Mark points corresponding to a local minimum of $f(x)$ with a B.

(c) Mark points corresponding to a point of inflexion of $f(x)$ with a C.

(d) Mark points corresponding to a zero of $f''(x)$ with a D.

25. The graph shows $y = f''(x)$.

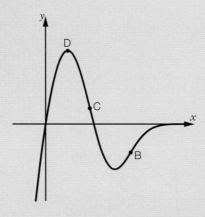

(a) On the graph, mark points corresponding to a point of inflexion of $f(x)$ with an A.

(b) State whether at the point B, the graph of $y = f(x)$ is concave up or concave down.

(c) Is $f'(x)$ increasing or decreasing at the point C?

(d) Given that the graph of $y = f(x)$ has a stationary point with the same x-coordinate as the point marked D, state the nature of this stationary point and justify your answer.

9.9 RELATED RATES OF CHANGE

WORKED EXAMPLE 9.9

The volume of a spherical snowball is increasing at a constant rate of $12\,\text{cm}^3\,\text{s}^{-1}$.
At what rate is the radius increasing when the radius is $4\,\text{cm}$?

Let V = volume in cm^3, r = radius in cm and t = time in seconds.

$\dfrac{dV}{dt} = 12$ and $\dfrac{dr}{dt}$ is needed.

> We start by defining the variables and writing down the given rate of change and the required rate of change.

By the chain rule:

$\dfrac{dr}{dt} = \dfrac{dr}{dV} \times \dfrac{dV}{dt}$

> Set the required rate of change as the subject of the chain rule.
>
> $\dfrac{dV}{dt}$ is known but $\dfrac{dr}{dV}$ is not.

Since the snowball is spherical,

$V = \dfrac{4}{3}\pi r^3 \implies \dfrac{dV}{dr} = 4\pi r^2$

$\therefore \dfrac{dr}{dV} = \dfrac{1}{4\pi r^2}$

> Use the geometric context to establish a link that enables us to find the unknown derivative.

$\therefore \dfrac{dr}{dt} = \dfrac{1}{4\pi r^2} \times 12 = \dfrac{3}{\pi r^2}$

> Substitute into the chain rule.

So, when $r = 4$:

$\dfrac{dr}{dt} = \dfrac{3}{16\pi} = 0.0597\ (3\ \text{SF})$

> Evaluate when the radius is $4\,\text{cm}$.

The radius is increasing at $0.0597\,\text{cm}\,\text{s}^{-1}$.

Practice questions 9.9

26. Oil is flowing into a conical container with vertex on the bottom which has height $10\,\text{m}$ and maximum radius $3\,\text{m}$. The oil is flowing into the cone at a rate of $2\,\text{m}^3\,\text{s}^{-1}$. At what rate is the height of the oil increasing when the petrol tank is filled to half of its capacity?

27. A hot air balloon rises vertically upwards from point L with a constant speed of $6\,\text{m}\,\text{s}^{-1}$.
An observer stands at point P, $100\,\text{m}$ from L.
He observes the balloon at an angle of elevation θ.
Find the rate of change of θ when the balloon is $50\,\text{m}$ above the ground.

9.10 KINEMATICS

WORKED EXAMPLE 9.10

 If the displacement, s, at time t is given by $s = 4t^2 - 3e^{-3t}$, find the time when the minimum velocity occurs in the form $\ln k$ where k is a rational number.

$$v = \frac{ds}{dt} = 8t + 9e^{-3t}$$

○— We first need to find an expression for the velocity.

$$\frac{dv}{dt} = 8 - 27e^{-3t}$$

At a local minimum, $\dfrac{dv}{dt} = 0$:

○— If there is a local minimum, it will occur when $\dfrac{dv}{dt} = 0$.

$$8 - 27e^{-3t} = 0 \Rightarrow e^{3t} = \frac{27}{8}$$

$$\Rightarrow t = \frac{1}{3}\ln\left(\frac{27}{8}\right) = \ln\left(\frac{3}{2}\right)$$

○— Use the laws of logarithms to put the result into the required form.

◄◄ **Laws of logarithms are covered in Chapter 2.**

$$\frac{d^2v}{dt^2} = 81e^{-3t} > 0 \text{ for all } t$$

Therefore $t = \ln\left(\dfrac{3}{2}\right)$ is a minimum.

○— We now need to check that this is a local minimum (rather than a maximum or point of inflexion). If it is not a minimum, the minimum velocity would occur at the end point.

Practice questions 9.10

28. A hiker has a displacement s km, at a time t hours, modelled by $s = t^3 - 4t$, $t \geq 0$.

(a) Find the time it takes for the hiker to return to his original position (where he stops).

(b) Find the maximum displacement from the starting point.

(c) Find the maximum speed of the hiker.

 29. A small ball oscillates on a spring so that its displacement from the starting position depending on time is given by $s = \dfrac{2}{3}\sin\left(\dfrac{3\pi t}{2}\right)$.

(a) Find expressions for the velocity and acceleration of the ball at time t.

(b) Find the first two values of t for which the speed of the ball equals $\dfrac{\pi}{2}$.

Mixed practice 9

1. The radius of a circle is increasing at the constant rate of $3\,\mathrm{cm\,s^{-1}}$.
   Find the rate of increase of the area when the radius is $20\,\mathrm{cm}$.

2. If $h(x) = f(x) + g(x)$, prove from first principles that $h'(x) = f'(x) + g'(x)$.

3. A rectangle has perimeter $40\,\mathrm{cm}$. One side of the rectangle has length $x\,\mathrm{cm}$.

   (a) Find an expression for the area of the rectangle in terms of x.

   (b) Prove that the rectangle with the largest area is a square.

4. Find the equation of the normal to the curve $y = 5\sin 3x + x^2$ when $x = \pi$, giving your answer in the form $y = mx + c$.

5. A particle is moving with displacement s at time t.

   (a) A model of the form $s = at^2 + bt$ is applied. Show that the particle moves with constant acceleration.

   It is known that when $t = 1$, $v = 1$, and when $t = 2$, $v = 5$.

   (b) Find a and b.

6. Show that the curve $x^3 + y^3 = 3$ is always decreasing.

7. (a) State the Fundamental Theorem of Algebra.

   (b) Explain why a polynomial of degree n can have at most $n - 1$ stationary points.

   (c) The cubic graph $y = ax^3 + bx^2 + cx + d$ has one stationary point. Show that $b^2 - 3ac = 0$.

8. Consider $f(x) = x^4 - x$.

   (a) Find the zeros of $f(x)$.

   (b) Find the region in which $y = f(x)$ is decreasing.

   (c) Solve the equation $f''(x) = 0$.

   (d) Find the region in which $y = f(x)$ is concave up.

   (e) Hence explain why $y = f(x)$ has no points of inflexion.

   (f) Sketch the curve $y = f(x)$.

9. The point P lies on the curve $y = \dfrac{1}{x}$ with $x = p$, $p > 0$.

   (a) Show that the equation of the tangent to the curve at P is $p^2 y + x = 2p$.

   The tangent to the curve at P meets the y-axis at Q and meets the x-axis at R.

   (b) Show that the area of the triangle OQR (where O is the origin) is independent of p.

   (c) Show that the distance QR is given by $2\sqrt{p^2 + p^{-2}}$.

   (d) Find the value of p that minimises the distance QR.

Going for the top 9

1. Find the stationary points on the curve $y^2 + 4xy - x^2 = 20$.

2. If $x^2 + y^2 = 9$, show that $\dfrac{d^2y}{dx^2} = -\dfrac{9}{y^3}$ (for $y \neq 0$).

3. Find the point(s) on the curve $y = x^2$ closest to $(0, 9)$.

4. Prove that all cubic curves have a point of inflexion.

5. An object has speed v at a displacement s, linked by $v = s^2 + s$.
   Find an expression for the acceleration in terms of the displacement.

6. An isosceles triangle has two equal sides of length l with angle θ between them. The length of the equal sides is increasing at a rate of $0.4\,\mathrm{m\,s^{-1}}$, and the angle is decreasing at a rate of 0.01 radians per second. Find the rate of change of the area of the triangle when $l = 4$ and $\theta = \dfrac{\pi}{4}$.

7. By differentiating $x \times \dfrac{1}{x}$ using the product rule, prove that $\dfrac{d}{dx}(x^{-1}) = -x^{-2}$.

8. The point P lies on the curve $y = e^x$ with $x = p$, $p > 0$. O is the origin.

   (a) Find the angle that [OP] makes with the positive x-axis.

   (b) Find the equation of the tangent to the curve at P.

   (c) The tangent intersects the x-axis at Q. Find the coordinates of Q.

   (d) Find the angle that [QP] makes with the positive x-axis.

   (e) Sketch the graph of angle $O\hat{P}Q$ against p, stating the intersections with any axes and the equations of any asymptotes.

   (f) Find the maximum value of the angle $O\hat{P}Q$ when $p > 1$.

   (g) The equation $e^x = kx$ has one solution with $k > 0$. Find the exact value of k.

10 INTEGRATION

WHAT YOU NEED TO KNOW

- Integration is the reverse process of differentiation.
- The basic rules of integration:
  - For all rational $n \neq -1$, $\int x^n \, dx = \dfrac{x^{n+1}}{n+1} + C$, where C is the constant of integration.
  - $\int kf(x) \, dx = k \int f(x) \, dx$ for any constant k.
  - $\int f(x) + g(x) \, dx = \int f(x) \, dx + \int g(x) \, dx$
- Definite integration deals with integration between two points.
  - If $\int f(x) \, dx = F(x)$ then $\int_a^b f(x) \, dx = F(b) - F(a)$, where a and b are the limits of integration.
  - $\int_a^b f(x) \, dx + \int_b^c f(x) \, dx = \int_a^c f(x) \, dx$
  - $\int_a^b f(x) \, dx = -\int_b^a f(x) \, dx$
- These integrals are given in the Formula booklet:

Function	Integral
$\dfrac{1}{x}$	$\ln|x| + C$
$\sin x$	$-\cos x + C$
$\cos x$	$\sin x + C$
e^x	$e^x + C$
a^x	$\dfrac{1}{\ln a} a^x + C$
$\dfrac{1}{a^2 + x^2}$	$\dfrac{1}{a} \arctan\left(\dfrac{x}{a}\right) + C$
$\dfrac{1}{\sqrt{a^2 - x^2}}$	$\arcsin\left(\dfrac{x}{a}\right) + C, \; |x| < a$

- The following integrals of common functions composed with linear expressions are very useful. (They are not in the Formula booklet but can be obtained from those that are by reversing the chain rule.)

Function	Integral
$\dfrac{1}{ax+b}$	$\dfrac{1}{a}\ln|ax+b|+C$
$\sin kx$	$-\dfrac{1}{k}\cos kx+C$
$\cos kx$	$\dfrac{1}{k}\sin kx+C$
$\sec^2 kx$	$\dfrac{1}{k}\tan kx+C$
e^{kx}	$\dfrac{1}{k}e^{kx}+C$

- Further integration methods:

  - Integration by substitution can be useful in a variety of circumstances. One particularly common case is where there is a composite function and (a multiple of) *the derivative of the inner part* of that function. (This can also be achieved by simply reversing the chain rule.)

    - Two useful substitutions are: (1) if a function involves $a^2 - x^2$, try $x = a\sin u$; (2) if a function involves $a^2 + x^2$, try $x = a\tan u$.

  - Integration by parts can be used on some integrals involving the product of functions:
  $$\int u\frac{\mathrm{d}v}{\mathrm{d}x}\mathrm{d}x = uv - \int v\frac{\mathrm{d}u}{\mathrm{d}x}\mathrm{d}x$$

  - Some integrals may require the use of trigonometric identities. Common examples are:

    - $\int \sin^2 x\ \mathrm{d}x = \int \dfrac{1}{2}(1 - \cos 2x)\mathrm{d}x$

    - $\int \cos^2 x\ \mathrm{d}x = \int \dfrac{1}{2}(1 + \cos 2x)\mathrm{d}x$

    - $\int \tan^2 x\ \mathrm{d}x = \int \sec^2 x - 1\ \mathrm{d}x$

- Integration can be used to calculate areas:

  - The area between a curve and the x-axis from $x = a$ to $x = b$ is given by $\int_a^b y\ \mathrm{d}x$.

  - The area between a curve and the y-axis from $y = a$ to $y = b$ is given by $\int_a^b x\ \mathrm{d}y$.

  - The area between two curves is given by $\int_a^b f(x) - g(x)\mathrm{d}x$, where $f(x) > g(x)$ and a and b are the intersection points.

- The volume of revolution is given by:
  - $V = \int_a^b \pi y^2 \, dx$ for rotation around the x-axis from $x = a$ to $x = b$
  - $V = \int_a^b \pi x^2 \, dy$ for rotation around the y-axis from $y = a$ to $y = b$
  - $V = \int_a^b \pi \left(f(x)^2 - g(x)^2 \right) dx$, where $f(x) > g(x)$ and a and b are the intersection points, for rotation of the region between two curves around the x-axis.
- Integrate with respect to time to change an expression for acceleration (a) into an expression for velocity (v) and then into one for displacement (s):
  - $v = \int a \, dt$
  - $s = \int v \, dt$
    - The displacement between times a and b is $\int_a^b v \, dt$.
    - The distance travelled between times a and b is $\int_a^b |v| \, dt$.

⚠ EXAM TIPS AND COMMON ERRORS

- Don't forget the '+ C' for indefinite integration – it is part of the answer and you must write it every time. However, it can be ignored for definite integration.
- Make sure you know how to use your calculator to evaluate definite integrals. You can also check your answer on the calculator when you are asked to find the exact value of the integral.
- Always look out for integrals which are in the Formula booklet. Don't forget that $\dfrac{1}{\cos^2 x}$ is $\sec^2 x$.
- You cannot integrate products or quotients by integrating each part separately.
- When integrating fractions, always check whether the numerator is the derivative of the denominator. If this is the case, the answer is the natural logarithm of the denominator: $\int \dfrac{f'(x)}{f(x)} dx = \ln |f(x)| + C$.
- You may have to simplify a fraction before integrating. This can be achieved by splitting into separate fractions or by polynomial division (or equivalent method).
- If you have a product of functions to integrate, try substitution unless you recognise the situation as a typical 'integration by parts' integral (where the two functions are often of different 'types', such as $\int x \sin x \, dx$, $\int x^2 e^x \, dx$). One important example of integration by parts that you should remember is $\int \ln x \, dx$, which is split into the product $\int 1 \times \ln x \, dx$.

10.1 INTEGRATING EXPRESSIONS

WORKED EXAMPLE 10.1

Find $\int x\left(e^{x}+e^{x^{2}}\right)dx$.

$$\int x\left(e^{x}+e^{x^{2}}\right)dx=\int xe^{x}dx+\int xe^{x^{2}}dx$$

> We can split up the integral of a sum.

For $\int xe^{x}dx$:

$$u=x \text{ and } \frac{dv}{dx}=e^{x}$$

$$\Rightarrow \frac{du}{dx}=1 \text{ and } v=e^{x}$$

> This is a product of two functions and is therefore a good candidate for integration by parts. Choose the function that is simpler to integrate as $\frac{dv}{dx}$ (here this should be e^{x} as its integral is the same as itself).

$$\therefore \int xe^{x}dx=xe^{x}-\int 1\times e^{x}dx$$
$$=xe^{x}-e^{x}+c$$

> Apply the integration by parts formula
> $$\int u\frac{dv}{dx}dx=uv-\int v\frac{du}{dx}dx$$

For $\int xe^{x^{2}}dx$: Let $u=x^{2}$; then

$$\frac{du}{dx}=2x \Rightarrow dx=\frac{du}{2x}$$

$$\int xe^{x^{2}}dx=\int xe^{u}\frac{du}{2x}$$

$$=\frac{1}{2}\int e^{u}du$$

$$=\frac{1}{2}e^{u}+c'$$

$$=\frac{1}{2}e^{x^{2}}+c'$$

> This product has one part (x) that is a multiple of the derivative of the 'inner function' x^{2} of the other part, which makes it ideal for substitution. Make the substitution $u=$ 'inner function'.

 When a product consists of a composite function and (a multiple of) the derivative of the 'inner part' of that function, always use substitution rather than integration by parts. So always check for this situation before trying integration by parts.

Therefore

$$\int x\left(e^{x}+e^{x^{2}}\right)dx=xe^{x}-e^{x}+\frac{1}{2}e^{x^{2}}+C$$

> Put the two integrals together.

Practice questions 10.1

1. Find $\int x\sin(x^{2})+x^{2}\sin x\,dx$.

2. Find $\int 1+x\ln x\,dx$.

3. Find $\int \dfrac{e^{x}}{1-3e^{x}}dx$.

4. Find $\int \csc x\cot x\,dx$.

5. Find $\int \dfrac{7^{x}}{3^{2x}}dx$.

6. Find $\int \dfrac{\sqrt{x}+1}{x}dx$.

10.2 FINDING AREAS

WORKED EXAMPLE 10.2

Find the area enclosed between the curves $y = x^2 - 5x$ and $y = 7x - x^2$.

Using GDC:

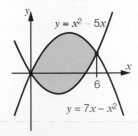

> Sketch the graph on the GDC and use it to find the intersection points.

Intersections: $x = 0$ and $x = 6$

So area $= \displaystyle\int_0^6 (7x - x^2) - (x^2 - 5x)\,dx$

$\qquad = \displaystyle\int_0^6 12x - 2x^2\,dx$

$\qquad = \left[6x^2 - \dfrac{2}{3}x^3 \right]_0^6 = 72$

> Write down the integral representing the area and carry out the definite integration.

 The integral can be checked using your calculator.

Practice questions 10.2

7. Find the area enclosed by the curves $y = \sin x$ and $y = \cos x$ between $x = \dfrac{\pi}{4}$ and $x = \dfrac{3\pi}{4}$.

8. The diagram shows the graph of $y = \ln x$. Find the shaded area.

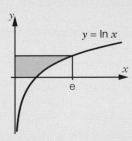

9. The diagram shows the graph of $y = x^2 - 3x + 2$. Find the shaded area.

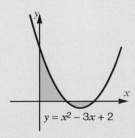

10.3 VOLUMES OF REVOLUTION

WORKED EXAMPLE 10.3

Find the volume of revolution when the curve $y = \arcsin x$ is rotated $360°$ about the y-axis.

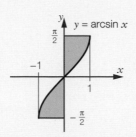

Sketch the graph to find the end points; since the volume of revolution is about the y-axis, y limits will be required.

When $x = -1$, $y = -\dfrac{\pi}{2}$. When $x = 1$, $y = \dfrac{\pi}{2}$.

$$\text{Volume} = \int_{-\pi/2}^{\pi/2} \pi x^2 \, dy$$

$$= \int_{-\pi/2}^{\pi/2} \pi (\sin y)^2 \, dy$$

Use the formula for the volume of revolution for rotation around the y-axis. Rearrange the equation to get x in terms of y: $y = \arcsin x \Rightarrow x = \sin y$

$$= \frac{\pi}{2} \int_{-\pi/2}^{\pi/2} 1 - \cos 2y \, dy$$

Use the cosine double angle identity for the integration:

$$\cos 2y = 1 - 2\sin^2 y \Rightarrow \sin^2 y = \frac{1}{2}(1 - \cos 2y)$$

$$= \frac{\pi}{2} \left[y - \frac{1}{2}\sin 2y \right]_{-\frac{\pi}{2}}^{\frac{\pi}{2}} = \frac{\pi^2}{2}$$

▶ Trigonometric identities are covered in Chapter 6.

Practice questions 10.3

10. Find the exact volume generated when $y = e^{3x}$, for $1 < x < 3$, is rotated $360°$ around the x-axis.

11. Find the volume of revolution formed when the curve $y = \cos x$ between $x = 0$ and $x = \dfrac{\pi}{2}$ is rotated $180°$ around the x-axis.

12. The diagram shows the graph of $y = \dfrac{1}{x} - 2$.

Find the volume generated when the shaded area is rotated 2π radians about the y-axis.

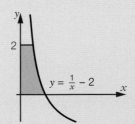

13. The diagram shows the graph of $y = x^2$.
Find the volume generated when the shaded area is rotated 2π radians about the y-axis.

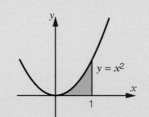

10.4 KINEMATICS

WORKED EXAMPLE 10.4

The velocity, $v\,\mathrm{m\,s^{-1}}$, of a ball is given by $v = t^2 - 4t$, where t is measured in seconds. Initially the displacement is zero.

(a) Find the displacement when $t = 10$.

(b) Find the distance travelled in the first 10 seconds.

(a) $s = \displaystyle\int_0^{10} v\,dt$

$= \displaystyle\int_0^{10} t^2 - 4t\,dt$

$= \dfrac{400}{3}\,\mathrm{m}$ (from GDC)

> 'Initially' means when $t = 0$, so we integrate between the limits $t = 0$ and $t = 10$.

(b) Distance $= \displaystyle\int_0^{10} |v|\,dt$

> To find the distance travelled, we need to take the modulus before integrating, as the velocity may be negative for part of the journey.

$= \displaystyle\int_0^{10} |t^2 - 4t|\,dt$

$= \dfrac{464}{3}\,\mathrm{m}$ (from GDC)

 To answer a question of this type without a GDC, first sketch the velocity–time graph and then separate out the parts above the axis and below the axis.

Practice questions 10.4

14. The acceleration of a car for $0 \le t \le 5$ is modelled by $a = 5(1 - e^{-2t})$, where a is measured in $\mathrm{m\,s^{-2}}$ and t is measured in seconds. The car is initially at rest.

   (a) Find the velocity of the car after t seconds.

   (b) Find the displacement from the initial position after t seconds.

   (c) Find the maximum velocity of the car.

15. The velocity of a wave is modelled by $v = \cos 5t$. When $t = 0$, $s = 0$. Show that the acceleration a and displacement s are related by $a = ks$, where k is a constant to be determined.

16. A bird has acceleration modelled by $2e^{-t}\,\mathrm{m\,s^{-2}}$ due north, where t is the time in seconds. The bird is initially travelling with speed $8\,\mathrm{m\,s^{-1}}$ north and is $100\,\mathrm{m}$ south of a tree.

   (a) Find an expression for the velocity of the bird at time t.

   (b) According to the model, when does the bird reach the tree?

Mixed practice 10

1. Find: (a) $\displaystyle\int \sqrt{e^x}\, dx$ (b) $\displaystyle\int_0^{\ln 2} \frac{e^x}{\sqrt{e^x+1}}\, dx$

2. Find the exact value of $\displaystyle\int_0^\pi \cos^2 5x\, dx$.

3. Use a substitution to find $\displaystyle\int x\sqrt{4-x}\, dx$.

4. (a) Show that $\displaystyle\int \tan x\, dx = \ln|\sec x| + c$.

   (b) Find the following integrals:

      (i) $\displaystyle\int \tan^2 x\, dx$ (ii) $\displaystyle\int \sec x\tan x\, dx$ (iii) $\displaystyle\int \sec^2 x\tan x\, dx$

5. (a) Write $x^2 - 4x + 5$ in the form $(x-p)^2 + q$.

   The velocity of a ball is given by $v = \dfrac{1}{t^2 - 4t + 5}$, where v is measured in $\mathrm{m\,s^{-1}}$ and t is measured in seconds. The ball is initially $5\,\mathrm{m}$ away from a flag.

   (b) Find the displacement of the ball from the flag after t seconds.

   (c) Find the acceleration of the ball after t seconds.

   (d) Find the maximum velocity of the ball.

6. Find the area enclosed by the curves $y = \dfrac{1}{1+x^2}$ and $y = \dfrac{1}{2}x^2$.

7. Evaluate $\displaystyle\int_0^1 e^{\sin x}\, dx$.

8. A ball's velocity, $v\,\mathrm{m\,s^{-1}}$, after time t seconds is given by $v = t\sin t$.

   (a) Find the displacement of the ball from the initial position when $t = \dfrac{3\pi}{2}$ seconds.

   (b) After how long has the ball reached its maximum displacement in the first $\dfrac{3\pi}{2}$ seconds?

   (c) Find the distance travelled by the ball in the first $\dfrac{3\pi}{2}$ seconds.

9. Find a if $\displaystyle\int_0^a \sin 2x\, dx = \dfrac{3}{4}$, $0 < a \le \pi$.

10. (a) Show that $\int 2^x \, dx = \dfrac{1}{\ln 2} 2^x + c$.

(b) Find $\dfrac{d}{dx}(x \log_2 x)$.

(c) Find $\int \log_2 x \, dx$.

11. The region between the curves $y = x + \dfrac{2}{x}$ and $y = 5 - x$ is labelled R.

(a) Find the exact area of R.

(b) Find the exact volume generated when R is rotated a full turn around the x-axis.

12. Find the exact value of $\displaystyle\int_0^{\pi/4} x^2 \cos 2x \, dx$.

13. (a) Find constants A, B and C such that $\dfrac{x^2 + 3}{x + 2} = Ax + B + \dfrac{C}{x + 2}$.

(b) Hence find $\displaystyle\int \dfrac{x^2 + 3}{x + 2} \, dx$.

14. (a) Find the volume generated when the region marked A is rotated 2π radians around the y-axis.

(b) Find the volume generated when the region marked B is rotated 2π radians around the y-axis.

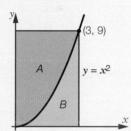

15. Consider the functions $f(x) = \sin x$ and $g(x) = 2 \sin^2 x$ over the domain $0 \leq x \leq \dfrac{\pi}{2}$.

(a) Show that $\int 2 \sin^2 x \, dx = x - \sin x \cos x + c$.

(b) Find the exact coordinates of the points of intersection of $f(x)$ and $g(x)$.

The region enclosed between the two curves is labelled R.

(c) Find the exact area of R.

(d) Find the volume of the solid generated when R is rotated $360°$ around the x-axis.

(e) Use integration by parts to find $\int \arcsin x \, dx$.

(f) Find the area enclosed by $g(x)$, the y-axis and the line $y = 1$.

(g) Find the shaded area in terms of p.

(h) Hence find $\int \arcsin \sqrt{x} \, dx$ for $0 < x < 1$.

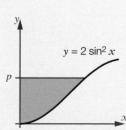

Going for the top 10

1. Find $\int \sqrt{1-x^2}\,dx$.

2. Let $S = \int \dfrac{\sin x}{\cos x + \sin x}\,dx$ and $C = \int \dfrac{\cos x}{\cos x + \sin x}\,dx$.

   (a) Find an expression for $C - S$.

   (b) Hence find $\int \dfrac{\sin x}{\cos x + \sin x}\,dx$.

3. Find $\int \cos^3 x\,dx$.

4. Consider the region bounded by the curve $y = \sin x$ and the line $y = \dfrac{1}{2}$ between $x = \dfrac{\pi}{3}$ and $x = \dfrac{2\pi}{3}$. Find the volume generated when the region is rotated a full turn around:

   (a) the x-axis

   (b) the line $y = \dfrac{1}{2}$.

5. Use integration by parts to find $\int e^x \sin x\,dx$.

6. (a) (i) Show that $\sqrt{\dfrac{1-3x}{1+3x}} = \dfrac{1-3x}{\sqrt{1-9x^2}}$.

      (ii) Hence find $\int \sqrt{\dfrac{1-3x}{1+3x}}\,dx$.

   (b) (i) Use integration by parts to find $\int \sec^3 x\,dx$.

      (ii) Hence find $\int_0^1 \sqrt{x^2+3}\,dx$, giving your answer in the form $a + b\ln 3$ where a and b are rational numbers.

11 PROBABILITY AND STATISTICS

WHAT YOU NEED TO KNOW

- Standard deviation, σ, is a measure of how spread out the data is relative to the mean, μ. The square of the standard deviation is called the variance, and it has the formula:

$$\sigma^2 = \frac{\sum_{i=1}^{k} f_i x_i^2}{n} - \mu^2 \text{ where } \mu = \frac{\sum_{i=1}^{k} f_i x_i}{n}, \; n = \sum_{i=1}^{k} f_i \text{ and } f_i \text{ is the frequency of the } i\text{th data value.}$$

- The probability of an event can be found by listing or counting all possible outcomes. The probabilities of combined events are often best found using Venn diagrams or tree diagrams.

  - Venn diagrams are often useful when the question involves a union of events.

    - The union of events A and B can be found using the formula:

    $$P(A \cup B) = P(A) + P(B) - P(A \cap B)$$

    - For mutually exclusive events, the formula becomes $P(A \cup B) = P(A) + P(B)$.

  - Tree diagrams can be used when the question involves a sequence of events.

- The probability of event A happening given that an event B has already happened is known as conditional probability and is given by:

$$P(A \mid B) = \frac{P(A \cap B)}{P(B)}$$

  - Events A and B are independent if $P(A \mid B) = P(A)$ or $P(A \cap B) = P(A)\,P(B)$.

- Bayes' theorem is a formula for relating conditional probabilities:

  - When there are only two outcomes: $P(B \mid A) = \dfrac{P(B)\,P(A \mid B)}{P(B)\,P(A \mid B) + P(B')\,P(A \mid B')}$

  - When there are more than two outcomes for event B:

  $$P(B_i \mid A) = \frac{P(A \mid B_i)P(B_i)}{P(A \mid B_1)P(B_1) + P(A \mid B_2)P(B_2) + \cdots + P(A \mid B_n)P(B_n)}$$

- A discrete random variable can be described by its probability distribution, which is the list of all possible values and their probabilities.

  - The total of all the probabilities must always equal 1.

  - The expected value is $E(X) = \mu = \sum_x x\,P(X = x)$.

  - The variance is $\mathrm{Var}(X) = E(X - \mu)^2 = E(X^2) - \left[E(X)\right]^2$.

- If there is a fixed number of trials (n) with constant and independent probability of success (p) in each trial, the number of successes follows a binomial distribution: $X \sim B(n, p)$.

  - $E(X) = np$

  - $\mathrm{Var}(X) = np(1 - p)$

- If successes occur independently and at a constant average rate (m), the number of successes in a given period follows a Poisson distribution: $X \sim \text{Po}(m)$.
  - $\text{E}(X) = m$
  - $\text{Var}(X) = m$
- A continuous random variable X can be described by its probability density function, $f(x)$.
  - Its probability is found by integration: $P(a < X < b) = \int_{a}^{b} f(x)\, dx$.
  - The total probability over all cases must equal 1: $\int_{-\infty}^{\infty} f(x)\, dx = 1$.
  - The expected value is $\text{E}(X) = \mu = \int_{-\infty}^{\infty} x\, f(x)\, dx$.
  - The variance is $\text{Var}(X) = \text{E}(X^2) - \left[\text{E}(X)\right]^2$ where $\text{E}(X^2) = \int_{-\infty}^{\infty} x^2 f(x)\, dx$.
- The normal distribution is determined by its mean (μ) and variance (σ^2): $X \sim \text{N}(\mu, \sigma^2)$.
  - The inverse normal distribution is used to find the value of x which corresponds to a given cumulative probability: $p = P(X \leq x)$.
  - If μ or σ is unknown, use the standard normal distribution to replace the values of X with their Z-scores, $z = \dfrac{x - \mu}{\sigma}$, which satisfy $Z \sim \text{N}(0, 1)$.

⚠ EXAM TIPS AND COMMON ERRORS

- Make sure that you do not confuse standard deviation and variance, especially when working with the normal distribution.

- When interpreting probability questions, pay particular attention to whether the required probability is conditional or not.

- When you use your GDC to find probabilities, you must write the results using the correct mathematical notation, **not** calculator notation.

- If a question mentions average rate of success, or events occurring at a constant rate, you should use the Poisson distribution. If you can identify a fixed number of trials, then the binomial distribution is appropriate.

- With the Poisson distribution, make sure that you are using the correct mean for the time (or spatial) interval.

11.1 CALCULATING THE MEAN AND STANDARD DEVIATION FROM SUMMARY STATISTICS

WORKED EXAMPLE 11.1

A teacher records the time, t minutes, it takes her to drive to work every morning. The times for 12 days are summarised by: $\sum t_i = 256$ and $\sum t_i^2 = 5963$. She then adds the time for the 13th day, which was 24 minutes. Calculate the mean and standard deviation of all 13 times.

The new sums are:

$\sum t_i = 256 + 24 = 280$

$\sum t_i^2 = 5963 + 24^2 = 6539$

> Find the new totals including the extra data value of 24 minutes.

$\bar{t} = \dfrac{280}{13} = 21.5 \ (3\,SF)$

> Find the new mean.

$s_n^2 = \dfrac{6539}{13} - \left(\dfrac{280}{13}\right)^2 = 39.0946\ldots$

$\therefore s_n = \sqrt{39.0946\ldots} = 6.25 \ (3\,SF)$

> Find the new variance and take its square root to find the standard deviation.

 For a question involving several steps, do not use a rounded value before reaching the final answer.

Practice questions 11.1

1. The ages, y years, of 42 children are summarised by $\sum y_i = 483$ and $\sum y_i^2 = 6015$. Find the mean and the standard deviation of the children's ages.

2. The mean height of a group of 15 basketball players is 207.2 cm. When another player joins the group, the mean height decreases to 206.5 cm. Find the height of the new player.

3. In her first five attempts at long jump, Greta's mean jump length was 4.80 m and the standard deviation of the lengths was 0.2 m. After her sixth jump the mean increased to 4.85 m. Find the standard deviation of all six jumps.

11.2 FREQUENCY TABLES AND GROUPED DATA

WORKED EXAMPLE 11.2

The heights of 50 trees (measured to the nearest metre) are summarised below.

Height (m)	2–5	6–10	11–15	16–22	23–30
Frequency	5	11	17	14	3

Estimate the mean and variance of the heights.

h_i	3.5	8	13	19	26.5
f_i	5	11	17	14	3

From GDC:

$\bar{h} = 13.4\,cm$ (3 SF)

$s_n = 5.9453\ldots$

$\Rightarrow s_n^2 = 35.3\,cm^2$ (3 SF)

 Use the mid-interval value for each group.

> ⚠ When using a calculator in statistics questions, make sure you show the numbers being entered into your GDC.

Practice questions 11.2

4. The cumulative frequency diagram shows the test scores of a group of students.

Test score, S	Frequency
$0 \le S \le 20$	7
$20 < S \le 35$	q
$35 < S \le 50$	r
$50 < S \le p$	17
$p < S \le 75$	8

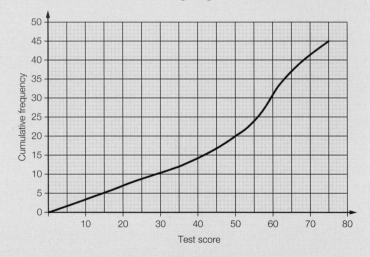

(a) Estimate the median and the interquartile range of the scores.

(b) Find the values of p, q and r to complete the frequency table.

(c) Hence estimate the mean and standard deviation of the scores.

5. The results of a group of students on a mathematics test are summarised below.

Score	20–30	31–40	41–55	56–70	71–82	83–100
Frequency	6	13	k	25	11	9

(a) Given that the mean score is 59 (rounded to the nearest integer), find the value of k.

(b) Find the standard deviation of the results.

11.3 CALCULATING PROBABILITIES BY CONSIDERING POSSIBLE OUTCOMES

WORKED EXAMPLE 11.3

A cubical die has the numbers 1, 1, 2, 3, 3, 3 written on its faces. The die is rolled twice. Find the probability that the sum of the two scores is greater than 4.

The possible sums are $S = 5$ and $S = 6$.

$$P(S=6) = P(3 \cap 3)$$
$$= P(3) \times P(3)$$
$$= \frac{1}{2} \times \frac{1}{2} = \frac{1}{4}$$

> The scores on the two rolls of the die are independent, so $P(3 \cap 3) = P(3) \times P(3)$.

There are two ways of getting a sum of 5: $2 + 3$ and $3 + 2$.
$$P(S=5) = P(2 \text{ then } 3) \text{ OR } (3 \text{ then } 2)$$
$$= (P(2) \times P(3)) + (P(3) \times P(2))$$
$$= \frac{1}{6} \times \frac{1}{2} + \frac{1}{2} \times \frac{1}{6} = \frac{1}{6}$$

> The event 'a 2 followed by a 3' has to be counted as a separate event from 'a 3 followed by a 2'.

The total probability is $\dfrac{1}{4} + \dfrac{1}{6} = \dfrac{5}{12}$.

> The two events $S = 5$ and $S = 6$ are mutually exclusive, so we use $P(A \cup B) = P(A) + P(B)$.

Practice questions 11.3

6. The random variable X has probability distribution as shown in the table below.

x	1	2	3
$P(X = x)$	0.4	0.3	0.3

Find the probability that the sum of two independent observations of X is 4.

7. Seven students are randomly arranged in a line. Find the probability that Anne and Beth are standing next to each other.

◀◀ Counting principles can be used to calculate probabilities. Counting principles are covered in Chapter 1.

8. A bag contains seven caramels and one chocolate. Three children, Peng, Quinn and Raul, take turns to pick a sweet out of the bag at random. If the sweet is a chocolate, they take it; if it is a caramel, they put it back and pass the bag around.
   (a) Find the probability that Raul gets the chocolate on his second turn.
   (b) Find the probability that the chocolate is still in the bag when it gets to Quinn for the fifth time.

11.4 VENN DIAGRAMS

WORKED EXAMPLE 11.4

The events A and B are such that $P(A \cup B) = \dfrac{3}{5}$, $P(B) = \dfrac{2}{5}$ and $P(B \mid A) = \dfrac{3}{7}$.

(a) State, with a reason, whether A and B are independent.

(b) Find $P(A)$.

(a) The events A and B are not independent because $P(B \mid A) \neq P(B)$.

> For independent events, knowing that A has occurred has no impact on the probability of B occurring, i.e. $P(B \mid A) = P(B)$.

(b) Let $P(A \cap B) = x$. Then $P(B \cap A') = \dfrac{2}{5} - x$ and

$$P(A \cap B') = \dfrac{3}{5} - \left(\dfrac{2}{5} - x\right) - x = \dfrac{1}{5}$$

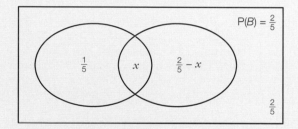

> ⚠ Venn diagrams are a useful way of representing information when you are given information about the union. Label the intersection x and work outwards.

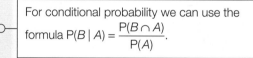

$$P(B \mid A) = \dfrac{P(B \cap A)}{P(A)}$$

$$\therefore \dfrac{3}{7} = \dfrac{x}{\dfrac{1}{5} + x}$$

$$\Rightarrow x = \dfrac{3}{20}$$

Hence $P(A) = \dfrac{1}{5} + \dfrac{3}{20} = \dfrac{7}{20}$.

> For conditional probability we can use the formula $P(B \mid A) = \dfrac{P(B \cap A)}{P(A)}$.

Practice questions 11.4

9. Given that $P(B) = 0.5$, $P(A' \cap B') = 0.2$ and $P(B \mid A) = 0.4$, find $P(A)$.

10. All of the 100 students at a college take part in at least one of three activities: chess, basketball and singing. 10 play both chess and basketball, 12 play chess and sing, and 7 take part in both singing and basketball. 40 students play basketball, 62 play chess and 22 sing.

    (a) How many students take part in all three activities?

    (b) A student is chosen at random. Given that this student plays basketball and sings, what is the probability that she also plays chess?

11.5 BAYES' THEOREM AND TREE DIAGRAMS

WORKED EXAMPLE 11.5

 The events A and B are such that $P(A) = \dfrac{1}{3}$, $P(B \mid A) = \dfrac{1}{3}$ and $P(B \mid A') = \dfrac{1}{2}$. Find $P(A \mid B)$.

⚠️ This type of question can be done using Bayes' theorem or by drawing a tree diagram.

$$P(A \mid B) = \frac{P(A)P(B \mid A)}{P(A)P(B \mid A) + P(A')P(B \mid A')}$$

$$= \frac{\dfrac{1}{3} \times \dfrac{1}{3}}{\dfrac{1}{3} \times \dfrac{1}{3} + \dfrac{2}{3} \times \dfrac{1}{2}} = \frac{1}{4}$$

○── Write out Bayes' theorem in terms of the events mentioned.

Practice questions 11.5

11. The events A and B are such that $P(B \mid A) = 0.2$, $P(B' \mid A') = 0.3$, $P(A \mid B) = 0.4$ and $P(A) = x$.

    (a) Complete the following tree diagram.

    (b) Find the value of x.

    (c) State, with a reason, whether the events A and B are independent.

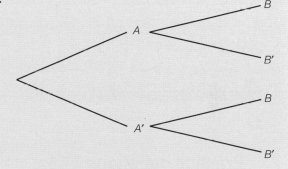

12. Given that $P(B) = 0.3$, $P(A \mid B) = 0.6$ and $P(A \mid B') = 0.4$, find $P(B \mid A)$.

13. Every morning I either walk or cycle to school, with equal probability. If I walk, the probability that I am late is 0.2. If I cycle, the probability that I am late is 0.4. Given that I was late for school yesterday, what is the probability that I walked?

14. A large box contains three different types of toys. One third of the toys are cars, one quarter are yo-yos and the rest are balloons. 20% of the cars, 30% of the yo-yos and 40% of the balloons are pink. A toy is selected at random from the box. Given that the toy is pink, find the probability that it is a balloon.

11.6 EXPECTATION AND VARIANCE OF DISCRETE RANDOM VARIABLES

WORKED EXAMPLE 11.6

A discrete random variable Y has probability distribution as shown in the table below.

y	2	3	4	5
$P(Y=y)$	k	$\dfrac{2}{5}$	$\dfrac{1}{4}$	$2k$

(a) Find the exact value of k.

(b) Find the variance of Y.

(a) $k+\dfrac{2}{5}+\dfrac{1}{4}+2k=1 \Rightarrow k=\dfrac{7}{60}$

> We use the fact that the probabilities must add up to 1.

(b) $E(Y)=2\left(\dfrac{7}{60}\right)+3\left(\dfrac{2}{5}\right)+4\left(\dfrac{1}{4}\right)+5\left(\dfrac{14}{60}\right)=3.6$

> First, find the expectation using the formula $E(Y) = \sum y P(Y = y)$.

$E(Y^2)=2^2\left(\dfrac{7}{60}\right)+3^2\left(\dfrac{2}{5}\right)+4^2\left(\dfrac{1}{4}\right)+5^2\left(\dfrac{14}{60}\right)$

$\qquad =13.9$

$Var(Y)=13.9-3.6^2=0.94$

> To find the variance, use the formula $Var(Y) = E(Y^2) - [E(Y)]^2$.

Practice questions 11.6

15. Find the expected value and the variance of the following discrete random variable.

z	11	13	17	19	23
$P(Z=z)$	0.2	0.1	0.1	0.2	0.4

16. The random variable X has probability distribution as shown in the table below.

x	1	2	3	4
$P(X=x)$	c	p	0.4	0.2

Given that $E(X) = 2.6$, find the values of c and p.

11.7 THE BINOMIAL AND POISSON DISTRIBUTIONS

WORKED EXAMPLE 11.7

Sandra receives 8 emails per day on average. It is assumed that the number of emails follows a Poisson distribution.

(a) Find the probability that Sandra receives more than 10 emails in one day.

(b) Find the probability that Sandra receives more than 10 emails on two out of seven days.

(a) Let X = number of emails received in a day.
Then $X \sim Po(8)$.

> We start by defining the random variable and stating the probability distribution.

$$P(X > 10) = 1 - P(X \leq 10)$$
$$= 1 - 0.81588\ldots \quad \text{(from GDC)}$$
$$= 0.184 \text{ (3 SF)}$$

> Write down the probability required. To use the calculator we must relate it to $P(X \leq k)$.

(b) Let Y = number of days out of 7 with more than 10 emails. Then $Y \sim B(7, 0.184)$.
$$P(Y = 2) = 0.257 \text{ (3 SF) from GDC}$$

> There is a fixed number of days, so we need to use the binomial distribution this time.

 When using your GDC, always state the distribution used and the probability calculated, and give the answer to 3 SF.

Practice questions 11.7

17. A fair six-sided die is rolled 16 times. Find the probability it lands on a '4' more than five times.

18. During the winter months, snowstorms occur at a constant rate of 1.2 per week, independently of each other.

    (a) Find the probability that no snowstorms occur in a given week.

    (b) Find the probability that in seven consecutive weeks there is at least one week with no snowstorms.

19. The random variable X has distribution $B(n, p)$. The mean of X is equal to three times its variance, and $P(X = 2) = 0.0384$ (to three significant figures). Find the values of n and p.

20. Rebekah recorded the number of cars in the school car park over a period of 14 days. The results are summarised by $\sum x_i = 245$ and $\sum x_i^2 = 4462$.

    (a) Find the mean and variance of the number of cars in the car park.

    (b) State, with a reason, whether a Poisson distribution would be an appropriate model for the number of cars in the car park.

11.8 EXPECTATION AND VARIANCE OF CONTINUOUS RANDOM VARIABLES

WORKED EXAMPLE 11.8

A continuous random variable X has probability density function

$$f(x) = \begin{cases} 3x^2 + \dfrac{7}{4} & \text{for } 0 \le x \le \dfrac{1}{2} \\ 0 & \text{otherwise} \end{cases}$$

(a) Find the value of q such that $P(X < q) = 0.25$.

(b) Given that $E(X) = \dfrac{17}{64}$, calculate $\text{Var}(X)$.

(a) $\displaystyle\int_0^q 3x^2 + \dfrac{7}{4}\, dx = 0.25$

$\left[x^3 + \dfrac{7}{4}x \right]_0^q = 0.25$

$\Rightarrow q^3 + \dfrac{7}{4}q - 0.25 = 0$

$\Rightarrow q = 0.141 \text{ (from GDC)}$

> $P(X < q)$, or equivalently the probability that X lies in $[0, q]$, is given by $\int_0^q f(x)\, dx$.

> Make sure you know how to use your GDC to solve polynomial equations.

(b) $\text{Var}(X) = \displaystyle\int_0^{\frac{1}{2}} 3x^4 + \dfrac{7x^2}{4}\, dx - \left(\dfrac{17}{64} \right)^2$

$= 0.0211 \text{ (from GDC)}$

> $\text{Var}(X) = E(X^2) - [E(X)]^2$ where $E(X^2) = \int_{-\infty}^{\infty} x^2 f(x)\, dx$.
> We can use the GDC to evaluate the integral.

Practice questions 11.8

21. The continuous random variable X is defined for $-2 \le x \le 2$ and has the probability density function $f(x) = ke^{2x}$.

(a) Find the exact value of k.

(b) Find the median of X.

> ⚠ The median, m, of a continuous random variable satisfies $\int_{-\infty}^{m} f(x)\, dx = \dfrac{1}{2}$.
> The mode is the value of x at the maximum of $f(x)$.

22. A continuous random variable X has probability density function $f(x) = \dfrac{1}{9}(4 - x^2)$ for $x \in [-1, 2]$.

(a) Show that $E(X) = \dfrac{1}{4}$.

(b) Find the probability that X takes on a value between the mean and the mode.

11.9 THE NORMAL AND INVERSE NORMAL DISTRIBUTIONS

WORKED EXAMPLE 11.9

Test scores are normally distributed with mean 62 and standard deviation 12.

(a) Find the percentage of candidates who scored below 50.

(b) It is known that 44% of candidates scored between 62 and p. Find the value of p.

(a) Let X = test score, so $X \sim N(62, 12^2)$.

> We start by defining the random variable and stating the distribution used.

$P(X < 50) = 0.159$ (3 SF) from GDC
So 15.9% of candidates scored below 50.

> For a normal distribution you must be able to use a GDC to find a probability.

(b) $P(62 < X < p) = 0.44$

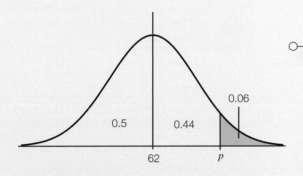

> Sketching a diagram allows us to see more clearly exactly what we need to find from the GDC.
>
> As the probability is known, we need to use the inverse normal distribution.

> On some calculators it is necessary to change problems like this into the form $P(X \le x) = p$ (i.e. a left-tail calculation).

From the diagram, $P(X > p) = 0.06$
From GDC, $p = 80.7$ (3 SF)

Practice questions 11.9

23. The random variable Y follows a normal distribution with mean 7.5 and variance 1.44. Find:

(a) $P(6 < Y < 7)$

(b) $P(Y \ge 8.5)$

(c) the value of k such that $P(Y \le k) = 0.35$.

24. The weights, W kg, of babies born at a certain hospital satisfy $W \sim N(3.2, 0.7^2)$. Find the value of m such that 35% of the babies weigh between m kg and 3.2 kg.

25. The time a laptop battery can last before needing to be recharged is assumed to be normally distributed with mean 4 hours and standard deviation 20 minutes.

(a) Find the probability that a laptop battery will last more than 4.5 hours.

(b) A manufacturer wants to ensure that 95% of batteries will last for $4 \pm x$ hours. Find x.

11.10 USING THE STANDARD NORMAL DISTRIBUTION WHEN μ OR σ ARE UNKNOWN

WORKED EXAMPLE 11.10

It is known that the average height of six-year-old boys is 105 cm and that 22% of the boys are taller than 110 cm. Find the standard deviation of the heights.

Let X = height of a six-year-old boy.
Then $X \sim N(105, \sigma^2)$.

> We start by defining the random variable and stating the distribution.

The standardised variable is $Z = \dfrac{X-105}{\sigma}$ and $Z \sim N(0,1)$.

> As σ is unknown, we need to use the standard normal distribution, $Z \sim N(0, 1)$ where $Z = \dfrac{X-\mu}{\sigma}$.

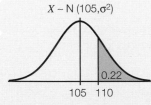
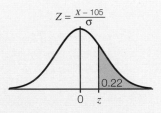

> ⚠ It is always a good idea to sketch a normal distribution diagram to help you visualise the solution.

$P(Z > z) = 0.22$
$\Rightarrow z = 0.7722$ (from GDC)

> As the probability is known (22% = 0.22), we need to use the inverse normal distribution.

$z = \dfrac{x-105}{\sigma}$

$\therefore 0.7722 = \dfrac{110-105}{\sigma}$

$\Rightarrow \sigma = 6.48\,\text{cm}$

> We can now find σ from z.

Practice questions 11.10

26. The weights of apples sold at a market are normally distributed with mean weight 125 g. It is found that 26% of the apples weigh less than 116 g. Find the standard deviation of the weights.

27. A machine dispenses cups of coffee. The volume of coffee in a cup is normally distributed with standard deviation 5.6 ml. If 10% of cups contain more than 160 ml, find to one decimal place the mean volume of coffee in a cup.

28. It is known that the scores on a test follow a normal distribution $N(\mu, \sigma^2)$. 20% of the scores are above 82 and 10% are below 47.

(a) Show that $\mu + 0.8416\sigma = 82$.

(b) By writing a similar equation, find the mean and standard deviation of the scores.

Mixed practice 11

1. The heights of trees in a forest are normally distributed with mean height 26.2 m and standard deviation 5.6 m.

   (a) Find the probability that a tree is more than 30 m tall.

   (b) What is the probability that among 16 randomly selected trees at least 2 are more than 30 m tall?

2. A discrete random variable X is given by $P(X = n) = kn^2$ for $n = 1, 2, 3, 4$.

   Find the expected value and variance of X.

3. If $P(A) = 0.3$, $P(B \mid A') = 0.5$ and $P(A \mid B) = \dfrac{7}{16}$, find $P(B \mid A)$.

4. The discrete random variable Y has probability distribution as shown in the table below.

y	1	2	3	4
$P(Y = y)$	0.1	0.2	p	q

   Given that $E(Y) = 3.1$, find the values of p and q.

5. A continuous random variable X has probability density function $f(x) = k(4 - x^2)$ for $0 \le x \le 2$.

   (a) Find the value of k.

   (b) Show that the median satisfies $m^3 - 12m + 8 = 0$.

6. A cat visits my garden at random, at the constant average rate of four times a day.

   (a) What is the probability that the cat visits my garden at least once on a given day?

   (b) What is the probability that the cat visits my garden at least once every day in a seven-day week?

   (c) Given that the cat has already visited my garden once today, what is the probability that it will visit the garden at least five times?

7. A continuous random variable X has probability density function

   $$f(x) = \begin{cases} ke^{-x^2} & \text{for } 0 \le x \le 2 \\ 0 & \text{otherwise} \end{cases}$$

   (a) Find:

      (i) the value of k

      (ii) the lower quartile

      (iii) the mean of X.

   (b) Two independent observations of X are recorded.

      (i) Find the probability that one of them is above and the other is below the mean.

      (ii) Given that exactly one of the observations is above the mean, find the probability that it is the first one.

8. A company hires out vans on a daily basis. It has three vans it can hire out. The number of requests it gets for hiring a van can be modelled by a Poisson distribution with a mean of 1.8 requests per day.

(a) Find the probability that in one day some requests have to be turned down.

(b) Given that some requests have to be turned down, find the probability that there were exactly four requests.

(c) Find the probability that there are more than six requests in two days.

(d) Find the probability that in a seven-day week there are at least two days in which requests are rejected.

(e) Find the probability distribution of the number of vans which are hired out each day.

(f) The price of hiring a van is $120. Find the expected daily takings of the company.

(g) The number of kilometres travelled by each van can be modelled by a normal distribution with mean 150 km. 10% of vans travel more than 200 km. Find the standard deviation of the normal distribution.

(h) If two vans are hired, find the probability that each travels less than 100 km.

Going for the top 11

1. The continuous random variable X has probability density function

$f(x) = kx \sin x$ for $x \in [0, \pi]$.

(a) Show that $k = \dfrac{1}{\pi}$.

(b) Find the interquartile range of X.

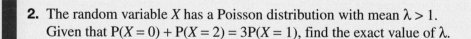

2. The random variable X has a Poisson distribution with mean $\lambda > 1$.
Given that $P(X = 0) + P(X = 2) = 3P(X = 1)$, find the exact value of λ.

3. Three basketball players, Annie, Brent and Carlos, try to shoot a free throw. Annie shoots first, then Brent, then Carlos. The probability that Annie scores is 0.6, the probability that Brent scores is 0.5, and the probability that Carlos scores is 0.8. The shots are independent of each other and the first player to score wins.

(a) Find the probability that Annie wins with her second shot.

(b) What is the probability that Carlos gets a second shot?

(c) (i) Show that the probability of Brent winning with his kth shot is $0.2 \times 0.04^{k-1}$.

(ii) Hence find the probability that Brent wins.

12 MATHEMATICAL INDUCTION

WHAT YOU NEED TO KNOW

- Proof by mathematical induction always follows the same basic steps:
  - Show that the statement is true for the base case. This is *usually* done by substituting $n = 1$ into the given expression.
  - Assume that the statement is true for $n = k$ and write down what this means (this is called the inductive hypothesis).
  - Link the kth case to the $(k + 1)$th case.
  - Show that if the statement is true for $n = k$ then it is also true for $n = k + 1$.
  - Write a conclusion using the standard formulation:
    The statement is true for $n = 1$, and if true for $n = k$ it is also true for $n = k + 1$. Hence, the statement is true for all $n \geq 1$ by the principle of mathematical induction.

- The inductive step depends on the problem type:
  - For series, the sum of k terms is linked to the sum of $k + 1$ terms by adding the $(k + 1)$th term of the series: $S_{k+1} = S_k + u_{k+1}$.
  - For sequences, use the recurrence relation that relates the kth term to the $(k + 1)$th term. If a recurrence relation involves two previous terms, check two base cases, $n = 1$ and $n = 2$.
  - For differentiation, find the $(k + 1)$th derivative by differentiating the kth derivative.
  - For divisibility, form an equation for the inductive hypothesis by making the given expression equal to a multiple of the number it should be divisible by; for example, $3A, A \in \mathbb{Z}$, for divisibility by 3. Then substitute from this equation into the expression for $n = k + 1$.
  - For inequalities, substitute from the inductive hypothesis into the left-hand side of the expression for $n = k + 1$.

EXAM TIPS AND COMMON ERRORS

- When carrying out the inductive step, make it clear where you have used the result for $n = k$ in your working.
- In the conclusion **do not** write 'The statement is true for $n = k$ and for $n = k + 1$'. You must understand the correct logic: '*Assuming* it is true for $n = k$, it can *then* be shown that it is also true for $n = k + 1$.'
- You can pick up marks for writing the statements for $n = 1$ and $n = k$ and the conclusion, even if you cannot complete the calculation in the inductive step.
- Induction problems involving differentiation may require the use of the product or quotient rules.

 The product and quotient rules are covered in Chapter 9.

12.1 SERIES AND SEQUENCES

WORKED EXAMPLE 12.1

Prove by induction that $\dfrac{1}{2!} + \dfrac{2}{3!} + \dfrac{3}{4!} + \ldots + \dfrac{n}{(n+1)!} = \dfrac{(n+1)!-1}{(n+1)!}$.

When $n = 1$:

$\text{LHS} = \dfrac{1}{2!} = \dfrac{1}{2}; \text{RHS} = \dfrac{2!-1}{2!} = \dfrac{1}{2}$

So the statement is true for $n = 1$.

> Show that the statement is true for $n = 1$.

> ⚠ Make it clear that you have evaluated each side separately.

Assume it is true for $n = k$:

$\dfrac{1}{2!} + \dfrac{2}{3!} + \dfrac{3}{4!} + \ldots + \dfrac{k}{(k+1)!} = \dfrac{(k+1)!-1}{(k+1)!} \quad \ldots (*)$

> Clearly state the inductive hypothesis (the statement for $n = k$ that is assumed to be true).

> ⚠ It is a good idea to label this equation so that it can be referred to later.

Let $n = k + 1$. Working towards:

$\dfrac{1}{2!} + \dfrac{2}{3!} + \dfrac{3}{4!} + \ldots + \dfrac{k+1}{(k+2)!} = \dfrac{(k+2)!-1}{(k+2)!}$

> This is the start of the inductive step. Writing down what we are working towards will help us see how to simplify the expression.

$\text{LHS} = \dfrac{1}{2!} + \dfrac{2}{3!} + \dfrac{3}{4!} + \ldots + \dfrac{k}{(k+1)!} + \dfrac{k+1}{(k+2)!}$

$= \dfrac{(k+1)!-1}{(k+1)!} + \dfrac{k+1}{(k+2)!} \quad (\text{using } (*))$

> We start from the LHS and simplify until we get to the RHS expression that we are working towards.
>
> We use the statement of the inductive hypothesis (equation $(*)$) and add the next term, $\dfrac{k+1}{(k+2)!}$, to get the sum for $n = k + 1$.

$= \dfrac{(k+2)(k+1)!-(k+2)}{(k+2)!} + \dfrac{(k+1)}{(k+2)!}$

$= \dfrac{(k+2)!-k-2+k+1}{(k+2)!}$

$= \dfrac{(k+2)!-1}{(k+2)!} = \text{RHS}$

> The expression we are working towards has $(k + 2)!$ in the denominator, so we write the two fractions with a common denominator $(k + 2)!$
>
> We then use the fact that $(k + 2)! = (k + 2)(k + 1)!$

So the statement is true for $n = k + 1$.

> We must state what we have shown.

The statement is true for $n = 1$, and if true for $n = k$ it is also true for $n = k + 1$. Hence, the statement is true for all $n \geq 1$ by the principle of mathematical induction.

> Write a conclusion using the standard formulation.

Practice questions 12.1

1. Use the principle of mathematical induction to show that

$$\sum_{r=1}^{n} r^3 = \left(\frac{n(n+1)}{2} \right)^2$$

2. Prove using induction that $1 + r + r^2 + \ldots + r^n = \dfrac{r^{n+1} - 1}{r - 1}$ for $n \in \mathbb{Z}^+$.

3. Use the principle of mathematical induction to show that

$$\sum_{r=1}^{n} \frac{1}{4r^2 - 1} = \frac{n}{2n+1}$$

4. Prove by induction that $\displaystyle\sum_{r=1}^{n} r(r!) = (n+1)! - 1$.

5. Use the principle of mathematical induction to show that for any integer $n \geq 1$:

$$1 + \frac{3}{2} + \frac{5}{4} + \ldots + \frac{2n-1}{2^{n-1}} = 6 - \frac{2n+3}{2^{n-1}}$$

6. Prove by induction that

$$\sum_{r=0}^{n-1} \frac{1}{(2r+1)(2r+3)} = \frac{n}{2n+1}$$

7. A sequence is given by the recurrence relation $u_{n+1} = 5u_n - 8$ with $u_1 = 7$. Prove by induction that the general term of the sequence is $u_n = 5^n + 2$.

 Be clear that you are trying to prove the formula for the general term, **not** the recurrence relation formula. The general term formula with $n = k$ will form the inductive hypothesis, and the recurrence relation will only be used to move from this to the $n = k + 1$ case.

8. Given that $u_{n+1} = 2u_n + 1$ and $u_1 = 3$, prove by induction that $u_n = 2^{n+1} - 1$.

9. Given that $u_1 = 8$, $u_2 = 34$ and $u_{n+2} = 8u_{n+1} - 15u_n$, use the principle of mathematical induction to show that $u_n = 5^n + 3^n$.

 If the recurrence relation involves the previous two terms of the sequence, you need to check two base cases ($n = 1$ and $n = 2$) and you need to assume that two statements are true (one for u_k and one for u_{k+1}) in the inductive hypothesis.

12.2 DIFFERENTIATION

WORKED EXAMPLE 12.2

Let $f(x) = xe^{3x}$. Prove by induction that $f^{(n)}(x) = (3^n x + n3^{n-1})e^{3x}$ for $n \geq 1$.

When $n = 1$:
$$f'(x) = e^{3x} + x(3e^{3x})$$
$$= e^{3x}(3x+1)$$
$$= (3^1 x + 1 \times 3^0)e^{3x} = \text{RHS}$$

So the statement is true for $n = 1$.

 Show that the statement is true for $n = 1$.

⚠ Make sure that the expression for $f'(x)$ is written explicitly in the required form.

Assume it is true for $n = k$:
$$f^{(k)}(x) = (3^k x + k3^{k-1})e^{3x} \quad \cdots (*)$$

Clearly state the inductive hypothesis (the statement for $n = k$ that is assumed to be true).

Let $n = k + 1$. Working towards:
$$f^{(k+1)}(x) = (3^{k+1} x + (k+1)3^k)e^{3}$$

Writing down what we are working towards will help us see how to simplify after differentiation.

$$f^{(k+1)}(x) = \frac{d}{dx}(f^{(k)}(x))$$
$$= \frac{d}{dx}((3^k x + k3^{k-1})e^{3x}) \quad (\text{using}(*))$$
$$= (3^k + 0)e^{3x} + (3^k x + k3^{k-1})(3e^{3x})$$
$$= [3^k + (3^k x + k3^{k-1}) \times 3]e^{3x}$$
$$= (3^k + 3^{k+1} x + k3^k)e^{3x}$$
$$= (3^{k+1} x + (k+1)3^k)e^{3x}$$

This is the inductive step.
We find $f^{(k+1)}$ by differentiating the expression for $f^{(k)}$ in equation $(*)$, and then simplify until we get to the RHS expression that we are working towards.

⚠ Make sure that all the steps are clearly shown.

So the statement is true for $n = k + 1$.

 We must state what we have shown.

The statement is true for $n = 1$, and if true for $n = k$ it is also true for $n = k + 1$. Hence, the statement is true for all $n \geq 1$ by the principle of mathematical induction.

Write a conclusion using the standard formulation.

Practice questions 12.2

10. The function f is defined by $f(x) = xe^{kx}$. Use mathematical induction to show that
$$f^{(n)}(x) = e^{kx}(k^n x + nk^{n-1}).$$

11. If $y = \dfrac{1}{1-2x}$, prove by induction that $\dfrac{d^n y}{dx^n} = \dfrac{2^n n!}{(1-2x)^{n+1}}$.

12.3 DIVISIBILITY

WORKED EXAMPLE 12.3

Use mathematical induction to show that $9^n - 7^n - 2^n$ is divisible by 14 for $n \in \mathbb{Z}^+$.

When $n = 1$, $9^1 - 7^1 - 2^1 = 0 \ (= 0 \times 14)$, which is divisible by 14.

So the statement is true for $n = 1$.

> Show that the statement is true for $n = 1$ by evaluating the expression and checking that it is divisible by 14.

Assume it is true for $n = k$:

$9^k - 7^k - 2^k = 14A$ for some $A \in \mathbb{Z}^+ \ldots (*)$

> Clearly state the inductive hypothesis (the statement for $n = k$ that is assumed to be true). A number being divisible by 14 means that it can be written as a multiple of 14 (i.e. $14A$).

Let $n = k + 1$. Then

$9^{k+1} - 7^{k+1} - 2^{k+1}$

$= 9(9^k) - 7^{k+1} - 2^{k+1}$

$= 9(14A + 7^k + 2^k) - 7^{k+1} - 2^{k+1} \ \left(\text{using } (*)\right)$

> This is the start of the inductive step.
> We can write $9^{k+1} = 9 \times 9^k$ and then substitute for 9^k from equation $(*)$.

$= 9A(14) + 9(7^k) + 9(2^k) - 7^{k+1} - 2^{k+1}$

$= 9A(14) + 7^k(9-7) + 2^k(9-2)$

$= 9A(14) + 7^k(2) + 2^k(7)$

> Multiply out the bracket and take out a factor of 7^k and 2^k from the relevant terms.

⚠️ It is always a good idea to group together powers of the same number.

$= 9A(14) + 7^{k-1}(7 \times 2) + 2^{k-1}(2 \times 7) \ \ (\text{as } k \geq 1)$

$= 9A(14) + 7^{k-1}(14) + 2^{k-1}(14)$

$= 14(9A + 7^{k-1} + 2^{k-1})$

> To make each term a multiple of 14, we can 'borrow' a factor of 7 from 7^k and a factor of 2 from 2^k. Note, however, that this is only possible because $k \geq 1$.

So the statement is true for $n = k + 1$.

> We must state what we have shown.

The expression is divisible by 14 for $n = 1$, and if it is divisible by 14 for $n = k$ then it is also divisible by 14 for $n = k + 1$. Hence, the expression is divisible by 14 for all $n \geq 1$ by the principle of mathematical induction.

> Write a conclusion using the standard formulation.

Practice questions 12.3

12. Use the principle of mathematical induction to show that $3^{2n} - 1$ is divisible by 8 for all $n \geq 1$.

13. Prove by induction that $13^n - 4^n$ is divisible by 9 for all $n \geq 0$.

14. Use mathematical induction to prove that $(3n + 1)7^n - 1$ is divisible by 9 for all $n \in \mathbb{Z}^+$.

12.4 INEQUALITIES

WORKED EXAMPLE 12.4

Use induction to show that $2^n \geq n^2$ for all $n \geq 4$.

When $n = 4$:

LHS $= 2^4 = 16$

RHS $= 4^2 = 16$

LHS $\geq$ RHS, so the inequality holds for $n = 4$.

> Show that the inequality is true for the starting value $n = 4$.

 Make sure you identify the correct base case.

Assume it is true for $n = k$, where $k \geq 4$:

$$2^k \geq k^2 \cdots (*)$$

> Clearly state the inductive hypothesis (the statement for $n = k$ that is assumed to be true).

Let $n = k + 1$. Working towards:

$$2^{k+1} \geq (k+1)^2$$

> This is the start of the inductive step. Writing down what we are working towards will help us see how to simplify the expression.

LHS $= 2 \times 2^k$

$\geq 2 \times k^2 \quad \left(\text{using } (*)\right)$

$= k^2 + k^2$

> We use the result from inequality $(*)$ and then write $2k^2$ as $k^2 + k^2$ in order to move towards the RHS of $k^2 + 2k + 1$ (when expanded).

Then

$k^2 \geq 2k + 1 \Leftrightarrow k^2 - 2k - 1 \geq 0$

$\Leftrightarrow k \leq 1 - \sqrt{2}$ or $k \geq 1 + \sqrt{2}$

> We need to show that $k^2 \geq 2k + 1$.

> ▶ Solving quadratic inequalities is covered in Prior learning.

Since $4 > 1 + \sqrt{2}$, the inequality $k^2 \geq 2k + 1$ holds for $k \geq 4$, so:

LHS $\geq k^2 + k^2$

$\geq k^2 + (2k + 1)$

$= (k + 1)^2 = $ RHS

> Use the fact that $k \geq 4$ to show that the inequality $k^2 \geq 2k + 1$ holds in the circumstances of the question.

So the inequality holds for $n = k + 1$.

> We must state what we have shown.

The inequality holds for $n = 4$, and if it holds for $n = k$ then it also holds for $n = k + 1$. Hence, the inequality holds for all $n \geq 4$ by the principle of mathematical induction.

> Write a conclusion using the standard formulation.

Practice questions 12.4

15. Use induction to show that $2^n \geq n + 1$ for all positive integers n.

16. Prove by induction that $n! > 3^n$ for all $n > 6$.

Mixed practice 12

1. Use mathematical induction to show that the sum of the first n odd numbers is n^2.

2. Prove by induction that $3^{4n+2} + 2^{6n+3}$ is divisible by 17 for all $n \geq 0$.

3. (a) Find the smallest positive integer M such that $3^M > M + 5$.
   (b) Use the principle of mathematical induction to show that $3^n > n + 5$ for all integers $n \geq M$.

4. Consider the function $f(x) = x \cos x$.
   (a) Find $f'(x)$ and $f''(x)$.
   (b) Use the principle of mathematical induction to show that $f^{(2n)}(x) = (-1)^n (x \cos x + 2n \sin x)$.

5. Let $f(n) = n^3 - 4n$.
   (a) Show that $f(n + 1) - f(n) = 3n^2 + 3n - 3$.
   (b) Use induction to show that $f(n)$ is divisible by 3 for $n \in \mathbb{Z}^+$.

6. Prove, using the principle of mathematical induction, that $10^{n+1} - 9n - 10$ is divisible by 81 for all positive integers n.

7. Given that $u_1 = 2$ and $u_n = \sqrt{1 + 2u_{n-1}}$ for $n > 1$, prove that $u_n < 4$.

8. Given that $u_1 = -1$, $u_2 = 7$ and $u_{n+2} = 8u_{n+1} - 15u_n$, prove by induction that $u_n = 5^n - 2 \times 3^n$.

9. Prove De Moivre's theorem: $\left[r(\cos\theta + i\sin\theta)\right]^n = r^n(\cos n\theta + i\sin n\theta)$ for all $n \in \mathbb{Z}^+$.

Going for the top 12

1. Prove that $(n^2 + 3)(n^2 + 15)$ is divisible by 32 for all odd positive integers n.

2. Use the principle of mathematical induction to show that
$$(n + 1) + (n + 2) + (n + 3) + \ldots + (2n) = \frac{1}{2}n(3n + 1)$$

3. (a) (i) Use the principle of mathematical induction to show that
$$\cos\theta + \cos 3\theta + \cos 5\theta + \ldots + \cos(2n - 1)\theta = \frac{\sin(2n\theta)}{2\sin\theta} \text{ for } n \in \mathbb{Z}^+$$

   (ii) Hence find the exact value of $\cos\dfrac{\pi}{7} + \cos\dfrac{3\pi}{7} + \ldots + \cos\dfrac{13\pi}{7}$.

   (b) Prove by induction that $\displaystyle\sum_{r=1}^{n} \csc(2^r \theta) = \cot\theta - \cot(2^n \theta)$.

13 EXAMINATION SUPPORT

COMMON ERRORS

There are several very common errors which you need to be aware of.

- Making up rules which don't exist, such as:

    - $\ln(x + y) = \ln x + \ln y$
    [*Note*: $\ln(x + y)$ cannot be simplified.]

    - $(x + y)^2 = x^2 + y^2$
    [*Note*: The correct expansion is $x^2 + 2xy + y^2$.]

    - $\dfrac{\mathrm{d}}{\mathrm{d}x}\big(f(x) \times g(x)\big) = \dfrac{\mathrm{d}}{\mathrm{d}x}\big(f(x)\big) \times \dfrac{\mathrm{d}}{\mathrm{d}x}\big(g(x)\big)$
    [*Note*: You cannot differentiate products by finding the derivatives of the factors and multiplying them together.]

- Algebraic errors, especially involving minus signs and brackets, such as:

    - $3 - (1 - 2x) = 3 - 1 - 2x$
    [*Note*: The correct expansion is $3 - 1 + 2x$.]

    - $(5x)^3 = 5x^3$
    [*Note*: The correct expansion is $125x^3$.]

- Arithmetic errors, especially involving fractions, such as:

    - $3 \times \dfrac{2}{5} = \dfrac{6}{15}$
    [*Note*: The correct answer is $\dfrac{6}{5}$.]

Spot the common errors

Find the errors in the solutions below.

1. Find $\int x^2 \mathrm{e}^{2x}\, \mathrm{d}x$.

Solution: $\int x^2 \mathrm{e}^{2x}\, \mathrm{d}x = \dfrac{x^3}{3} \times 2\mathrm{e}^{2x}$

2. Solve $\ln x - \ln(10 - x) = \ln\left(\dfrac{x}{2}\right)$.

Solution: $\ln x - \ln 10 - \ln x = \ln\left(\dfrac{x}{2}\right)$

$-\ln 10 = \ln\left(\dfrac{x}{2}\right)$

$-10 = \dfrac{x}{2}$ so $x = -20$

3. If $f(x) = \dfrac{1}{3-x}$, find $f \circ f(x)$.

    Solution: $f \circ f(x) = \dfrac{1}{3 - \dfrac{1}{3-x}} = \dfrac{3-x}{3(3-x)-1} = \dfrac{1}{3-1} = \dfrac{1}{2}$

HOW TO CHECK YOUR ANSWERS
What you need to know

Checking questions by reading through your previous working is usually not very effective. You need to try more subtle methods such as:

- using your calculator to check a solution you obtained algebraically, and vice versa

- estimating the answer

- substituting numbers into algebraic expressions.

It is vital that you know how to use your calculator to check work. It often requires a little imagination.

Example 1: Definite integration

Suppose you were asked to find $\int xe^{2x}\,dx$ and you said that the answer was $e^{2x}(2x-1)+c$. To check this, turn it into a definite integral.

According to your answer:

$$\int_3^4 xe^{2x}\,dx = \left[e^{2x}(2x-1)\right]_3^4 = 7e^8 - 5e^6 \approx 18\,850$$

 The numbers 3 and 4 were randomly chosen. Most numbers would be suitable, but try to keep them simple while avoiding 0, 1 and any numbers given in the question; all of which might lead to errors not getting caught.

But according to the definite integral function on your calculator, $\int_3^4 xe^{2x}\,dx \approx 4712$, so you have made a mistake! This does not necessarily mean, however, that you have to go all the way back to the beginning. Inspecting the two numbers shows that your answer is exactly four times too big, so you have a hint as to what the correct answer should be!

Example 2: Algebraic manipulation

Suppose you were asked to expand $(1+2x)^4$ and you got $1 + 8x + 12x^2 + 8x^3 + 2x^4$.

Substituting $x = 1$ into the original expression gives $3^4 = 81$. Substituting $x = 1$ into your answer gives 31, so something has gone wrong.

 This method (substitution) can be used to check each line of working to identify where the mistake occurred. It can also be used to check the steps when you are proving an identity.

Example 3: Differentiation

Suppose you were asked to differentiate $x^2 \sin x$ and you said that the answer was $2x \sin x + x^2 \cos x$.

If this is the derivative, then the gradient at $x = 3$ would be $6 \sin 3 + 9 \cos 3$, which is -8.06. According to the differentiation function on the calculator, the gradient at $x = 3$ is -8.06, so your answer is plausible.

 Just because these numbers agree doesn't mean the answer is correct; it could simply be a coincidence. However, it should certainly give you the confidence to move on and check another question!

 If you are finding the equation of a tangent, you should also plot it and the original curve on the same graph to make sure it looks like a tangent.

Example 4: Problems involving parameters

Many questions try to eliminate the option of using a calculator by putting an additional unknown into the question. For example, suppose a question asked you to find the range of the function $f(x) = x^2 - 2ax + 3a^2$, giving your answer in terms of a.

If you thought the answer was $f(x) \geq 2a^2$, then you could check this by sketching the graph with $a = 3$. The minimum point on this graph turns out to be 18, which is consistent with the range being $f(x) \geq 2a^2$.

14 THINGS YOU NEED TO KNOW HOW TO DO ON YOUR CALCULATOR

CASIO CALCULATOR

Note: These instructions were written based on the calculator model fx-9860G SD and may not be applicable to other models. If in doubt, refer to your calculator's manual.

Skill	On a Casio calculator	
Store numbers as variables	In the RUN menu use the → button and then key in a letter.	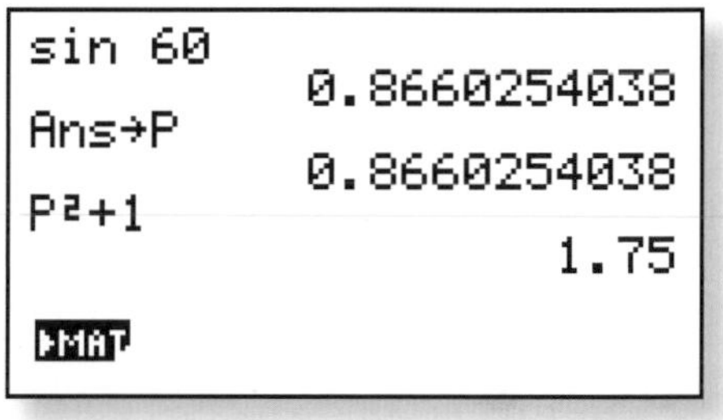 sin 60 0.8660254038 Ans→P 0.8660254038 P²+1 1.75 ▶MAT
Solve equations graphically	In the GRAPH menu input one equation into Y1 and the other into Y2. Go to the G-Solv menu (F5), and use the ISCT (F5) function to find the intersection. If there is more than one intersection, press across (F6) to move the cursor to the next intersection point.	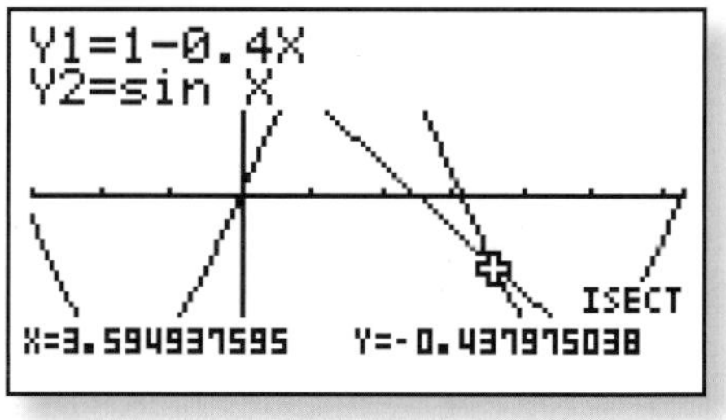 Y1=1-0.4X Y2=sin X ISECT X=3.594937595 Y=-0.437975038
Solve equations numerically	In the RUN menu press OPTN, CALC (F4) and then SolveN (F5). Put in the equation you want to solve.	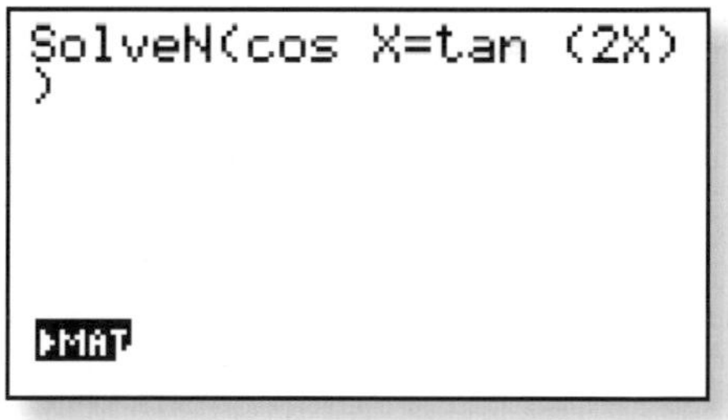 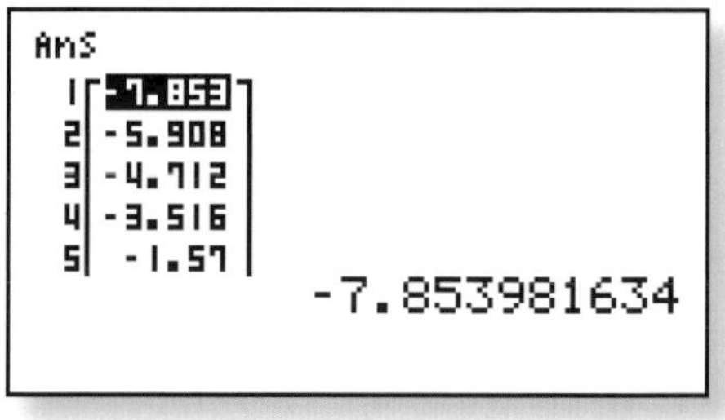 SolveN(cos X=tan (2X)) ▶MAT Ans 1 [-7.853] 2 -5.908 3 -4.712 4 -3.516 5 -1.57 -7.853981634

Skill	On a Casio calculator
Solve linear simultaneous equations	In the EQUA menu press F1 for simultaneous equations. Rearrange the equations into the form $ax + by + cz = d$ and input all the coefficients.
Use modulus functions	In the RUN or GRAPH menu press OPTN then across (F6) and NUM (F4). Abs (F1) is the modulus function.
Work with complex numbers	In the RUN menu, using SHIFT 0 allows you to enter 'i' and use it for calculations. By pressing OPTN, CPLX (F3) you can access a list of functions which can be applied to complex numbers, such as finding the modulus or the argument. You can enter complex numbers in polar form by using the $re^{i\theta}$ notation.
Put sequences into lists	Go to the STAT menu. With the cursor over List 1 press OPTN, List (F1) and then Seq (F5). The syntax is Seq(*expression*, X, *lowest value*, *highest value*, *increment*). To find the sum of the sequence, go to List 2 and, using the same menu as before, go across to get Cuml and then List 1.

Skill	On a Casio calculator

Find numerical derivatives	In the RUN menu press OPTN, CALC (F4) and then d/dx (F2).
	
	Input the expression you want to differentiate followed by a comma and the value at which you want to evaluate the derivative.
	
	If you want to sketch a derivative you can use this expression in a graph too.
		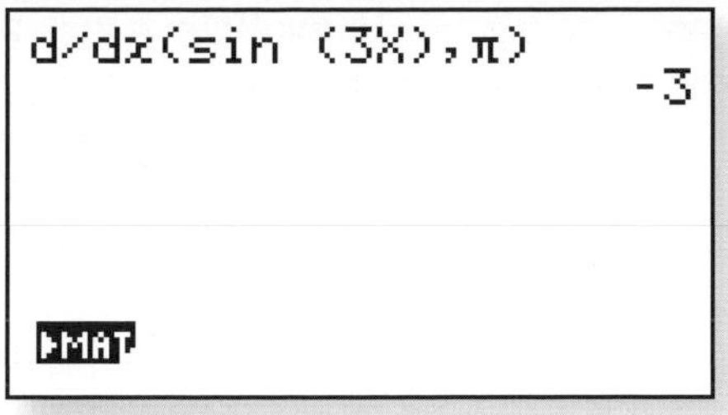 ```d/dx(sin (3X),π)```
		``` -3```
		
		```▶MAT``` 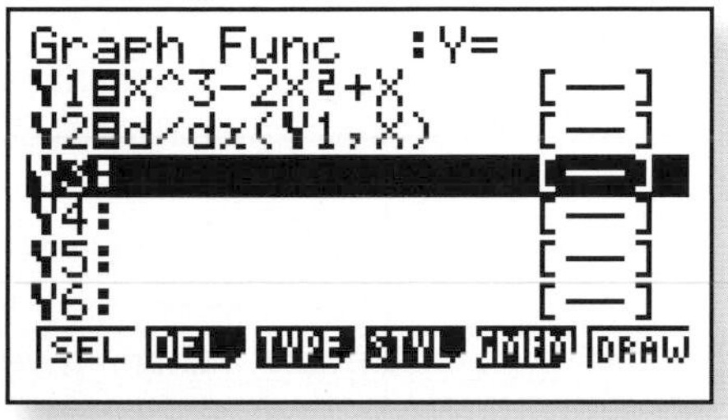
		
		```Graph Func :Y=```
		```Y1⬛X^3-2X²+X [—]```
		```Y2⬛d/dx(Y1,X) [—]```
		```Y3: [ ]```
		```Y4: [—]```
		```Y5: [—]```
		```Y6: [—]```
		```SEL DEL TYPE STYL GMEM DRAW```

Find numerical integrals	In the RUN menu press OPTN, CALC (F4) and then $\int dx$ (F4). Input the expression you want to integrate followed by the lower and upper limits, all separated by commas.	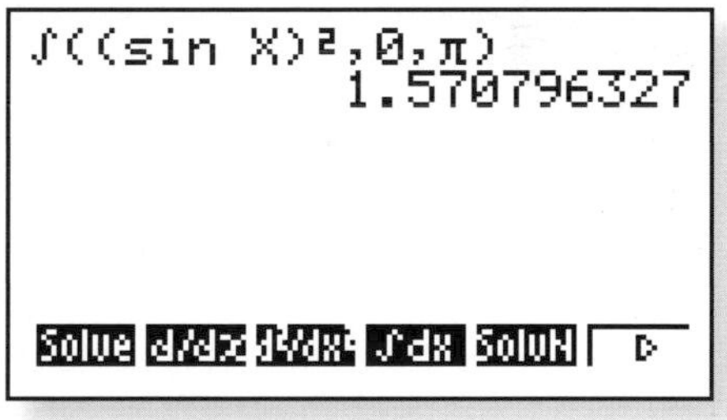 ```∫((sin X)²,0,π)```
		``` 1.570796327```
		
		```Solve d/dx d²/dx² ∫dx SolvN ▷```

Find maximum and minimum points on a graph	In the GRAPH menu, plot the graph and press G-Solv (F5).
	
	Then press Max (F2) or Min (F3).
		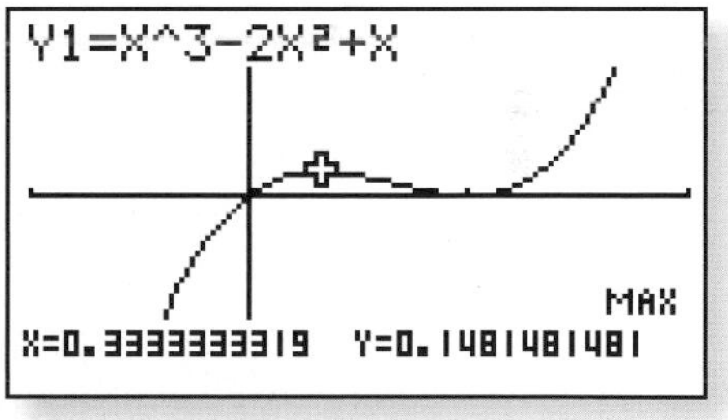 ```Y1=X^3-2X²+X```
		
		``` MAX```
		```X=0.333333319 Y=0.148148148```

Find sample statistics	In the STAT menu enter the data in List 1 and, if required, the frequencies in List 2. Press CALC (F2). Use SET (F6) to make sure that the 1-Var XList is List 1 and that 1-Var Freq is either 1 or List 2, as appropriate. Then exit and press 1-Var (F1). Scrolling down shows the median and quartiles.	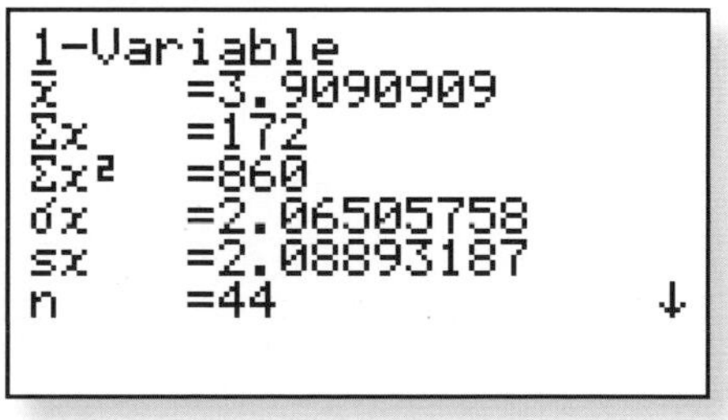 ```1-Variable```
		```x̄ =3.9090909```
		```Σx =172```
		```Σx² =860```
		```σx =2.06505758```
		```sx =2.08893187```
		```n =44 ↓```

Skill	On a Casio calculator		
Find probabilities in distributions	In the RUN menu, press OPTN, STAT (F5) and then DIST (F3). There are several options:		

Name	Description	Syntax
Ncd	Probability from a normal N(μ, σ^2) distribution	NormalCD(*lower limit, upper limit*, μ, σ)
Bpd	Probability from a binomial B(n, p) distribution	BinomialPD(x, n, p)
Bcd	Cumulative probability, P($X \le x$), from a binomial B(n, p) distribution	BinomialCD(x, n, p)
Ppd	Probability from a Poisson Po(m) distribution	PoissonPD(x, m)
Pcd	Cumulative probability, P($X \le x$), from a Poisson Po(m) distribution	PoissonCD(x, m)

```
BinominalCD(1,3,0.5)
                 0.5
PoissonPD(2,2.4
       0.2612677055


Ppd Pcd InvP
```

Use inverse normal functions	To find the boundaries of a region with a specified probability, go to the STAT menu, then DIST (F5), NORM (F1) and InvN (F3). Input the data as a variable.

Depending on the information you have, you can use different 'tails': for P($X < x$) use the left tail, for P($X > x$) use the right tail, and for P($-x < X < x$) use the central tail.

Input the mean and standard deviation. Use $\mu = 0$ and $\sigma = 1$ if you do not know the mean or standard deviation and want to find a Z-score.

```
Inverse Normal
Data    :Variable
Tail    :Left
Area    :0.95
σ       :1
μ       :0
Save Res:None        ↓
```

TEXAS CALCULATOR

Note: These instructions were written based on the calculator model TI-84 Plus Silver Edition and may not be applicable to other models. If in doubt, refer to your calculator's manual.

Skill	On a Texas calculator	
Store numbers as variables	In the RUN menu, use the STO► button and then key in a letter.	sin(60) .8660254038 Ans→P .8660254038 P²+1 1.75
Solve equations graphically	In the Y= menu, input one equation into Y1 and the other into Y2. Then press the GRAPH button. You may need to use the WINDOW or ZOOM functions to find an appropriate scale. To look for intersections, press CALC (2nd, F4) then intersect (F5). You must select the two graphs you want to intersect and move the cursor close to the intersection point you are interested in.	Intersection X=3.5949376 Y=-.437975
Solve equations numerically	In the MATH menu press Solve (0). You must rearrange your equation into the form …= 0. Input this and press Solve (ALPHA, ENTER) when the cursor is above the X value. To find other values, change the bounds within which you want the calculator to search. For polynomial equations, you can find all solutions by using the solver in the PolySmlt 2 APP (which is recommended by the IB).	cos(X)-tan(2X)=0 ■ X=.37473443270… bound={-1E99,1… ■ left-rt=0

Skill	On a Texas calculator
Solve linear simultaneous equations	In the PolySmlt APP select 'SimultEqn-Solver' (2). You can change the number of equations and the number of unknowns. Rearrange the equations into the form $ax + by + cz = d$ and input all the coefficients. If the solution is not unique, a parametric representation of the solution will be given.
Use modulus functions	In the MATH menu, go across to NUM; the first option is ABS, which is the calculator notation for the modulus function.
Work with complex numbers	2nd, . (decimal point) allows you to enter 'i' and use it for calculations. By pressing MATH and going across to CPX you can access a list of functions which can be applied to complex numbers, such as finding the modulus (abs) or the argument (angle). You can enter complex numbers in polar form by using the $re^{i\theta}$ notation.
Put sequences into lists	Press LIST (2nd, STAT) and move across to OPS. Option 5 is seq, an operation which puts a sequence into a list. The syntax is seq(*rule*, X, *lower limit*, *upper limit*, *step*). You can store this sequence in a list using the STO▶ button. To look at the cumulative sum of your sequence, use the cumSum function from the same menu.

Skill	On a Texas calculator
Find numerical derivatives	In the MATH menu, option 8 is the numerical derivative, nDeriv. The syntax is nDeriv(*function*, X, *value of interest*). If you want to sketch the derivative function, you can graph Y1 = nDeriv(*function*, X, X).
	nDeriv(sin(3X),X,π) -2.9999955
Find numerical integrals	In the MATH menu, option 9 is numerical integration, fnInt. The syntax is fnInt(*function*, X, *lower limit*, *upper limit*). If you want to see how the value of the integral changes with the upper limit, you can graph Y1 = fnInt(*function*, X, *lower limit*, X).
	fnInt((sin(X))²,X,0,π) 1.570796327
Find maximum and minimum points on a graph	When viewing a graph in the CALC menu (2nd, F4), press minimum (3) or maximum (4). Use the cursor to describe the left and right sides of the region you want to look in and then click the cursor close to the stationary point.
	Maximum X=.33333265 Y=.14814815
Find sample statistics	In the STAT menu, use the edit function to enter the data in List 1 and, if required, the frequencies in List 2. Press STAT and CALC, then 1-Var Stats (1) as appropriate. Give the name of the list which holds the data and, if required, the list which holds the frequencies. Scrolling down shows the median and quartiles.
	1-Var Stats X̄=9.868421053 Σx=375 Σx²=5161 Sx=6.282412399 σx=6.199197964 ↓n=38

Skill	On a Texas calculator
Find probabilities in distributions	Probabilities from different distributions can be found using the DISTR menu (2nd, VARS). There are several options:

Name	Description	Syntax
normalcdf	Probability from a normal $N(\mu, \sigma^2)$ distribution	normalcdf(*lower limit*, *upper limit*, μ, σ)
binomialpdf	Probability from a binomial $B(n, p)$ distribution	binompdf(n, p, x)
binomialcdf	Cumulative probability, $P(X \leq x)$, from a binomial $B(n, p)$ distribution	binomcdf(n, p, x)
poissonpdf	Probability from a Poisson $Po(m)$ distribution	poissonpdf(m, x)
poissoncdf	Cumulative probability, $P(X \leq x)$, from a Poisson $Po(m)$ distribution	poissoncdf(m, x)

```
normalcdf(-1E99,
150,160,10)
        .1586552596
binompdf(12,0.4,
5)
        .2270303355
```

Use inverse normal functions	If you know the probability of an event being below a particular point of a normal distribution, you can find the value of that point. In the DISTR menu (2nd, VARS), use the invNorm function with the syntax invNorm(*probability*, μ, σ). Use $\mu = 0$ and $\sigma = 1$ if you do not know the mean or standard deviation and want to find a Z-score.

```
invNorm(0.6,0,1)
        .2533471011
```

15 WORKED SOLUTIONS

1 COUNTING PRINCIPLES

Mixed practice 1

1. (a) $\dbinom{12}{5} = 792$

(b) Fixing Jonny and Lin among the choice of 5 leaves 3 other spaces to be chosen from the remaining 10 students. This can be done in

$$\dbinom{10}{3} = 120 \text{ ways.}$$

So $P(\text{selecting both Jonny and Lin}) = \dfrac{120}{792} = \dfrac{5}{33}$

2. The two different letters can be selected in $^{26}P_2$ ways. There are 9 different ways of selecting the first digit; then, since numbers can be repeated, there are also 9 ways of selecting the second, third, fourth, fifth and sixth digits.

So the total number of different registration numbers is $^{26}P_2 \times 9 \times 9 \times 9 \times 9 \times 9 \times 9 = 345\,436\,650$.

3. $\dbinom{n}{2} = 210$

$\Leftrightarrow \dfrac{n(n-1)}{2} = 210$

$\Leftrightarrow n^2 - n = 420$

$\Leftrightarrow n^2 - n - 420 = 0$

$\Leftrightarrow (n - 21)(n + 20) = 0$

$\therefore \; n = 21$ (n cannot be negative)

4. The following number of selections for each position are possible:

- goalkeepers: $\dbinom{3}{1} = 3$
- defenders: $\dbinom{7}{4} = 35$
- midfielders: $\dbinom{9}{4} = 126$
- strikers: $\dbinom{3}{2} = 3$

In total, therefore, there are $3 \times 35 \times 126 \times 3 = 39\,690$ ways.

5. (a) $^7P_3 = 210$

(b) $7 \times 7 \times 7 = 343$

6. (a) Number of ways of choosing:

- 2 green pens is $\dbinom{5}{2} = 10$
- 2 purple pens is $\dbinom{3}{2} = 3$

Therefore, the number of ways of choosing 2 green and 2 purple pens is $10 \times 3 = 30$.

(b) Number of ways of choosing:

- 4 pens of any colour (from 8) is $\dbinom{8}{4} = 70$
- 4 green pens (and therefore no purple pens) is $^5C_4 = 5\dbinom{5}{4} = 5$

Therefore, the number of ways of choosing at least 1 purple pen is $70 - 5 = 65$.

7. Number of permutations of:

- a consonant for the beginning and another for the end is $^3P_2 = 6$
- the remaining 4 letters in between is $4! = 24$

Therefore, the number of such words is $6 \times 24 = 144$.

Number of arrangements without constraint $= 6! = 720$. Therefore the probability of starting and ending with a consonant is $\dfrac{144}{720} = \dfrac{1}{5}$.

8. (a) $^nP_3 = \dfrac{n!}{(n-3)!} = n(n-1)(n-2)$

(b) Without arranging them, Theo can make

$$\dbinom{n}{3} = \dfrac{n(n-1)(n-2)}{3!} \text{ selections.}$$

$\therefore \; n(n-1)(n-2) = \dfrac{n(n-1)(n-2)}{6} + 50$

$\Leftrightarrow 6n(n-1)(n-2) = n(n-1)(n-2) + 300$

$\Leftrightarrow 6n^3 - 18n^2 + 12n = n^3 - 3n^2 + 2n + 300$

$\Leftrightarrow 5n^3 - 15n^2 + 10n - 300 = 0$

$\Rightarrow n^3 - 3n^2 + 2n - 60 = 0$

So $n = 5$ (from GDC)

9. (a) $8! = 40\,320$

(b) Treating the 3 vowels as one 'block', there are now only 6 items to permute, which can be done in $6! = 720$ ways. However, the 3 vowels themselves can be permuted within their 'block' in $3! = 6$ ways. Therefore, there are $720 \times 6 = 4320$ such arrangements.

(c) Fixing TER in the last 3 positions leaves 5 letters to be permuted in front of them. This can be done in $5! = 120$ ways.

(d) Just as for the 3 vowels together in a 'block' in part (b), this can be done in 4320 ways.

10. (a) (i) $22!$

(ii) There are $\binom{22}{11}$ ways of choosing 11 people to be in the first line (which fixes the other 11 in the second line).

There are then $11!$ ways of arranging the 11 people in each line separately.

Therefore, there are $\binom{22}{11} \times 11! \times 11!$

$= \dfrac{22!}{11! \times 11!} \times 11! \times 11! = 22!$ ways in total, i.e. the same as the number of ways the 22 could be arranged in a single line.

(b) Fixing Max, Lizzie and Jessie on the committee leaves 2 others to be selected from the remaining 19. Since order doesn't matter, this can be done in

$\binom{19}{2} = 171$ ways.

(c) (i) Treating all 3 boys as one cluster gives 4 items to be arranged (the 3 girls and this cluster). This can be done in $4!$ ways. But the 3 boys in the cluster can be arranged in $3!$ different ways, giving a total of $4! \times 3! = 144$ ways.

(ii) If all the boys are to be kept apart, then they must be placed in 3 of the following 4 vacant positions, separated by the girls:

_ G _ G _ G _

This is the same as saying that the boys and girls must be arranged in one of the following ways:

GBGBGB BGBGBG BGBGGB BGGBGB

There are:

- $3! = 6$ ways of permuting the girls in their 3 positions
- $^4P_3 = 24$ ways of selecting (in order) boys in 3 of the 4 gaps

Therefore, there are $3! \times 24 = 144$ ways in total.

(d) The number of ways of awarding the medals (where the order clearly matters) is $^nP_3$. So

$^nP_3 = 1320$

$\Leftrightarrow \dfrac{n!}{(n-3)!} = 1320$

$\Leftrightarrow n(n-1)(n-2) = 1320$

$\therefore n = 12$ (from GDC)

Going for the top 1

1. To have the vowels separated, they must occupy 4 of the 6 spaces shown below (where each C stands for one of the 5 consonants):

_ C _ C _ C _ C _ C _

There are:

- $5! = 120$ ways of permuting the consonants
- $\dfrac{4!}{2!} = 12$ different ways of permuting the vowels (since the E is repeated)
- $^6C_4 = 15$ ways of choosing 4 of the 6 gaps to fill

Therefore, there are $120 \times 12 \times 15 = 21\,600$ ways in total.

2. (a) $^5P_4 = 120$

(b) There are 5 possible choices for the first digit, and since numbers can be repeated there are also 5 choices for the second digit and the third and the fourth.

That is, $5 \times 5 \times 5 \times 5 = 625$.

(c) To be greater than 3000 and even, the following are possibilities (the vacant positions in the middle can be filled by any 2 of the remaining 3 numbers):

- 3 _ _ 2 ($3 \times 2 = 6$ ways) or 3 _ _ 4 ($3 \times 2 = 6$ ways)
- 4 _ _ 2 ($3 \times 2 = 6$ ways)
- 5 _ _ 2 ($3 \times 2 = 6$ ways) or 5 _ _ 4 ($3 \times 2 = 6$ ways)

So in total there are $6 + 6 + 6 + 6 + 6 = 30$ such numbers.

3. As there are 3 repeated As and 4 repeated Bs, the total number of distinct ways of arranging these 7 letters is

$\dfrac{7!}{3!4!} = 35.$

4. (a)
$$\binom{n}{3} = \binom{n+1}{2} - 5$$
$$\Leftrightarrow \frac{n(n-1)(n-2)}{3!} = \frac{(n+1)n}{2!} - 5$$
$$\Leftrightarrow n(n-1)(n-2) = 3(n+1)n - 30$$
$$\Leftrightarrow n^3 - 3n^2 + 2n = 3n^2 + 3n - 30$$
$$\Leftrightarrow n^3 - 6n^2 - n + 30 = 0$$

(b) Let $f(x) = x^3 - 6x^2 - x + 30$. Then
$$f(-2) = (-2)^3 - 6(-2)^2 - (-2) + 30$$
$$= -8 - 24 + 2 + 30$$
$$= 0$$
Therefore $(x + 2)$ is a factor of $f(x)$.

(c) $n^3 - 6n^2 - n + 30 = (n+2)(n^2 - 8n + 15)$
$$= (n+2)(n-3)(n-5)$$

So $n = 3$ or 5 (as n cannot be negative).

2 EXPONENTS AND LOGARITHMS

Mixed practice 2

1.
$$3 \times 9^x - 10 \times 3^x + 3 = 0$$
$$\Leftrightarrow 3 \times \left(3^2\right)^x - 10 \times 3^x + 3 = 0$$
$$\Leftrightarrow 3 \times \left(3^x\right)^2 - 10 \times 3^x + 3 = 0$$

Let $3^x = y$. Then

$$3y^2 - 10y + 3 = 0$$
$$\Leftrightarrow (3y - 1)(y - 3) = 0$$
$$\Leftrightarrow y = \frac{1}{3} \quad \text{or} \quad y = 3$$

So $3^x = \frac{1}{3} \Rightarrow x = -1 \quad \text{or} \quad 3^x = 3 \Rightarrow x = 1$

2.
$$2^{3x+1} = 5^{5-x}$$
$$\Rightarrow \ln\left(2^{3x+1}\right) = \ln\left(5^{5-x}\right)$$
$$\Rightarrow (3x + 1)\ln 2 = (5 - x)\ln 5$$
$$\Rightarrow (3\ln 2)x + \ln 2 = 5\ln 5 - x\ln 5$$
$$\Rightarrow (3\ln 2)x + x\ln 5 = 5\ln 5 - \ln 2$$
$$\Rightarrow x(3\ln 2 + \ln 5) = 5\ln 5 - \ln 2$$
$$\Rightarrow x = \frac{5\ln 5 - \ln 2}{3\ln 2 + \ln 5}$$

3. From the first equation:

$$\ln\left(x^2 y\right) = 15$$
$$\Rightarrow x^2 y = e^{15}$$
$$\Rightarrow y = \frac{e^{15}}{x^2}$$

Substituting this into the second equation gives

$$\ln x + \ln\left(\frac{e^{15}}{x^2}\right)^3 = 10$$
$$\Rightarrow \ln\left(x \times \frac{e^{45}}{x^6}\right) = 10$$
$$\Rightarrow \frac{e^{45}}{x^5} = e^{10}$$
$$\Rightarrow x^5 = e^{35}$$
$$\Rightarrow x = e^7$$

Then, substituting back to find y:

$$y = \frac{e^{15}}{x^2} = \frac{e^{15}}{e^{14}} = e$$

So the solution is $x = e^7$, $y = e$.

4.
$$y = \ln x - \ln(x + 2) + \ln\left(x^2 - 4\right)$$
$$= \ln\left(\frac{x}{x + 2}\right) + \ln\left(x^2 - 4\right)$$
$$= \ln\left(\frac{x\left(x^2 - 4\right)}{x + 2}\right)$$
$$= \ln\left(\frac{x(x - 2)(x + 2)}{x + 2}\right)$$
$$= \ln\left(x(x - 2)\right)$$

$$\therefore x(x - 2) = e^y$$
$$\Rightarrow x^2 - 2x - e^y = 0$$
$$\Rightarrow x = \frac{2 \pm \sqrt{4 + 4e^y}}{2} = 1 \pm \sqrt{1 + e^y}$$

So $x = 1 + \sqrt{1 + e^y}$ (as $x > 0$)

5. Substituting $x = 5$ and $y = \ln 16$ into the equation:
$$\ln 16 = 4\ln(5 - a)$$
$$\Rightarrow \ln 16 = \ln(5 - a)^4$$
$$\Rightarrow 16 = (5 - a)^4$$
$$\Rightarrow 5 - a = \pm 2$$
$$\Rightarrow a = 3 \text{ or } 7$$

Putting each of these values into the original equation and checking that $(5, \ln 16)$ is a solution shows that $a = 7$ is not valid, because in that case we would get $\ln(5 - 7) = \ln(-2)$, which is not real.

So $a = 3$.

6. (a) (i) After 10 days the rate of increase is 325 per day, so $\frac{dD}{dt} = 325$ when $t = 10$:

$$\frac{dD}{dt} = 0.2Ce^{-0.2t}$$
$$325 = 0.2Ce^{-2}$$
$$\therefore C = 1625e^2$$

(ii) After 10 days the demand is 15 000, so we have $D = 15\,000$ when $t = 10$:

$$15\,000 = A - Ce^{-2}$$
$$15\,000 = A - \left(1625e^2\right)e^{-2}$$
$$\therefore A = 16\,625$$

The initial demand, D_0, is the value of D when $t = 0$:

$$D_0 = A - C = 16\,625 - 1625e^2 = 4618$$
(to the nearest integer)

(iii) As $t \to \infty$, $e^{-0.2t} \to 0$. Therefore
$$D \to A = 16\,625$$

(b) (i) We are given that $D = 16\,625 - 1625\mathrm{e}^2$ when $t = 0$, so

$$16\,625 - 1625\mathrm{e}^2 = B\ln\left(\frac{0+10}{5}\right)$$

$$\therefore B = \frac{16\,625 - 1625\mathrm{e}^2}{\ln 2} = 6662 \ (4\ \text{SF})$$

(ii) As $t \to \infty$, $\ln\left(\dfrac{t+10}{5}\right) \to \infty$. Therefore $D \to \infty$.

(c) We need to find the first t for which

$$B\ln\left(\frac{t+10}{5}\right) > A - C\mathrm{e}^{-0.2t};\ \text{that is, we need to solve}$$

$$B\ln\left(\frac{t+10}{5}\right) = A - C\mathrm{e}^{-0.2t}.\ \text{From GDC, } t = 50.6,$$

i.e. after 51 days.

Going for the top 2

1. $2^{3x-4} \times 3^{2x-5} = 36^{x-2}$

$\Rightarrow \ln\left(2^{3x-4} \times 3^{2x-5}\right) = \ln\left(36^{x-2}\right)$

$\Rightarrow \ln\left(2^{3x-4}\right) + \ln\left(3^{2x-5}\right) = \ln\left(36^{x-2}\right)$

$\Rightarrow (3x-4)\ln 2 + (2x-5)\ln 3 = (x-2)\ln 36$

$\Rightarrow (3\ln 2)x - 4\ln 2 + (2\ln 3)x - 5\ln 3 = x\ln 36 - 2\ln 36$

$\Rightarrow (3\ln 2 + 2\ln 3 - \ln 36)x = 4\ln 2 + 5\ln 3 - 2\ln 36$

$\Rightarrow (\ln 8 + \ln 9 - \ln 36)x = \ln 2^4 + \ln 3^5 - \ln 36^2$

$\Rightarrow x\ln\left(\frac{8 \times 9}{36}\right) = \ln\left(\frac{2^4 \times 3^5}{36^2}\right)$

$\Rightarrow x\ln 2 = \ln\left(\frac{6^4 \times 3}{6^4}\right)$

$\Rightarrow x = \dfrac{\ln 3}{\ln 2}$

2. Changing base a into base b, we have

$$\log_a b = \frac{\log_b b}{\log_b a} = \frac{1}{\log_b a},\ \text{so}$$

$$\log_a b^2 = c^2$$

$$\Leftrightarrow 2\log_a b = c^2$$

$$\Leftrightarrow 2\left(\frac{1}{\log_b a}\right) = c^2$$

Then, substituting $\log_b a = c+1$ from the other equation gives

$$2\left(\frac{1}{c+1}\right) = c^2$$

$$\Leftrightarrow \frac{2}{c+1} = c^2$$

$$\Leftrightarrow 2 = c^3 + c^2$$

$$\Leftrightarrow c^3 + c^2 - 2 = 0$$

$$\Leftrightarrow (c-1)(c^2 + 2c + 2) = 0$$

$$\therefore\ c = 1$$

Therefore, $\log_b a = 1 + 1 = 2$ and hence $a = b^2$.

3. Gradient of the line through $(2, 4.5)$ and $(4, 7.2)$ is

$$m = \frac{7.2 - 4.5}{4 - 2} = 1.35$$

So

$$\ln F - 4.5 = 1.35\left(\ln x - 2\right)$$

$$\ln F = 1.35\ln x + 1.8$$

$$= \ln x^{1.35} + 1.8$$

and therefore $F = \mathrm{e}^{\ln x^{1.35} + 1.8} = \mathrm{e}^{1.8}x^{1.35}$.

3 POLYNOMIALS

Mixed practice 3

1. The function has a repeated root at $x = -2$, so it has a factor $(x+2)^2$; it has another repeated root at $x = 3$, and hence also a factor $(x-3)^2$.

This would give a y-intercept of $2^2 \times (-3)^2 = 36$, so a factor of 2 is also needed. Therefore

$$y = 2(x+2)^2(x-3)^2$$

$$= 2(x^2 + 4x + 4)(x^2 - 6x + 9)$$

$$= 2x^4 - 4x^3 - 22x^2 + 24x + 72$$

2. The general term of this binomial expansion is

$$\binom{8}{r}(x^3)^{8-r}\left(\frac{3}{x}\right)^r = \binom{8}{r}x^{24-3r}x^{-r}3^r = \binom{8}{r}x^{24-4r}3^r$$

The term independent of x will have power 0 for x; that is, $24 - 4r = 0$, so $r = 6$. The term is

$$\binom{8}{6}(x^3)^2\left(\frac{3}{x}\right)^6 = 28x^6\left(\frac{729}{x^6}\right) = 20\,412$$

3. Because it has a factor of $(x+1)$:

$$(-1)^3 + 10(-1)^2 + c(-1) + d = 0$$

$$\Leftrightarrow -1 + 10 - c + d = 0$$

$$\Leftrightarrow c - d = 9$$

As it has a remainder of 5 when divided by $(x-2)$:

$$2^3 + 10(2)^2 + c(2) + d = 5$$

$$\Leftrightarrow 8 + 40 + 2c + d = 5$$

$$\Leftrightarrow 2c + d = -43$$

Solving these equations simultaneously gives $c = -\dfrac{34}{3}$ and $d = -\dfrac{61}{3}$.

4. $y = x^2 + kx + 2$ never touches the x-axis and so has no real roots. Therefore

$b^2 - 4ac < 0$

$k^2 - 4 \times 1 \times 2 < 0$

$k^2 < 8$

$-2\sqrt{2} < k < 2\sqrt{2}$

5. Let the 3 roots be α, β and γ.

Then $\alpha + \beta + \gamma = \dfrac{-b}{1} = -b$.

Since α, β, γ form an arithmetic sequence:

$\beta - \alpha = \gamma - \beta$

$\Leftrightarrow 2\beta = \alpha + \gamma$

$\Leftrightarrow 3\beta = \alpha + \beta + \gamma$

$\therefore \beta = \dfrac{\alpha + \beta + \gamma}{3} = \dfrac{-b}{3}$

6. Using the binomial theorem:

$$(2 + x)(3 - 2x)^5 = (2 + x)\left(3^5 + \binom{5}{1}3^4(-2x) \right.$$

$$\left. + \binom{5}{2}3^3(-2x)^2 + ... \right)$$

$$= (2 + x)(243 - 810x + 1080x^2 + ...)$$

The quadratic term will be

$2 \times 1080x^2 + x \times (-810x) = 2160x^2 - 810x^2 = 1350x^2$

7. Solving simultaneously for the intersection point:

$x^2 + (x + k)^2 = 9$

$\Leftrightarrow x^2 + x^2 + 2kx + k^2 = 9$

$\Leftrightarrow 2x^2 + 2kx + k^2 - 9 = 0$

As $y = x + k$ is a tangent, there is only one solution to this quadratic, so the discriminant is 0:

$b^2 - 4ac = 0$

$(2k)^2 - 4 \times 2(k^2 - 9) = 0$

$4k^2 - 8k^2 + 72 = 0$

$4k^2 = 72$

$k^2 = 18$

$k = \pm 3\sqrt{2}$

8. (a) Using the binomial theorem:

$$(2 - x)^5 = 2^5 + \binom{5}{1}2^4(-x) + \binom{5}{2}2^3(-x)^2$$

$$+ \binom{5}{3}2^2(-x)^3 \quad + ...$$

$$= 32 - 80x + 80x^2 - 40x^3 + ...$$

(b) Let $x = 0.01$ so that $(2 - x)^5 = 1.99^5$. Then

$1.99^5 \approx 32 - 80 \times 0.01 + 80 \times 0.01^2 - 40 \times$

$0.01^3 = 31.20796$

9. From the original equation, $\alpha + \beta = -\dfrac{b}{a}$ and $\alpha\beta = \dfrac{c}{a}$

The sum of the roots of the new equation is

$(\alpha + 2\beta) + (2\alpha + \beta) = 3\alpha + 3\beta$

$= 3(\alpha + \beta)$

$= -\dfrac{3b}{a}$

The product of the roots of the new equation is

$(\alpha + 2\beta)(2\alpha + \beta) = 2\alpha^2 + 5\alpha\beta + 2\beta^2$

$= 2(\alpha + \beta)^2 + \alpha\beta$

$= 2\left(\dfrac{-b}{a} \right)^2 + \dfrac{c}{a}$

$= \dfrac{2b^2}{a^2} + \dfrac{c}{a}$

$= \dfrac{2b^2 + ac}{a^2}$

Therefore, taking the coefficient of x^2 to be 1 in the new quadratic, a suitable equation is

$x^2 + \dfrac{3b}{a}x + \dfrac{2b^2 + ac}{a^2} = 0$

Or, multiplying through by a^2:

$a^2x^2 + 3abx + 2b^2 + ac = 0$

10. (a) Given that the polynomial has repeated roots α and β:

$x^4 + bx^3 + cx^2 + dx + e = (x - \alpha)^2(x - \beta)^2$

$\therefore e = (-\alpha)^2(-\beta)^2 = (\alpha\beta)^2 \geq 0$

(b) Sum of the roots: $\alpha + \alpha + \beta + \beta = \dfrac{-b}{1}$

$\Rightarrow 2(\alpha + \beta) = -b$

Product of the roots: $\alpha\alpha\beta\beta = \dfrac{e}{1} \Rightarrow (\alpha\beta)^2 = e$

$\alpha^2 + \beta^2 = (\alpha + \beta)^2 - 2\alpha\beta$

$= \left(\dfrac{-b}{2} \right)^2 - 2\sqrt{e}$

$= \dfrac{b^2}{4} - 2\sqrt{e}$

(c) $(\beta - \alpha)^2 = \beta^2 + \alpha^2 - 2\alpha\beta$

$= \dfrac{b^2}{4} - 2\sqrt{e} - 2\sqrt{e}w$

$= \dfrac{b^2}{4} - 4\sqrt{e}$

$\therefore \beta - \alpha = \sqrt{\dfrac{b^2}{4} - 4\sqrt{e}}$

(take the positive square root as $\beta > \alpha$)

11. **(a)** Using the binomial expansion:

$$(1+x)^n = \binom{n}{0} + \binom{n}{1}x + \binom{n}{2}x^2 + \ldots + \binom{n}{n-1}x^{n-1} + \binom{n}{n}x^n$$

$$= 1 + nx + \frac{n(n-1)}{2}x^2 + \ldots + nx^{n-1} + x^n$$

Then

$$(1+x)^n = k$$

$$\Leftrightarrow (1+x)^n - k = 0$$

$$\Leftrightarrow 1 - k + nx + \frac{n(n-1)}{2}x^2 + \ldots + nx^{n-1} + x^n = 0$$

Sum of roots $= -\dfrac{a_{n-1}}{a_n} = -\dfrac{n}{1} = -n$, which is independent of k.

Product of roots $= (-1)^n \dfrac{a_0}{a_n} = (-1)^n \dfrac{1-k}{1}$

$$= (-1)^n (1-k),$$

which has modulus $|1-k|$ independent of n.

(b) **(i)**

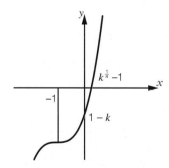

(ii)

(c) By the remainder theorem, $f(1) = 16$. That is,

$$(1+1)^n = 16$$

$$\Rightarrow 2^n = 16$$

$$\Rightarrow n = 4 \quad (\text{as } n \in \mathbb{Z}^+)$$

(d) From the expansion above, the coefficient of x^2 is $\dfrac{n(n-1)}{2}$. So

$$\frac{n(n-1)}{2} = 136$$

$$\Leftrightarrow n^2 - n - 272 = 0$$

$$\Leftrightarrow (n-17)(n+16) = 0$$

$$\therefore n = 17 \quad (\text{as } n \in \mathbb{Z}^+)$$

(e) Substitute $x = 1$ into the expansion of $f(x)$:

$$(1+1)^n = \binom{n}{0} + \binom{n}{1}1 + \binom{n}{2}1^2 + \ldots + \binom{n}{n-1}1^{n-1} + \binom{n}{n}1^n$$

$$\Rightarrow \binom{n}{0} + \binom{n}{1} + \binom{n}{2} + \ldots + \binom{n}{n-1} + \binom{n}{n} = 2^n$$

Going for the top 3

1. Since the remainder when divided by $x^2 + 7x + 12$ is $3x + 2$:

$$\frac{f(x)}{x^2 + 7x + 12} = g(x) + \frac{3x + 2}{x^2 + 7x + 12}$$

$$\Rightarrow f(x) = (x^2 + 7x + 12)g(x) + 3x + 2$$

for some polynomial $g(x)$.

Then, by the remainder theorem, the remainder, r, when divided by $x + 4$ is given by

$$r = f(-4)$$

$$= \left((-4)^2 + 7(-4) + 12\right)g(-4) + 3(-4) + 2$$

$$= 0 \times g(-4) - 10$$

$$= -10$$

2. $(1+ax)^n = 1 + nax + \dfrac{n(n-1)}{2}(ax)^2 + \ldots$

$$= 1 + nax + \frac{n(n-1)}{2}a^2x^2 + \ldots$$

So we have

$$\frac{n(n-1)}{2}a^2 = 54 \quad \cdots (1)$$

$$na = 12 \quad \cdots (2)$$

From (2), $a = \dfrac{12}{n}$. Substituting this into (1) gives

$$\frac{n(n-1)}{2}\left(\frac{12}{n}\right)^2 = 54$$

$$\Leftrightarrow \frac{72n^2 - 72n}{n^2} = 54$$

$$\Leftrightarrow 72n^2 - 72n = 54n^2$$

$$\Leftrightarrow 18n(n-4) = 0$$

$$\therefore \ n = 4$$

Then, substituting back into (2) gives $a = 3$.

3. The polynomial has a:

- single root at $x = -1$ and therefore a factor of $(x+1)$

- triply repeated root at $x = 1$ and therefore a factor of $(x-1)^3$

$y = (x+1)(x-1)^3$ has constant term $1(-1)^3 = -1$, but the graph has y-intercept at -3.

So $y = 3(x+1)(x-1)^3$ is a possible polynomial that fits the graph.

It is also possible that the root at $x = 1$ is repeated five times, so another function that has these properties would be $y = 3(x+1)(x-1)^5$.

4. Let $x^2 = y$. Then the quartic becomes $y^2 + by + c = 0$.

For the quartic to have 4 roots, this quadratic needs to have 2 *positive* roots.

So, firstly,

$$b^2 - 4c > 0$$

$$\Rightarrow b^2 > 4c$$

The smaller root of the quadratic in y is $\dfrac{-b - \sqrt{b^2 - 4c}}{2}$, and this needs to be positive:

$$\frac{-b - \sqrt{b^2 - 4c}}{2} > 0$$

$$\Rightarrow -b - \sqrt{b^2 - 4c} > 0$$

$$\Rightarrow -b > \sqrt{b^2 - 4c}$$

(Note that this means b must be negative, so that $-b$ is positive.) Hence, squaring gives

$$b^2 > b^2 - 4c$$

$$\therefore \ 4c > 0$$

Therefore, $b^2 > 4c > 0$.

4 FUNCTIONS, GRAPHS AND EQUATIONS

Mixed practice 4

1. For an even function, $f(-x) = f(x)$, so for any point x in the domain there exists a second point $-x$ that maps to the same value in the range. Therefore the function is not one-to-one and so doesn't have an inverse.

2. (a)

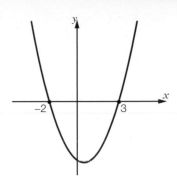

(b) $x < -2$ or $x > 3$

3.
$$\begin{cases} x - 2y + z = 2 & \cdots \ (1) \\ x + y - 3z = k & \cdots \ (2) \\ 2x - y - 2z = k^2 & \cdots \ (3) \end{cases}$$

$$(2)+(3) \ \begin{cases} x - 2y + z = 2 & \cdots \ (1) \\ x + y - 3z = k & \cdots \ (2) \\ 3x - 5z = k^2 + k & \cdots \ (4) \end{cases}$$

$$(1)+2\times(2) \ \begin{cases} 3x \quad 5z = 2 + 2k & \cdots \ (5) \\ x + y - 3z = k & \cdots \ (2) \\ 3x - 5z = k^2 + k & \cdots \ (4) \end{cases}$$

$$(4)-(5) \ \begin{cases} 3x - 5z = 2 + 2k & \cdots \ (5) \\ x + y - 3z = k & \cdots \ (2) \\ 0 = k^2 - k - 2 & \cdots \ (6) \end{cases}$$

From (6), there will be infinitely many solutions if:

$$k^2 - k - 2 = 0$$

$$\Leftrightarrow (k-2)(k+1) = 0$$

$$\Leftrightarrow k = 2 \ \text{or} \ -1$$

4.

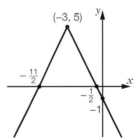

5. $x^2 - a^2 \geq 0 \Rightarrow x \geq a \ \text{or} \ x \leq -a$

6. (a)

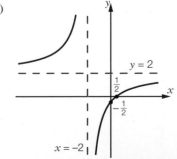

(b) $y = \dfrac{2x-1}{x+2}$

$\Rightarrow y(x+2) = 2x-1$

$\Rightarrow xy + 2y = 2x-1$

$\Rightarrow 2x - xy = 2y+1$

$\Rightarrow x(2-y) = 2y+1$

$\Rightarrow x = \dfrac{2y+1}{2-y}$

$\therefore f^{-1}(x) = \dfrac{2x+1}{2-x}$

Range is $y \in \mathbb{R}$, $y \neq -2$.

(c) $g(x) = f^{-1}(2-x)$

$= \dfrac{2(2-x)+1}{2-(2-x)}$

$= \dfrac{5-2x}{x}$

Therefore, the domain is $x \in \mathbb{R}$, $x \neq 0$.

(d) $f(x) = g(x)$

$\dfrac{2x-1}{x+2} = \dfrac{5-2x}{x}$

$\Leftrightarrow x(2x-1) = (5-2x)(x+2)$

$\Leftrightarrow 2x^2 - x = 10 + x - 2x^2$

$\Leftrightarrow 4x^2 - 2x - 10 = 0$

$\Leftrightarrow 2x^2 - x - 5 = 0$

$\Leftrightarrow x = \dfrac{1 \pm \sqrt{1 - 4 \times 2 \times (-5)}}{2 \times 2}$

$= \dfrac{1 \pm \sqrt{41}}{4}$

7. (a)

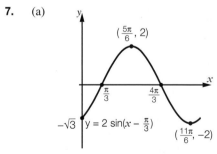

(b)

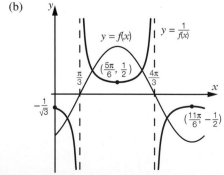

8. (a)

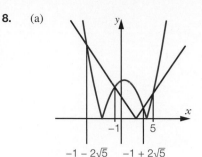

(b) The 4 points of intersection (from right to left on the graph) are given by the solutions to:

$x^2 - x - 12 = 3x - 7$ $\cdots$ (1)

$-(x^2 - x - 12) = 3x - 7$ $\cdots$ (2)

$-(x^2 - x - 12) = -(3x - 7)$ $\cdots$ (3)

$x^2 - x - 12 = -(3x - 7)$ $\cdots$ (4)

However, (1) and (3) are the same equation and (2) and (4) are the same, so just solve (1) and (2) to get 2 points of intersection from each:

$x^2 - x - 12 = 3x - 7$

$\Leftrightarrow x^2 - 4x - 5 = 0$

$\Leftrightarrow (x-5)(x+1) = 0$

$\Leftrightarrow x = 5, \ -1$

And

$-(x^2 - x - 12) = 3x - 7$

$\Leftrightarrow x^2 + 2x - 19 = 0$

$\Leftrightarrow x = \dfrac{-2 \pm \sqrt{2^2 - 4 \times 1 \times (-19)}}{2}$

$= \dfrac{-2 \pm 4\sqrt{5}}{2}$

$= -1 \pm 2\sqrt{5}$

From the graph the solution is therefore

$-1 - 2\sqrt{5} < x < -1$ or $-1 + 2\sqrt{5} < x < 5$

9. (a) $f(x) = \dfrac{ax - a^2 + 1}{x - a}$

$= \dfrac{a(x-a) + 1}{x - a}$

$= \dfrac{a(x-a)}{x-a} + \dfrac{1}{x-a}$

$= a + \dfrac{1}{x-a}$

So $p = a$ and $q = 1$.

(b) The graph $y = \dfrac{1}{x}$ has been translated up by a and to the right by a.

(c)

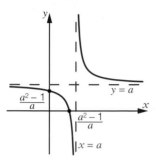

(d)

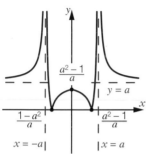

(e) $f\left(f\left(x\right)\right)=f\left(a+\dfrac{1}{x-a}\right)$

$=a+\dfrac{1}{\left(a+\frac{1}{x-a}\right)-a}$

$=a+\dfrac{1}{\frac{1}{x-a}}$

$=a+x-a$

$=x$

(f) Since $f\circ f(x)=x$, f is self-inverse and so

$f^{-1}\left(x\right)=a+\dfrac{1}{x-a}$.

(g) It is symmetric in the line $y=x$.

Going for the top 4

1. (a) $y=\dfrac{x^2-3x+3}{x-2}$

$\Rightarrow xy-2y=x^2-3x+3$

$\Rightarrow x^2-3x-xy+2y+3=0$

$\Rightarrow x^2-\left(3+y\right)x+\left(2y+3\right)=0$

$\Rightarrow x=\dfrac{3+y\pm\sqrt{\left(3+y\right)^2-4\left(2y+3\right)}}{2}$

$=\dfrac{3+y\pm\sqrt{y^2+6y+9-8y-12}}{2}$

$=\dfrac{3+y\pm\sqrt{y^2-2y-3}}{2}$

(b) For the square root to give a real number:

$y^2-2y-3\geq 0$

$\Leftrightarrow\left(y-3\right)\left(y+1\right)\geq 0$

$\therefore y\leq -1$ or $y\geq 3$

2. (a)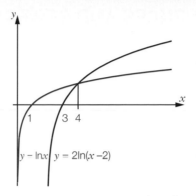

(b) Intersection when $\ln x=2\ln\left(x-2\right)$

$\Leftrightarrow \ln x=\ln\left(x-2\right)^2$

$\Leftrightarrow x=\left(x-2\right)^2$

$\Leftrightarrow x^2-5x+4=0$

$\Leftrightarrow \left(x-1\right)\left(x-4\right)=0$

$\therefore x=4$ (Reject $x=1$)

$2\ln(x-2)$ has no real value for $x\leq 2$

From the graph, $\ln x\geq 2\ln(x-2)$ for $2<x\leq 4$

3. Eliminating x and y from the last equation:

$\begin{cases}3x+2y-z=4 & \cdots\ (1)\\ 2x-4y+3z=1 & \cdots\ (2)\\ x+y+az=k & \cdots\ (3)\end{cases}$

$\begin{array}{l}\\ (2)-2\times(3)\\ 3\times(3)-(1)\end{array}\begin{cases}3x+2y-z=4 & \cdots\ (1)\\ -6y+\left(3-2a\right)z=1-2k & \cdots\ (4)\\ y+\left(3a+1\right)z=3k-4 & \cdots\ (5)\end{cases}$

$\begin{array}{l}\\ \\ (4)+6\times(5)\end{array}\begin{cases}3x+2y-z=4 & \cdots\ (1)\\ -6y+\left(3-2a\right)z=1-2k & \cdots\ (4)\\ \left(16a+9\right)z=16k-23 & \cdots\ (6)\end{cases}$

(a) The solution will be unique when the coefficient of z in the last equation is not 0:

$16a+9\neq 0$

$\therefore a\neq -\dfrac{9}{16}$

(b) There will be infinitely many solutions when the last equation is $0=0$, so:

$16k-23=0$

$\Rightarrow k=\dfrac{23}{16}$

The conditions for infinitely many solutions are $k=\dfrac{23}{16}$ and $a=-\dfrac{9}{16}$.

(c) There will be no solutions when the LHS of the last equation is 0 but the RHS isn't, i.e. when $a=-\dfrac{9}{16}$ and $k\neq\dfrac{23}{16}$.

5 SEQUENCES AND SERIES

Mixed practice 5

1. $u_4 = 17 \Rightarrow u_1 + 3d = 17 \qquad \cdots (1)$

$S_{20} = 990 \Rightarrow \dfrac{20}{2}\left[2u_1 + 19d\right] = 990$

$\Rightarrow 2u_1 + 19d = 99 \quad \cdots (2)$

From (1), $u_1 = 17 - 3d$; substituting this into (2) gives

$2(17 - 3d) + 19d = 99$

$\Leftrightarrow 34 + 13d = 99$

$\Leftrightarrow d = 5$

So $u_1 = 17 - 3d = 17 - 3 \times 5 = 2$.

2. The fourth, tenth and thirteenth terms of the geometric sequence are:

$u_4 = u_1 r^3$

$u_{10} = u_1 r^9$

$u_{13} = u_1 r^{12}$

As these form an arithmetic sequence:

$u_{10} - u_4 = u_{13} - u_{10}$

$\Rightarrow u_1 r^9 - u_1 r^3 = u_1 r^{12} - u_1 r^9$

$\Rightarrow r^{12} - 2r^9 + r^3 = 0 \quad (\text{as } u_1 \neq 0)$

$\Rightarrow r^9 - 2r^6 + 1 = 0 \quad (\text{as } r \neq 0)$

$\Rightarrow r = 1, \, 1.17, \, -0.852 \quad (\text{from GDC to 3 SF})$

$\therefore r = -0.852 \quad (\text{for sum to infinity to exist, } |r| < 1)$

3. $\displaystyle\sum_{r=1}^{12} 4r + \left(\dfrac{1}{3}\right)^r = 4\sum_{r=1}^{12} r + \sum_{r=1}^{12}\left(\dfrac{1}{3}\right)^r$

The first sum is an arithmetic series, and the second sum is a geometric series. So, using the formulae:

$4\left[\dfrac{12}{2}(2 \times 1 + (12-1) \times 1)\right] + \dfrac{\frac{1}{3}\left[1 - \left(\frac{1}{3}\right)^{12}\right]}{1 - \frac{1}{3}} = 312.5 \ (4 \text{ SF})$

4. For 20 terms of this series, i.e. with $n = 20$:

$\ln x + \ln x^4 + \ln x^7 + \ln x^{10} + \ldots = \ln x + 4\ln x + 7\ln x$

$+ 10\ln x + \ldots$

$= \ln x(1 + 4 + 7 + 10 + \ldots)$

$= \ln x\left(\dfrac{20}{2}(2 + 19 \times 3)\right)$

$= 590 \ln x$

$= \ln x^{590}$

5. We know that the total length of the pieces is 300, i.e. $S_n = 300$:

$S_n = \dfrac{n}{2}\left(u_1 + u_n\right)$

$300 = \dfrac{n}{2}(1 + 19)$

$\Leftrightarrow 300 = 10n$

$\Leftrightarrow n = 30$

So $u_{30} = 19$:

$u_n = u_1 + (n-1)d$

$19 = 1 + 29d$

$\Leftrightarrow d = \dfrac{18}{29}$ metres

6. The amount Aaron has in his account for the first few months is:

1st: 100
2nd: 100 + 110
3rd: 100 + 110 + 120

His monthly balance forms an arithmetic series with $a = 100$ and $d = 10$. So after n months he will have:

$S_n = \dfrac{n}{2}\left[2 \times 100 + (n-1)10\right]$

$= \dfrac{n}{2}\left[200 + 10n - 10\right]$

$= \dfrac{n}{2}\left[190 + 10n\right]$

$= 5n^2 + 95n$

The amount Blake has in his account for the first few months is:

1st: 50
2nd: 50×1.05
3rd: 50×1.05^2

His monthly balance forms a geometric series with $a = 50$ and $r = 1.05$. So after n months he will have:

$S_n = \dfrac{50(1.05^n - 1)}{1.05 - 1}$

$= 1000(1.05^n - 1)$

Therefore, Blake will have more in his account than Aaron does when:

$1000(1.05^n - 1) > 5n^2 + 95n$

$\therefore n = 73$ months (from GDC)

Going for the top 5

1. (a) (i) Writing out the sum from the first term, a, to the nth term, ar^{n-1}:

$S_n = a + ar + ar^2 + \ldots + ar^{n-2} + ar^{n-1} \quad (1)$

Multiplying through by r:

$rS_n = ar + ar^2 + ar^3 + \ldots + ar^{n-1} + ar^n \quad (2)$

We can see that (1) and (2) have many terms in common:

$S_n = a + ar + ar^2 + ar^3 + \ldots + ar^{n-2} + ar^{n-1} \qquad (1)$

$rS_n = \quad\ \ ar + ar^2 + ar^3 + \ldots + ar^{n-2} + ar^{n-1} + ar^n \quad (2)$

So (2) − (1) gives:

$$rS_n - S_n = ar^n - a$$
$$\Rightarrow S_n(r-1) = a(r^n - 1)$$
$$\Rightarrow S_n = \frac{a(r^n - 1)}{r-1}$$

(ii) If $-1 < r < 1$ (or equivalently $|r| < 1$), then as $n \to \infty$, $r^n \to 0$. So

$$S_n \to \frac{a(0-1)}{r-1} = \frac{-a}{r-1} = \frac{a}{1-r}$$

If $|r| \geq 1$, then r^n has no limit as $n \to \infty$, and so there is no finite limit for S_n.

Thus, $S_\infty = \dfrac{a}{1-r}$ only for $|r| < 1$.

(b) The sum of the first n terms is $S_n = \dfrac{u_1(1-r^n)}{1-r}$.

The sum of the next n terms is given by

$$S_{2n} - S_n = \frac{u_1(1-r^{2n})}{1-r} - \frac{u_1(1-r^n)}{1-r}$$
$$= \frac{u_1(1-r^{2n} - 1 + r^n)}{1-r}$$
$$= \frac{u_1(r^n - r^{2n})}{1-r}$$
$$= \frac{u_1 r^n(1-r^n)}{1-r}$$

So the ratio of the sum of the first n terms to the sum of the next n terms is

$$\frac{u_1(1-r^n)}{1-r} : \frac{u_1 r^n(1-r^n)}{1-r} = 1 : r^n$$

(c) (i) $u_7 + 4u_5 = u_8$

i.e. $u_1 r^6 + 4u_1 r^4 = u_1 r^7$
$$\Rightarrow r^2 + 4 = r^3 \quad (\text{since } u_1, r \neq 0)$$
$$\Rightarrow r^3 - r^2 - 4 = 0$$

To factorise this, substitute small positive and negative integers into $f(r) = r^3 - r^2 - 4$ until you find an r such that $f(r) = 0$:

$$f(1) = 1^3 - 1^2 - 4 = -4$$
$$f(-1) = (-1)^3 - (-1)^2 - 4 = -6$$
$$f(2) = 2^3 - 2^2 - 4 = 0$$

Therefore, by the factor theorem, $(x-2)$ is a factor and so by long division or equating coefficients we get:

$$r^3 - r^2 - 4 = (r-2)(r^2 + r + 2)$$
For the quadratic $r^2 + r + 2$,

$$\Delta = 1^2 - 4 \times 1 \times 2 = -7 < 0$$

Hence there are no real roots for this quadratic factor, and so the only root of $f(r)$ is $r = 2$.

Then, from part (b), the ratio is

$$1 : r^{10} = 1 : 2^{10} = 1 : 1024$$

(ii) No, because $r > 1$ in this case, and as shown in part (a)(ii), the condition for a sum to infinity to exist is that $|r| < 1$.

2. The integers from 1 to 1000 form an arithmetic sequence with $u_1 = 1$, $u_n = 1000$ and $n = 1000$. So

$$S_n = \frac{n}{2}(u_1 + u_n)$$
$$= \frac{1000}{2}(1 + 1000)$$
$$= 500\,500$$

The multiples of 7 between 1 and 1000 form an arithmetic sequence with $u_1 = 7$, $u_n = 994$ and $n = \dfrac{994}{7} = 142$. So

$$S_n = \frac{n}{2}(u_1 + u_n)$$
$$= \frac{142}{2}(7 + 994)$$
$$= 71\,071$$

Therefore the sum of the integers between 1 and 1000 that are not divisible by 7 is

$$500\,500 - 71\,071 = 429\,429.$$

6 TRIGONOMETRY

Mixed practice 6

1. $A = \dfrac{1}{2}ab\sin C$

$$12 = \frac{1}{2}x(x+2)\sin 30°$$
$$\Rightarrow 12 = \frac{1}{2}x(x+2)\frac{1}{2}$$
$$\Rightarrow 48 = x^2 + 2x$$
$$\Rightarrow x^2 + 2x - 48 = 0$$
$$\Rightarrow (x+8)(x-6) = 0$$
$$\therefore x = 6 \quad (\text{as } x > 0)$$

2. By the sine rule:

$$\frac{\sin\theta}{5} = \frac{\sin 2\theta}{7}$$
$$\Rightarrow 7\sin\theta = 5\sin 2\theta$$
$$\Rightarrow 7\sin\theta = 5(2\sin\theta\cos\theta)$$
$$\Rightarrow 7\sin\theta - 10\sin\theta\cos\theta = 0$$
$$\Rightarrow \sin\theta(7 - 10\cos\theta) = 0$$

$\Rightarrow \sin\theta = 0 \qquad$ or $\qquad \cos\theta = \dfrac{7}{10}$

$\Rightarrow \theta = 0°, 180° \quad$ or $\quad \theta = 45.6°$

$\therefore \ \theta = 45.6°$

3. (a) Shaded area = area of sector − area of triangle

$$6.2 = \dfrac{1}{2}r^2\theta - \dfrac{1}{2}ab\sin C$$

$$6.2 = \dfrac{1}{2}\times 5^2\theta - \dfrac{1}{2}\times 5 \times 5\sin\theta$$

$$6.2 = \dfrac{25}{2}(\theta - \sin\theta)$$

$$\therefore \ \theta - \sin\theta = \dfrac{12.4}{25} = 0.496$$

(b) From GDC, $\theta = 1.49$ (3 SF)

4. (a) Since $\widehat{\text{OTP}}$ is a right angle,

$$\text{Area} = \dfrac{1}{2}bh$$

$$= \dfrac{1}{2}\times 12 \times 7$$

$$= 42$$

(b) Let $\widehat{\text{POT}} = \theta$. Then

$$\tan\theta = \dfrac{12}{7}$$

$$\therefore \ \theta = \tan^{-1}\left(\dfrac{12}{7}\right) = 1.04 \ (3 \text{ SF})$$

(c) Shaded area = area of triangle OPT − area of sector

$$= 42 - \dfrac{1}{2}\times 7^2 \times \widehat{\text{POT}}$$

$$= 16.5 \ (3 \text{ SF})$$

5. (a) In triangle ABG, we know $\widehat{\text{GAB}} = 65°$ and $\widehat{\text{GBA}} = 80°$, so

$$\widehat{\text{AGB}} = 180° - 65° - 80° = 35°$$

By the sine rule:

$$\dfrac{\text{AG}}{\sin 80°} = \dfrac{20}{\sin 35°}$$

$$\Rightarrow \text{AG} = \dfrac{20}{\sin 35°}\times \sin 80°$$

$$= 34.3 \text{ m}$$

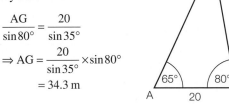

(b) In triangle AGT, we know the length AG and the angle $\widehat{\text{GAT}}$:

$$\tan 18° = \dfrac{\text{GT}}{\text{AG}}$$

$$\therefore \ \text{GT} = \text{AG}\times \tan 18°$$

$$= 11.2 \text{ m} \ (3 \text{ SF})$$

6. (a) $\cot x + \tan x = 4$

$$\Leftrightarrow \dfrac{1}{\tan x} + \tan x = 4$$

$$\Leftrightarrow 1 + \tan^2 x = 4\tan x$$

$$\Leftrightarrow \tan^2 x - 4\tan x + 1 - 0$$

$$\Leftrightarrow \tan x = \dfrac{4 \pm \sqrt{(-4)^2 - 4\times 1 \times 1}}{2 \times 1}$$

$$= \dfrac{4 \pm \sqrt{12}}{2}$$

$$= \dfrac{4 \pm 2\sqrt{3}}{2}$$

$$= 2 \pm \sqrt{3}$$

For $x \in \left[0, \dfrac{\pi}{4}\right[$, $0 \le \tan x < 1$, so only the smaller value is possible. Hence $\tan x = 2 - \sqrt{3}$.

(b) (i) $\cot x + \tan x = \dfrac{\cos x}{\sin x} + \dfrac{\sin x}{\cos x}$

$$= \dfrac{\cos^2 x}{\sin x\cos x} + \dfrac{\sin^2 x}{\sin x\cos x}$$

$$= \dfrac{\cos^2 x + \sin^2 x}{\sin x\cos x}$$

$$= \dfrac{1}{\sin x\cos x}$$

$$= \dfrac{1}{\frac{1}{2}\sin 2x}$$

$$= \dfrac{2}{\sin 2x}$$

$$= 2\csc 2x$$

(ii) $\cot x + \tan x = 4$

$$\Leftrightarrow 2\csc 2x = 4$$

$$\Leftrightarrow \csc 2x = 2$$

$$\Leftrightarrow \sin 2x = \dfrac{1}{2}$$

$$x \in [0, \pi] \Rightarrow 2x \in [0, 2\pi]$$

The graph shows that there are two solutions to $\sin\theta = \dfrac{1}{2}$ in $[0, 2\pi]$:

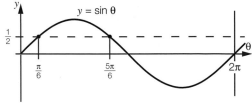

One solution is $\sin^{-1}\left(\dfrac{1}{2}\right) = \dfrac{\pi}{6}$

And another is $\pi - \dfrac{\pi}{6} = \dfrac{5\pi}{6}$

$$2x = \frac{\pi}{6}, \frac{5\pi}{6}$$

$$\therefore\ x = \frac{\pi}{12}, \frac{5\pi}{12}$$

(c) From (b)(ii), $x = \dfrac{\pi}{12}$ is a solution of the equation

$\cot x + \tan x = 4$, and it satisfies $x \in \left[0, \dfrac{\pi}{4}\right[$.

Therefore, from part (a), $\tan\left(\dfrac{\pi}{12}\right) = 2 - \sqrt{3}$.

7. $3\sin 2\theta = \tan 2\theta$

$\Leftrightarrow 3\sin 2\theta = \dfrac{\sin 2\theta}{\cos 2\theta}$

$\Leftrightarrow 3\sin 2\theta \cos 2\theta = \sin 2\theta$

$\Leftrightarrow 3\sin 2\theta \cos 2\theta - \sin 2\theta = 0$

$\Leftrightarrow \sin 2\theta(3\cos 2\theta - 1) = 0$

$\therefore\ \sin 2\theta = 0\quad$ or $\quad \cos 2\theta = \dfrac{1}{3}$

$\theta \in \left[-\dfrac{\pi}{2}, \dfrac{\pi}{2}\right] \Rightarrow 2\theta \in [-\pi, \pi]$

For $\sin 2\theta = 0$, the graph shows there to be three solutions in $[-\pi, \pi]$:

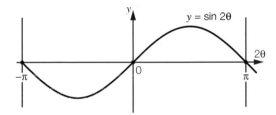

One solution is $\sin^{-1} 0 = 0$

Another is $\pi - 0 = \pi$

Then, adding/subtracting 2π gives one further value in the interval: $\pi - 2\pi = -\pi$

$\therefore\ 2\theta = 0, \pm\pi$

$\Rightarrow \theta = 0, \pm\dfrac{\pi}{2}$

For $\cos 2\theta = \dfrac{1}{3}$, the graph shows there to be two solutions:

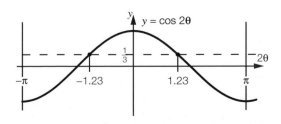

One solution is $\cos^{-1}\left(\dfrac{1}{3}\right) = 1.23$

$2\pi - 1.23 = 5.05$ is not in the interval $[-\pi, \pi]$,

but $5.05 - 2\pi = -1.23$ is in the interval.

$\therefore\ 2\theta = \pm 1.23$

$\Rightarrow \theta = \pm 0.615$

So the solutions are $\theta = 0, \pm 0.615, \pm\dfrac{\pi}{2}$

8. (a) $3x^2 - 2x + 5 = 3\left[x^2 - \dfrac{2}{3}x\right] + 5$

$$= 3\left[\left(x - \dfrac{1}{3}\right)^2 - \dfrac{1}{9}\right] + 5$$

$$= 3\left(x - \dfrac{1}{3}\right)^2 - \dfrac{1}{3} + 5$$

$$= 3\left(x - \dfrac{1}{3}\right)^2 + \dfrac{14}{3}$$

So the coordinates of the vertex are $\left(\dfrac{1}{3}, \dfrac{14}{3}\right)$.

(b) (i) $g(\theta) = 3\cos 2\theta - 4\cos\theta + 13$

$$= 3(2\cos^2\theta - 1) - 4\cos\theta + 13$$

$$= 6\cos^2\theta - 4\cos\theta + 10$$

(ii) Let $\cos\theta = x$. Then

$6\cos^2\theta - 4\cos\theta + 10 = 6x^2 - 4x + 10$

$$= 2(3x^2 - 2x + 5)$$

$$= 2f(x)$$

and $0 \le \theta \le 2\pi \Rightarrow -1 \le x \le 1$

Since the minimum value of $f(x)$ is $\dfrac{14}{3}$,

the minimum value of $2f(x)$ is $\dfrac{28}{3}$.

That is, the minimum value of $g(\theta)$ is $\dfrac{28}{3}$.

9. (a) In triangle ABD:

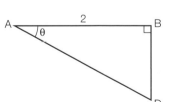

$\cos\theta = \dfrac{2}{AD}$

$\Rightarrow AD = \dfrac{2}{\cos\theta}$

Since AC is a diameter, $A\hat{E}C$ is a right angle.

So in triangle ACE:

$\sin\theta = \dfrac{CE}{3}$

$\Rightarrow CE = 3\sin\theta$

Therefore

$$R = AD - CE$$

$$= \frac{2}{\cos\theta} - 3\sin\theta$$

$$= 2\sec\theta - 3\sin\theta$$

(b) For stationary values, $\dfrac{dR}{d\theta} = 0$.

$$\frac{dR}{d\theta} = 2\sec\theta\tan\theta - 3\cos\theta$$

$$0 = 2\sec\theta\tan\theta - 3\cos\theta$$

$$\Rightarrow 2\sec\theta\tan\theta = 3\cos\theta$$

$$\Rightarrow 2 \times \frac{1}{\cos\theta} \times \frac{\sin\theta}{\cos\theta} = 3\cos\theta$$

$$\Rightarrow 2\sin\theta = 3\cos^3\theta$$

(c) From GDC, the minimum occurs at $\theta = 0.711$ and $R = 0.682$ (3 SF). So the smallest value of $AD - CE$ is 0.682.

Going for the top 6

1. (a) By the double angle formula:

$$\cos 2x = 2\cos^2 x - 1$$
$$= 2y^2 - 1$$

(b) $\cos 2x = 2y^2 - 1$

$$\Rightarrow 2x = \arccos(2y^2 - 1)$$

But $\cos x = y \Rightarrow x = \arccos y$

$$\therefore 2\arccos y = 2x = \arccos(2y^2 - 1)$$

(c) $y = \cos x \Rightarrow \arccos y = x$

Also, $y = \cos x = \sin\left(\dfrac{\pi}{2} - x\right) \Rightarrow \arcsin y = \dfrac{\pi}{2} - x$

$$\therefore \arcsin y + \arccos y = \left(\frac{\pi}{2} - x\right) + x = \frac{\pi}{2}$$

2. $\tan\alpha = \dfrac{AB}{AD} = \dfrac{2AD}{AD} = 2$

$$\tan\beta = \frac{AC}{AD} = \frac{3AD}{AD} = 3$$

By the compound angle formula:

$$\tan(\alpha + \beta) = \frac{\tan\alpha + \tan\beta}{1 - \tan\alpha\tan\beta}$$

$$= \frac{2 + 3}{1 - 2\times 3} = -1$$

$$\tan^{-1}(-1) = -\frac{\pi}{4}$$

$$\therefore \alpha + \beta = -\frac{\pi}{4} + \pi \quad (\text{as } \alpha + \beta > 0)$$

$$= \frac{3\pi}{4}$$

---

3. (a) $\cos\big[(A - B)x\big] - \cos\big[(A + B)x\big] = \cos(Ax - Bx) - \cos(Ax + Bx)$

$$= \cos Ax\cos Bx + \sin Ax\sin Bx - (\cos Ax\cos Bx - \sin Ax\sin Bx)$$

$$= 2\sin Ax\sin Bx$$

(b) Let $A = 1$ and $B = 2r - 1$.

Then, by (a), $2\sin x\sin[(2r - 1)x] = \cos\big[(1 - (2r - 1))x\big] - \cos\big[(1 + (2r - 1))x\big]$

$$\sum_{r=1}^{n} 2\sin x\sin(2r - 1)x = \sum_{r=1}^{n} \cos\big[(1 - (2r - 1))x\big] - \cos\big[(1 + (2r - 1))x\big]$$

$$= \sum_{r=1}^{n} \cos\big[2(1 - r)x\big] - \cos 2rx$$

$$= (\cos 0 - \cos 2x) + (\cos(-2x) + \cos 4x) + (\cos(-4x) + \cos 6x) + \ldots + \big(\cos\big[2(1 - n)x\big] + \cos 2nx\big)$$

$$= (\cos 0 - \cos 2x) + (\cos 2x - \cos 4x) + (\cos 4x - \cos 6x) + \ldots + \big(\cos\big[2(n - 1)x\big] - \cos 2nx\big)$$

$$= 1 - \cos 2nx \quad \text{(because all the terms in the middle cancel out)}$$

$$\therefore \sum_{r=1}^{n} \sin x\sin(2r - 1)x = \frac{1 - \cos 2nx}{2}$$

(c) Let $n = 2$ in part (b). Then

$$\sum_{r=1}^{2} \sin x \sin(2r-1)x = \frac{1-\cos 4x}{2}$$

$$\Leftrightarrow \sin x \sin x + \sin x \sin 3x = \frac{1-\cos 4x}{2}$$

$$\Leftrightarrow \sin^2 x + \sin x \sin 3x = \frac{1-\cos 4x}{2}$$

Therefore, solve

$$\frac{1-\cos 4x}{2} = \frac{1}{4}$$

$$\Leftrightarrow \cos 4x = \frac{1}{2}$$

$$0 < x < \pi \Rightarrow 0 < 4x < 4\pi$$

The graph shows there to be four solutions:

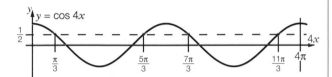

One solution is $\cos^{-1}\left(\frac{1}{2}\right) = \frac{\pi}{3}$

Another is $2\pi - \frac{\pi}{3} = \frac{5\pi}{3}$

Then, adding 2π to these gives two more solutions in $[0, 4\pi]$:

$$\frac{\pi}{3} + 2\pi = \frac{7\pi}{3}$$

$$\frac{5\pi}{3} + 2\pi = \frac{11\pi}{3}$$

$$\therefore 4x = \frac{\pi}{3}, \frac{5\pi}{3}, \frac{7\pi}{3}, \frac{11\pi}{3}$$

$$\Rightarrow x = \frac{\pi}{12}, \frac{5\pi}{12}, \frac{7\pi}{12}, \frac{11\pi}{12}$$

(d) Let $n = 5$ and $x = \frac{\pi}{5}$ in part (b). Then

$$\sum_{r=1}^{5} \sin\left(\frac{\pi}{5}\right)\sin\left[(2r-1)\frac{\pi}{5}\right] = \frac{1-\cos\left[2\times 5\left(\frac{\pi}{5}\right)\right]}{2}$$

$$\Rightarrow \sin\frac{\pi}{5}\sin\frac{\pi}{5} + \sin\frac{\pi}{5}\sin\frac{3\pi}{5} + \sin\frac{\pi}{5}\sin\frac{5\pi}{5} + \sin\frac{\pi}{5}\sin\frac{7\pi}{5} + \sin\frac{\pi}{5}\sin\frac{9\pi}{5} = \frac{1-\cos 2\pi}{2}$$

$$\Rightarrow \sin\frac{\pi}{5}\left(\sin\frac{\pi}{5} + \sin\frac{3\pi}{5} + \sin\frac{5\pi}{5} + \sin\frac{7\pi}{5} + \sin\frac{9\pi}{5}\right) = 0$$

$$\Rightarrow \sin\frac{\pi}{5} + \sin\frac{3\pi}{5} + \sin\frac{5\pi}{5} + \sin\frac{7\pi}{5} + \sin\frac{9\pi}{5} = 0$$

7 VECTORS

Mixed practice 7

1. (a) $a \times b = \begin{pmatrix} (-1) \times p - 2 \times 1 \\ 2 \times 1 - 3 \times p \\ 3 \times 1 - (-1) \times 1 \end{pmatrix}$

$$= \begin{pmatrix} -p-2 \\ 2-3p \\ 4 \end{pmatrix}$$

(or $-(p+2)\boldsymbol{i} + (2-3p)\boldsymbol{j} + 4\boldsymbol{k}$)

(b) If $a \times b$ is parallel to c, then $a \times b = \lambda c$ for some constant λ.

So $\begin{pmatrix} -p-2 \\ 2-3p \\ 4 \end{pmatrix} = \lambda \begin{pmatrix} 2 \\ 22 \\ 8 \end{pmatrix}$

The third component gives $4 = 8\lambda \Rightarrow \lambda = \frac{1}{2}$

And the first component gives

$$-p-2 = 2\lambda$$

$$\therefore p = -3$$

Check these values in the second equation: $2 - 3p = 11 = 22\lambda$, as stated.

2. If point D lies on the line, its position vector d satisfies

$$d = \begin{pmatrix} 1 \\ -1 \\ 5 \end{pmatrix} + \lambda \begin{pmatrix} -1 \\ 1 \\ -2 \end{pmatrix} = \begin{pmatrix} 1-\lambda \\ -1+\lambda \\ 5-2\lambda \end{pmatrix} \text{ for some value of } \lambda.$$

$$\therefore \overrightarrow{AD} = d - a = \begin{pmatrix} 1-\lambda \\ -1+\lambda \\ 5-2\lambda \end{pmatrix} - \begin{pmatrix} 3 \\ 2 \\ -1 \end{pmatrix} = \begin{pmatrix} -2-\lambda \\ -3+\lambda \\ 6-2\lambda \end{pmatrix}$$

For $\overrightarrow{AD}$ to be parallel to the x-axis,

$$\overrightarrow{AD} = \mu \begin{pmatrix} 1 \\ 0 \\ 0 \end{pmatrix} \quad \text{for some scalar } \mu$$

i.e. $\begin{pmatrix} -2-\lambda \\ -3+\lambda \\ 6-2\lambda \end{pmatrix} = \begin{pmatrix} \mu \\ 0 \\ 0 \end{pmatrix}$

$$\Rightarrow \begin{cases} -3+\lambda = 0 \\ 6-2\lambda = 0 \end{cases}$$

Both equations are satisfied when $\lambda = 3$.

3. Vectors a and b are perpendicular if

$a \cdot b = 0$

$\sin\theta\cos\theta + \cos\theta\sin 2\theta = 0$

$\Leftrightarrow \sin\theta\cos\theta + \cos\theta(2\sin\theta\cos\theta) = 0$

$\Leftrightarrow \sin\theta\cos\theta(1 + 2\cos\theta) = 0$

$\Leftrightarrow \sin\theta = 0 \quad \text{or} \quad \cos\theta = 0 \quad \text{or} \quad \cos\theta = -\dfrac{1}{2}$

$\therefore \theta = 0, \pi, 2\pi, \dfrac{\pi}{2}, \dfrac{3\pi}{2}, \dfrac{2\pi}{3}, \dfrac{4\pi}{3}$

4. (a) $\overrightarrow{AB} = b - a = \begin{pmatrix} 4-3 \\ 1-1 \\ 3-1 \end{pmatrix} = \begin{pmatrix} 1 \\ 0 \\ 2 \end{pmatrix}$

$$\overrightarrow{AC} = c - a = \begin{pmatrix} 3-3 \\ q+1-1 \\ q+1-1 \end{pmatrix} = \begin{pmatrix} 0 \\ q \\ q \end{pmatrix}$$

A vector perpendicular to both $\overrightarrow{AB}$ and $\overrightarrow{AC}$ is

$$\overrightarrow{AB} \times \overrightarrow{AC} = \begin{pmatrix} 0 \times q - 2q \\ 2 \times 0 - 1 \times q \\ 1 \times q - 0 \times 0 \end{pmatrix} = \begin{pmatrix} -2q \\ -q \\ q \end{pmatrix}$$

(b) The area of triangle ABC is

$$\dfrac{1}{2}\left|\overrightarrow{AB} \times \overrightarrow{AC}\right| = 6\sqrt{2}$$

$$\therefore \sqrt{4q^2 + q^2 + q^2} = 12\sqrt{2}$$

$\Leftrightarrow 6q^2 = \left(12\sqrt{2}\right)^2$

$\Leftrightarrow q^2 = \dfrac{144 \times 2}{6} = \dfrac{144}{3} = 48$

$\therefore q = 4\sqrt{3}$

(c) n is parallel to $\overrightarrow{AB} \times \overrightarrow{AC}$

$$\therefore n = \begin{pmatrix} -2 \\ -1 \\ 1 \end{pmatrix}$$

So the equation of the plane is

$$r \cdot n = a \cdot n$$

$$\begin{pmatrix} x \\ y \\ z \end{pmatrix} \cdot \begin{pmatrix} 2 \\ 1 \\ 1 \end{pmatrix} = \begin{pmatrix} 3 \\ 1 \\ 1 \end{pmatrix} \cdot \begin{pmatrix} 2 \\ 1 \\ 1 \end{pmatrix}$$

$-2x - y + z = -6 - 1 + 1$

$2x + y - z = 6$

5. (a) $d = \overrightarrow{PQ} = q - p = \begin{pmatrix} -4 \\ 2 \\ 5 \end{pmatrix}$

Then, using $r = a + \lambda d$ with $a = p$ and the d found above, we get the vector equation

$$r = \begin{pmatrix} 3 \\ -1 \\ 2 \end{pmatrix} + \lambda \begin{pmatrix} -4 \\ 2 \\ 5 \end{pmatrix}$$

(b) $\overrightarrow{PM} = m - p = \begin{pmatrix} 0 \\ -3 \\ -1 \end{pmatrix}$

So the angle θ between l and (PM) satisfies

$$\cos\theta = \dfrac{d \cdot \overrightarrow{PM}}{|d||\overrightarrow{PM}|} = \dfrac{\begin{pmatrix} -4 \\ 2 \\ 5 \end{pmatrix} \cdot \begin{pmatrix} 0 \\ -3 \\ -1 \end{pmatrix}}{\sqrt{16+4+25}\sqrt{0+9+1}}$$

$$= \dfrac{-11}{\sqrt{45}\sqrt{10}}$$

$$\therefore \theta = \cos^{-1}\left(\dfrac{-11}{\sqrt{45}\sqrt{10}}\right) = 121.2°$$

But since we are asked for the acute angle, it is $180° - 121.2° = 58.8°$.

(c) Let the shortest distance from M to the line be x.

From the diagram,

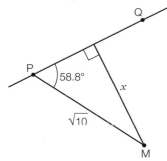

$$\sin 58.8° = \frac{x}{\left|\overrightarrow{PM}\right|} = \frac{x}{\sqrt{10}}$$

$$\therefore x = \sqrt{10}\sin 58.8° = 2.70$$

6. $\overrightarrow{BC} = c - b = \begin{pmatrix} -4-(-1) \\ 1-4 \\ 3-1 \end{pmatrix} = \begin{pmatrix} -3 \\ -3 \\ 2 \end{pmatrix}$

For ABCD to be a parallelogram, we must have $\overrightarrow{AD} = \overrightarrow{BC}$.

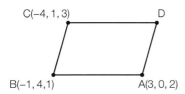

$\overrightarrow{AD} = d - a$

$\Rightarrow d = \overrightarrow{AD} + a$

$\quad = \overrightarrow{BC} + a$

$\quad = \begin{pmatrix} -3 \\ -3 \\ 2 \end{pmatrix} + \begin{pmatrix} 3 \\ 0 \\ 2 \end{pmatrix} = \begin{pmatrix} 0 \\ -3 \\ 4 \end{pmatrix}$

i.e. coordinates of D are $(0, -3, 4)$.

7. (a) (i) $\overrightarrow{AB} = b - a = \begin{pmatrix} 2-1 \\ 1-(-1) \\ 2-3 \end{pmatrix} = \begin{pmatrix} 1 \\ 2 \\ -1 \end{pmatrix}$

$\overrightarrow{AC} = c - a = \begin{pmatrix} 0-1 \\ 1-(-1) \\ 5-3 \end{pmatrix} = \begin{pmatrix} -1 \\ 2 \\ 2 \end{pmatrix}$

$\overrightarrow{AB} \times \overrightarrow{AC} = \begin{pmatrix} 2\times2-(-1)2 \\ (-1)(-1)-1\times2 \\ 1\times2-2(-1) \end{pmatrix} = \begin{pmatrix} 6 \\ -1 \\ 4 \end{pmatrix}$

(ii) For the plane ABC:

$$r \cdot n = a \cdot n$$

$$\begin{pmatrix} x \\ y \\ z \end{pmatrix} \cdot \begin{pmatrix} 6 \\ -1 \\ 4 \end{pmatrix} = \begin{pmatrix} 1 \\ -1 \\ 3 \end{pmatrix} \cdot \begin{pmatrix} 6 \\ -1 \\ 4 \end{pmatrix}$$

$$\Rightarrow 6x - y + 4z = 19$$

(b) (i) $r = \begin{pmatrix} 9 \\ 2 \\ 5 \end{pmatrix} + \lambda \begin{pmatrix} 6 \\ -1 \\ 4 \end{pmatrix}$

(ii) Writing $r = \begin{pmatrix} x \\ y \\ z \end{pmatrix}$ in the equation of part (b)(i):

$$\begin{pmatrix} x \\ y \\ z \end{pmatrix} = \begin{pmatrix} 9 \\ 2 \\ 5 \end{pmatrix} + \lambda \begin{pmatrix} 6 \\ -1 \\ 4 \end{pmatrix} \Rightarrow \begin{cases} x = 9 + 6\lambda \\ y = 2 - \lambda \\ z = 5 + 4\lambda \end{cases}$$

Substituting these expressions into the equation of the plane from part (a)(ii):

$$6(9 + 6\lambda) - (2 - \lambda) + 4(5 + 4\lambda) = 19$$

$$\Leftrightarrow 54 + 36\lambda - 2 + \lambda + 20 + 16\lambda = 19$$

$$\Leftrightarrow 53\lambda = -53$$

$$\Leftrightarrow \lambda = -1$$

Substituting $\lambda = -1$ back into the equation of the line:

$$x = 9 + 6\lambda = 3$$

$$y = 2 - \lambda = 3$$

$$z = 5 + 4\lambda = 1$$

i.e. the foot of the perpendicular, N, has coordinates $(3, 3, 1)$.

(iii) $\overrightarrow{MN} = n - m = \begin{pmatrix} 3-9 \\ 3-2 \\ 1-5 \end{pmatrix} = \begin{pmatrix} -6 \\ 1 \\ -4 \end{pmatrix}$

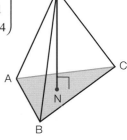

So the height, h, of the pyramid is

$$h = \left|\overrightarrow{MN}\right|$$

$$= \sqrt{(-6)^2 + 1^2 + (-4)^2} = \sqrt{53}$$

The area, A, of the (triangular) base is

$$A = \frac{1}{2}\left|\overrightarrow{AB} \times \overrightarrow{AC}\right|$$

$$= \frac{1}{2}\sqrt{6^2 + (-1)^2 + 4^2} \quad \text{(using part (a)(i))}$$

$$= \frac{1}{2}\sqrt{53}$$

Therefore the volume, V, of the tetrahedron is

$$V = \frac{1}{3}Ah$$

$$= \frac{1}{3}\left(\frac{1}{2}\sqrt{53}\right)\left(\sqrt{53}\right)$$

$$= \frac{53}{6}\left(\approx 8.83\right)$$

(c) The angle, θ, can be found from the right-angled triangle MNB.

$$\overrightarrow{BM} = m - b = \begin{pmatrix} 9-2 \\ 2-1 \\ 5-2 \end{pmatrix} = \begin{pmatrix} 7 \\ 1 \\ 3 \end{pmatrix}$$

$$\sin\theta = \frac{\left|\overrightarrow{MN}\right|}{\left|\overrightarrow{BM}\right|} = \frac{\sqrt{53}}{\sqrt{7^2 + 1^2 + 3^2}}$$

$$\therefore \theta = \sin^{-1}\left(\frac{\sqrt{53}}{\sqrt{59}}\right) = 71.4°$$

8. (a) $p \cdot q = |p||q|\cos 60°$

$$\therefore x + 2x + 4 = \sqrt{1^2 + 2^2 + 2^2}\sqrt{x^2 + x^2 + 4} \times \frac{1}{2}$$

$$\Rightarrow 3x + 4 = \sqrt{9}\sqrt{2x^2 + 4} \times \frac{1}{2}$$

$$\Rightarrow 3x + 4 = \frac{3}{2}\sqrt{2x^2 + 4}$$

$$\Rightarrow \left(3x + 4\right)^2 = \frac{9}{4}\left(2x^2 + 4\right)$$

$$\Rightarrow 9x^2 + 24x + 16 = \frac{9}{4}\left(2x^2 + 4\right)$$

$$\Rightarrow 18x^2 + 48x + 32 = 9x^2 + 18$$

$$\Rightarrow 9x^2 + 48x + 14 = 0$$

So $a = 9$, $b = 48$, $c = 14$.

(b) From GDC, $x = -0.3096...$ or $-5.0236...$

Let θ be the (acute) angle between vector q and the z-axis. Then

$$\cos\theta = \frac{\begin{pmatrix} x \\ x \\ 2 \end{pmatrix} \cdot \begin{pmatrix} 0 \\ 0 \\ 1 \end{pmatrix}}{\sqrt{x^2 + x^2 + 4}\,\sqrt{0^2 + 0^2 + 1^2}}$$

$$= \frac{2}{\sqrt{2x^2 + 4}}$$

$$= 0.977 \text{ or } 0.271$$

$$\therefore \theta = 12.3° \text{ or } 74.3°$$

9. (a) $\overrightarrow{AB} = \frac{1}{2}a + \frac{1}{2}b$

$$\overrightarrow{BC} = \frac{1}{2}b - \frac{1}{2}a$$

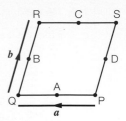

(b) (i) $a \cdot a = |a|^2$ and $b \cdot b = |b|^2$. Since PQRS is a rhombus, $|a| = |b|$ and therefore $a \cdot a = b \cdot b$.

(ii) $\overrightarrow{AB} \cdot \overrightarrow{BC} = \left(\frac{1}{2}a + \frac{1}{2}b\right)\cdot\left(\frac{1}{2}b - \frac{1}{2}a\right)$

$$= \frac{1}{4}a \cdot b - \frac{1}{4}a \cdot a + \frac{1}{4}b \cdot b - \frac{1}{4}b \cdot a$$

$$= \frac{1}{4}\left(a \cdot b - b \cdot a\right) + \frac{1}{4}\left(b \cdot b - a \cdot a\right)$$

$$= \frac{1}{4}\left(a \cdot b - a \cdot b\right) \qquad \text{since } a\cdot b = b\cdot a$$
$$\qquad\qquad\qquad\qquad \text{and } b\cdot b = a\cdot a$$

$$= 0$$

Therefore $\overrightarrow{AB}$ and $\overrightarrow{BC}$ are perpendicular.

(c) ABCD is a rectangle because $\overrightarrow{AB}$ and $\overrightarrow{BC}$ are perpendicular. (But since

$$\left|\overrightarrow{AB}\right|^2 = \left(\frac{1}{2}a + \frac{1}{2}b\right)\cdot\left(\frac{1}{2}a + \frac{1}{2}b\right) \text{ and}$$

$$\left|\overrightarrow{BC}\right|^2 = \left(\frac{1}{2}b - \frac{1}{2}a\right)\cdot\left(\frac{1}{2}b - \frac{1}{2}a\right) \text{ are not necessarily}$$

equal, ABCD is not necessarily a square.)

10. (a) $\overrightarrow{BA} = a - b = \begin{pmatrix} 4-1 \\ 1-5 \\ 2-1 \end{pmatrix} = \begin{pmatrix} 3 \\ -4 \\ 1 \end{pmatrix}$

$$\overrightarrow{BC} = c - b = \begin{pmatrix} \lambda-1 \\ \lambda-5 \\ 3-1 \end{pmatrix} = \begin{pmatrix} \lambda-1 \\ \lambda-5 \\ 2 \end{pmatrix}$$

If there is a right angle at B, $\overrightarrow{BA} \cdot \overrightarrow{BC} = 0$.

i.e. $\begin{pmatrix} 3 \\ -4 \\ 1 \end{pmatrix} \cdot \begin{pmatrix} \lambda-1 \\ \lambda-5 \\ 2 \end{pmatrix} = 0$

$$\Leftrightarrow 3\left(\lambda-1\right) - 4\left(\lambda-5\right) + 1 \times 2 = 0$$

$$\Leftrightarrow 3\lambda - 3 - 4\lambda + 20 + 2 = 0$$

$$\Leftrightarrow \lambda = 19$$

(b) $\overrightarrow{AD} = 2\overrightarrow{DC}$

$\Rightarrow \boldsymbol{d} - \boldsymbol{a} = 2(\boldsymbol{c} - \boldsymbol{d})$

$\Rightarrow 3\boldsymbol{d} = 2\boldsymbol{c} + \boldsymbol{a}$

$$= 2\begin{pmatrix} 19 \\ 19 \\ 3 \end{pmatrix} + \begin{pmatrix} 4 \\ 1 \\ 2 \end{pmatrix} = \begin{pmatrix} 42 \\ 39 \\ 8 \end{pmatrix}$$

$\Rightarrow \boldsymbol{d} = \begin{pmatrix} 14 \\ 13 \\ \frac{8}{3} \end{pmatrix}$

So the coordinates of D are $(14, 13, \frac{8}{3})$.

11. A normal to the plane $2x + 3y - 4z = 5$ is $\boldsymbol{n}_1 = \begin{pmatrix} 2 \\ 3 \\ -4 \end{pmatrix}$.

A normal to the plane $6x - 2y - 3z = 4$ is $\boldsymbol{n}_2 = \begin{pmatrix} 6 \\ -2 \\ -3 \end{pmatrix}$.

The angle between the planes, θ, is the same as the angle between the normals.

So

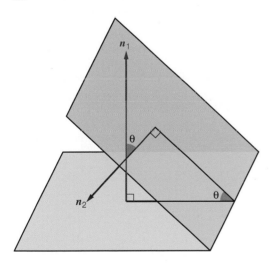

$\cos\theta = \dfrac{\boldsymbol{n}_1 \cdot \boldsymbol{n}_2}{|\boldsymbol{n}_1||\boldsymbol{n}_2|}$

$= \dfrac{\begin{pmatrix} 2 \\ 3 \\ -4 \end{pmatrix} \cdot \begin{pmatrix} 6 \\ -2 \\ -3 \end{pmatrix}}{\sqrt{4+9+16}\,\sqrt{36+4+9}}$

$= \dfrac{18}{\sqrt{29}\sqrt{49}}$

$\therefore \theta = \cos^{-1}\left(\dfrac{18}{7\sqrt{29}}\right) = 61.5°$

12. (a) If $(-1, 3, 5)$ lies on l, then there exists a λ such that

$$\begin{pmatrix} -1 \\ 5 \\ 3 \end{pmatrix} = \begin{pmatrix} -2 \\ 3 \\ 1 \end{pmatrix} + \lambda\begin{pmatrix} 1 \\ 2 \\ -1 \end{pmatrix}$$

$\begin{cases} -1 = -2 + \lambda & \cdots (1) \\ 5 = 3 + 2\lambda & \cdots (2) \\ 3 = 1 - \lambda & \cdots (3) \end{cases}$

$(1) \Rightarrow \lambda = 1;\ \ (2) \Rightarrow \lambda = 1;\ \ (3) \Rightarrow \lambda = -2.$

There is no consistent value of λ, so A does not lie on l.

(b) Since B lies on l, its position vector is

$\boldsymbol{b} = \begin{pmatrix} -2 \\ 3 \\ 1 \end{pmatrix} + \lambda\begin{pmatrix} 1 \\ 2 \\ -1 \end{pmatrix} = \begin{pmatrix} -2+\lambda \\ 3+2\lambda \\ 1-\lambda \end{pmatrix}$ for some value of λ.

Therefore $\overrightarrow{AB} = \begin{pmatrix} -2+\lambda \\ 3+2\lambda \\ 1-\lambda \end{pmatrix} - \begin{pmatrix} -1 \\ 5 \\ 3 \end{pmatrix} = \begin{pmatrix} -1+\lambda \\ -2+2\lambda \\ -2-\lambda \end{pmatrix}$

Since $\overrightarrow{AB}$ is perpendicular to l,

$\begin{pmatrix} -1+\lambda \\ -2+2\lambda \\ -2-\lambda \end{pmatrix} \cdot \begin{pmatrix} 1 \\ 2 \\ -1 \end{pmatrix} = 0$

$\Leftrightarrow -1 + \lambda - 4 + 4\lambda + 2 + \lambda = 0$

$\Leftrightarrow 6\lambda = 3$

$\Leftrightarrow \lambda = \dfrac{1}{2}$

Substituting back into the expression for $\boldsymbol{b}$ gives

$\boldsymbol{b} = \begin{pmatrix} -2+\lambda \\ 3+2\lambda \\ 1-\lambda \end{pmatrix} = \begin{pmatrix} -1.5 \\ 4 \\ 0.5 \end{pmatrix}$

So the coordinates of B are $(-1.5, 4, 0.5)$.

13. (a) Putting $\boldsymbol{r} = \begin{pmatrix} x \\ y \\ z \end{pmatrix}$ in the equation of the line:

$\begin{pmatrix} x \\ y \\ z \end{pmatrix} = \begin{pmatrix} 1 \\ -1 \\ 3 \end{pmatrix} + t\begin{pmatrix} 1 \\ 1 \\ 3 \end{pmatrix} \Rightarrow \begin{cases} x = 1 + t \\ y = -1 + t \\ z = 3 + 3t \end{cases}$

Substituting each of these expressions into the equation of the plane:

$(1+t) - 3(-1+t) + (3+3t) = 17$

$\Leftrightarrow 1 + t + 3 - 3t + 3 + 3t = 17$

$\Leftrightarrow t = 10$

Then, substituting $t = 10$ back into the equation of the line gives:

$$x = 1 + t = 11$$
$$y = -1 + t = 9$$
$$z = 3 + 3t = 33$$

so Q has coordinates (11, 9, 33).

(b) A direction vector of the line $\dfrac{x+1}{3} = \dfrac{2-y}{7} = \dfrac{z}{3}$

is $\begin{pmatrix} 3 \\ 7 \\ 3 \end{pmatrix}$.

So the equation of the line through Q in the same direction is $r = \begin{pmatrix} 11 \\ 9 \\ 33 \end{pmatrix} + t\begin{pmatrix} 3 \\ 7 \\ 3 \end{pmatrix}$

(c) The angle between l_1 and l_2 is the angle between their direction vectors:

$$\cos\theta = \dfrac{\begin{pmatrix} 1 \\ 1 \\ 3 \end{pmatrix} \cdot \begin{pmatrix} 3 \\ 7 \\ 3 \end{pmatrix}}{\sqrt{1+1+9}\sqrt{9+49+9}}$$

$$= \dfrac{19}{\sqrt{11}\sqrt{67}}$$

$$\therefore \theta = \cos^{-1}\left(\dfrac{19}{\sqrt{11}\sqrt{67}}\right) = 45.6°$$

14. (a) Equating the x, y and z components of l_1 and l_2:

$$\begin{cases} 3\lambda = 9 + 2\mu \\ 5\lambda = 15 \\ \lambda = 3 - \mu \end{cases}$$

From the second equation, $\lambda = 3$; then, from the third equation, $\mu = 0$.

Checking these values in the first equation: $3\lambda = 9 = 9 + 2\mu$, so the lines do intersect.

To find the coordinates of the point of intersection, substitute $\lambda = 3$ into the equation for l_1 (or substitute $\mu = 0$ into the equation for l_2) to get (9, 15, 3).

(b) The angle between l_1 and l_2 is the angle between their direction vectors:

$$\cos\theta = \dfrac{\begin{pmatrix} 3 \\ 5 \\ 1 \end{pmatrix} \cdot \begin{pmatrix} 2 \\ 0 \\ -1 \end{pmatrix}}{\sqrt{9+25+1}\sqrt{4+0+1}}$$

$$= \dfrac{5}{\sqrt{35}\sqrt{5}}$$

$$\therefore \theta = \cos^{-1}\left(\dfrac{5}{\sqrt{35}\sqrt{5}}\right) = 67.8°$$

(c) Velocity vector is $v = \begin{pmatrix} 3 \\ 5 \\ 1 \end{pmatrix}$ cm s^{-1}

Speed is the magnitude of velocity, so

$$\text{speed} = \left\|\begin{pmatrix} 3 \\ 5 \\ 1 \end{pmatrix}\right\| = \sqrt{9+25+1} = 5.92 \text{ cm s}^{-1}$$

(d) At time t, the position of the

- first fly is $r = t\begin{pmatrix} 3 \\ 5 \\ 1 \end{pmatrix}$

- second fly is $r = \begin{pmatrix} 9 \\ 15 \\ 3 \end{pmatrix} + t\begin{pmatrix} 2 \\ 0 \\ -1 \end{pmatrix}$

From part (a), both flies pass through the point (9, 15, 3), but the first fly is there when $t = 3$ and the second one when $t = 0$. As there can be only one possible intersection point of these two straight line paths, the flies do not meet.

(e) They are at the same height when their z-coordinates are the same:

$$t = 3 - t \Leftrightarrow t = 1.5$$

Substituting $t = 1.5$ into the two position vector expressions above gives:

- first fly: $r = t\begin{pmatrix} 3 \\ 5 \\ 1 \end{pmatrix} = \begin{pmatrix} 4.5 \\ 7.5 \\ 1.5 \end{pmatrix}$

- second fly: $r = \begin{pmatrix} 9 \\ 15 \\ 3 \end{pmatrix} + 1.5\begin{pmatrix} 2 \\ 0 \\ -1 \end{pmatrix} = \begin{pmatrix} 12 \\ 15 \\ 1.5 \end{pmatrix}$

i.e. the coordinates of the two flies are (4.5, 7.5, 1.5) and (12, 15, 1.5) when they are at the same height.

The distance between them is

$$d = \sqrt{(4.5-12)^2 + (7.5-15)^2 + (1.5-1.5)^2}$$
$$= \sqrt{112.5} = 10.6 \text{ cm}$$

(f) The displacement vector from the first fly to the second fly is

$$\begin{pmatrix} 9+2t \\ 15 \\ 3-t \end{pmatrix} - \begin{pmatrix} 3t \\ 5t \\ t \end{pmatrix} = \begin{pmatrix} 9-t \\ 15-5t \\ 3-2t \end{pmatrix}$$

The distance d between the flies at time t therefore satisfies

$$d^2 = \left\| \begin{pmatrix} 9-t \\ 15-5t \\ 3-2t \end{pmatrix} \right\|^2$$

$$= (9-t)^2 + (15-5t)^2 + (3-2t)^2$$

$$= 315 - 180t + 30t^2$$

Using a graph on the GDC (or by differentiation), the minimum value is $d^2 = 45$, i.e. $d = 6.71$ cm.

Going for the top 7

1. (a) $|\boldsymbol{a} + 2\boldsymbol{b}|^2 = |\boldsymbol{b} - 2\boldsymbol{a}|^2$

$\Leftrightarrow (\boldsymbol{a} + 2\boldsymbol{b}) \cdot (\boldsymbol{a} + 2\boldsymbol{b}) = (\boldsymbol{b} - 2\boldsymbol{a}) \cdot (\boldsymbol{b} - 2\boldsymbol{a})$

$\Leftrightarrow |\boldsymbol{a}|^2 + 4\boldsymbol{a} \cdot \boldsymbol{b} + 4|\boldsymbol{b}|^2 = |\boldsymbol{b}|^2 - 4\boldsymbol{a} \cdot \boldsymbol{b} + 4|\boldsymbol{a}|^2$

$\Leftrightarrow 1 + 4\boldsymbol{a} \cdot \boldsymbol{b} + 4 = 1 - 4\boldsymbol{a} \cdot \boldsymbol{b} + 4$ (using $|\boldsymbol{a}| = |\boldsymbol{b}| = 1$)

$\Leftrightarrow 8\boldsymbol{a} \cdot \boldsymbol{b} = 0$

$\Leftrightarrow \boldsymbol{a} \cdot \boldsymbol{b} = 0$

(b) Because $\boldsymbol{a} \cdot \boldsymbol{b} = 0$, the vectors $\boldsymbol{a}$ and $\boldsymbol{b}$ are perpendicular, so the angle between them is $90°$.

2. (a) As A lies on l_1, its position vector satisfies

$$\boldsymbol{a} = \begin{pmatrix} 1 \\ 3 \\ 1 \end{pmatrix} + \lambda \begin{pmatrix} 1 \\ -1 \\ 2 \end{pmatrix} = \begin{pmatrix} 1+\lambda \\ 3-\lambda \\ 1+2\lambda \end{pmatrix}$$ for some value of λ.

As B lies on l_2, its position vector satisfies

$$\boldsymbol{b} = \begin{pmatrix} 5 \\ -1 \\ -6 \end{pmatrix} + \mu \begin{pmatrix} 1 \\ 1 \\ 3 \end{pmatrix} = \begin{pmatrix} 5+\mu \\ -1+\mu \\ -6+3\mu \end{pmatrix}$$ for some value of μ.

$$\therefore \overrightarrow{AB} = \begin{pmatrix} 5+\mu \\ -1+\mu \\ -6+3\mu \end{pmatrix} - \begin{pmatrix} 1+\lambda \\ 3-\lambda \\ 1+2\lambda \end{pmatrix} = \begin{pmatrix} \mu-\lambda+4 \\ \mu+\lambda-4 \\ 3\mu-2\lambda-7 \end{pmatrix}$$

Since $\overrightarrow{AB}$ is perpendicular to l_1,

$$\begin{pmatrix} \mu-\lambda+4 \\ \mu+\lambda-4 \\ 3\mu-2\lambda-7 \end{pmatrix} \cdot \begin{pmatrix} 1 \\ -1 \\ 2 \end{pmatrix} = 0$$

$\Leftrightarrow (\mu-\lambda+4) - (\mu+\lambda-4) + 2(3\mu-2\lambda-7) = 0$

$\Leftrightarrow 6\mu - 6\lambda - 6 = 0$

$\Leftrightarrow \mu - \lambda = 1$

(b) Since $\overrightarrow{AB}$ is perpendicular to l_2,

$$\begin{pmatrix} \mu-\lambda+4 \\ \mu+\lambda-4 \\ 3\mu-2\lambda-7 \end{pmatrix} \cdot \begin{pmatrix} 1 \\ 1 \\ 3 \end{pmatrix} = 0$$

$\Leftrightarrow (\mu-\lambda+4) + (\mu+\lambda-4) + 3(3\mu-2\lambda-7) = 0$

$\Leftrightarrow 11\mu - 6\lambda - 21 = 0$

$\Leftrightarrow 11\mu - 6\lambda = 21$

(c) Solving the two equations in (a) and (b) simultaneously using the GDC gives $\mu = 3$, $\lambda = 2$.

$$\therefore \overrightarrow{AB} = \begin{pmatrix} 3-2+4 \\ 3+2-4 \\ 9-4-7 \end{pmatrix} = \begin{pmatrix} 5 \\ 1 \\ -2 \end{pmatrix}$$

The shortest distance is $|\overrightarrow{AB}| = \sqrt{25+1+4} = \sqrt{30}$.

3. (a) Eliminating x and y from the last equation:

$$\begin{cases} x - 2y + z = 0 & \cdots (1) \\ 3x - z = 4 & \cdots (2) \\ x + y - z = k & \cdots (3) \end{cases}$$

$(2) - 3 \times (1)$ $\begin{cases} x - 2y + z = 0 & \cdots (1) \\ 6y - 4z = 4 & \cdots (4) \\ 3y - 2z = k & \cdots (5) \end{cases}$

$(3) - (1)$

$2 \times (5) - (4)$ $\begin{cases} x - 2y + z = 0 & \cdots (1) \\ 6y - 4z = 4 & \cdots (4) \\ 0 = 2k - 4 & \cdots (6) \end{cases}$

Hence the system does not have a unique solution (as the last equation has no variables left in it).

(b) There are no solutions unless $2k - 4 = 0$, i.e. $k = 2$.

When $k = 2$, there are infinitely many solutions:

Let $z = t$. Then, from equation (4):

$6y - 4t = 4$

$\Rightarrow y = \dfrac{4+4t}{6} = \dfrac{2}{3} + \dfrac{2}{3}t$

From equation (1):

$x - 2y + t = 0$

$\therefore x = -t + 2\left(\dfrac{2}{3} + \dfrac{2}{3}t\right) = \dfrac{4}{3} + \dfrac{1}{3}t$

Therefore the equation of the line is $\boldsymbol{r} = \begin{pmatrix} \frac{4}{3} \\ \frac{2}{3} \\ 0 \end{pmatrix} + t \begin{pmatrix} \frac{1}{3} \\ \frac{2}{3} \\ 1 \end{pmatrix}$.

4. The two planes share a common normal, $\boldsymbol{n} = \begin{pmatrix} 1 \\ -2 \\ 3 \end{pmatrix}$, and so are parallel.

To find the (perpendicular) distance between the two parallel planes, consider the distance of each from the origin along this normal.

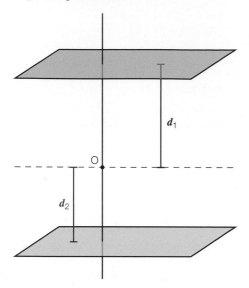

The equation of the line through $(0, 0, 0)$ along the normal is $r = \lambda \begin{pmatrix} 1 \\ -2 \\ 3 \end{pmatrix}$,

i.e. any point on this line has $\begin{cases} x = \lambda \\ y = -2\lambda \\ z = 3\lambda \end{cases}$

This line intersects the plane $x - 2y + 3z = 7$ when

$$\lambda - 2(-2\lambda) + 3(3\lambda) = 7$$
$$\Leftrightarrow 14\lambda = 7$$
$$\Leftrightarrow \lambda = \frac{1}{2}$$

Substituting $\lambda = \frac{1}{2}$ back into the equation of the line:

$$r = \frac{1}{2} \begin{pmatrix} 1 \\ -2 \\ 3 \end{pmatrix} = \begin{pmatrix} \frac{1}{2} \\ -1 \\ \frac{3}{2} \end{pmatrix}$$

so the coordinates of the point of intersection are

$$\left(\frac{1}{2}, -1, \frac{3}{2} \right).$$

Hence the distance between plane Π_1 and the origin is

$$d_1 = \sqrt{\left(\frac{1}{2} - 0 \right)^2 + \left(-1 - 0 \right)^2 + \left(\frac{3}{2} - 0 \right)^2} = \frac{1}{2}\sqrt{14}$$

Now we repeat the same process for the other plane (which is on the opposite side of the origin as the RHS is negative). The equation of the line through $(0, 0, 0)$ along the normal intersects the plane $x - 2y + 3z = -21$ when

$$\lambda - 2(-2\lambda) + 3(3\lambda) = -21$$
$$\Leftrightarrow 14\lambda = -21$$
$$\Leftrightarrow \lambda = -\frac{3}{2}$$

Substituting $\lambda = -\frac{3}{2}$ back into the equation of the line:

$$r = -\frac{3}{2} \begin{pmatrix} 1 \\ -2 \\ 3 \end{pmatrix} = \begin{pmatrix} -\frac{3}{2} \\ 3 \\ -\frac{9}{2} \end{pmatrix}$$

so the coordinates of the point of intersection are

$$\left(-\frac{3}{2}, 3, -\frac{9}{2} \right).$$

Hence the distance between plane Π_2 and the origin is

$$d_2 = \sqrt{\left(-\frac{3}{2} - 0 \right)^2 + \left(3 - 0 \right)^2 + \left(-\frac{9}{2} - 0 \right)^2} = \frac{3}{2}\sqrt{14}$$

Therefore, the distance between the two planes is

$$d_1 + d_2 = \frac{1}{2}\sqrt{14} + \frac{3}{2}\sqrt{14} = 2\sqrt{14}$$

8 COMPLEX NUMBERS

Mixed practice 8

1. (a) In polar form, $z = 2e^{i\frac{2\pi}{3}}$, so

$$z^2 = \left(2e^{i\frac{2\pi}{3}} \right)^2 = 4e^{i\frac{4\pi}{3}} = 4e^{-i\frac{2\pi}{3}}$$

$$z^3 = \left(2e^{i\frac{2\pi}{3}} \right)^3 = 8e^{i\frac{6\pi}{3}} = 8e^{i2\pi} = 8$$

$$z^4 = \left(2e^{i\frac{2\pi}{3}} \right)^4 = 16e^{i\frac{8\pi}{3}} = 16e^{i\frac{2\pi}{3}}$$

(b)

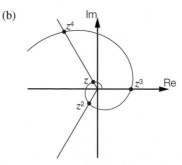

2. $z = 2i + \dfrac{1}{\sqrt{2} - i}$

$= 2i + \dfrac{1}{\sqrt{2} - i} \times \dfrac{\sqrt{2} + i}{\sqrt{2} + i}$

$= 2i + \dfrac{\sqrt{2} + i}{2 - (-1)}$

$= 2i + \dfrac{\sqrt{2} + i}{3}$

$= \dfrac{\sqrt{2}}{3} + \dfrac{7}{3}i$

3. $2iz + 5w = 6i \qquad \cdots (1)$

$3z + iw = 2 + 3i \qquad \cdots (2)$

$i \times (1): \quad -2z + 5iw = -6 \qquad \cdots (3)$

$5 \times (2): \quad 15z + 5iw = 10 + 15i \qquad \cdots (4)$

$(4) - (3): \quad 17z = 16 + 15i$

$\Leftrightarrow z = \dfrac{16}{17} + \dfrac{15}{17}i$

Substituting into (1):

$2i\left(\dfrac{16}{17} + \dfrac{15}{17}i\right) + 5w = 6i$

$\Leftrightarrow \dfrac{32}{17}i - \dfrac{30}{17} + 5w = 6i$

$\Leftrightarrow 5w = \dfrac{30}{17} + \dfrac{70}{17}i$

$\Leftrightarrow w = \dfrac{6}{17} + \dfrac{14}{17}i$

4. (a) $\left|\sqrt{3} - i\right| = \sqrt{\left(\sqrt{3}\right)^2 + (-1)^2} = \sqrt{3 + 1} = 2$

For $\arg\left(\sqrt{3} - i\right)$, consider the Argand diagram:

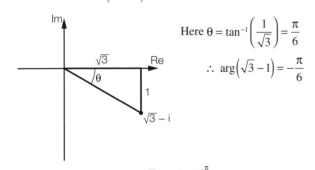

Here $\theta = \tan^{-1}\left(\dfrac{1}{\sqrt{3}}\right) = \dfrac{\pi}{6}$

$\therefore \arg\left(\sqrt{3} - 1\right) = -\dfrac{\pi}{6}$

(b) In polar form, $\sqrt{3} - i = 2e^{-i\frac{\pi}{6}}$, so

$\dfrac{1}{\left(\sqrt{3} - i\right)^9} = \dfrac{1}{\left(2e^{-i\frac{\pi}{6}}\right)^9} = \dfrac{1}{2^9 e^{-i\frac{9\pi}{6}}}$

$= \dfrac{1}{512 e^{-i\frac{3\pi}{2}}} = \dfrac{1}{512 e^{i\frac{\pi}{2}}}$

$= \dfrac{1}{512i} = \dfrac{-i}{512}$

5. $\dfrac{z^3}{w^2} = \dfrac{\left(5e^{i\frac{\pi}{4}}\right)^3}{\left(2e^{i\frac{\pi}{6}}\right)^2} = \dfrac{125 e^{i\frac{3\pi}{4}}}{4 e^{i\frac{2\pi}{6}}}$

$= \dfrac{125}{4} e^{i\left(\frac{3\pi}{4} - \frac{2\pi}{6}\right)} = \dfrac{125}{4} e^{i\frac{5\pi}{12}}$

$\therefore \left|\dfrac{z^3}{w^2}\right| = \dfrac{125}{4} \quad \text{and} \quad \arg\left(\dfrac{z^3}{w^2}\right) = \dfrac{5\pi}{12}$

6. $1 + 2i$ is a root $\Rightarrow 1 - 2i$ is also a root.

Therefore, one quadratic factor is given by

$\left(z - (1 + 2i)\right)\left(z - (1 - 2i)\right) = z^2 - z(1 - 2i) - z(1 + 2i)$

$\qquad\qquad + (1 + 2i)(1 - 2i)$

$= z^2 - z + 2iz - z - 2iz + 5$

$= z^2 - 2z + 5$

For the other quadratic factor:

$3 - i$ is a root $\Rightarrow 3 + i$ is also a root.

$\left(z - (3 - i)\right)\left(z - (3 + i)\right) = z^2 - z(3 + i) - z(3 - i)$

$\qquad\qquad + (3 - i)(3 + i)$

$= z^2 - 3z - iz - 3z + iz + 10$

$= z^2 - 6z + 10$

So $f(z) = \left(z^2 - 2z + 5\right)\left(z^2 - 6z + 10\right)$

7. (a) $(1 - \omega)\left(1 + \omega + \omega^2 + \omega^3 + \omega^4\right) = 1 + \omega + \omega^2 + \omega^3 + \omega^4$

$\qquad\qquad - \omega - \omega^2 - \omega^3 - \omega^4 - \omega^5$

$= 1 - \omega^5$

But since ω is a root of $z^5 = 1$:

$\omega^5 = 1$

$\Leftrightarrow \omega^5 - 1 = 0$

$\Leftrightarrow (1 - \omega)\left(1 + \omega + \omega^2 + \omega^3 + \omega^4\right) = 0$

$\therefore 1 + \omega + \omega^2 + \omega^3 + \omega^4 = 0$

(b) The fifth roots of unity will be evenly spaced around the unit circle, so ω will have argument $\dfrac{2\pi}{5}$ (and modulus 1); that is,

$\omega = \cos\dfrac{2\pi}{5} + i\sin\dfrac{2\pi}{5}$

(c) By De Moivre's theorem:

$\omega^2 = \cos\dfrac{4\pi}{5} + i\sin\dfrac{4\pi}{5}$

$\omega^3 = \cos\dfrac{6\pi}{5} + i\sin\dfrac{6\pi}{5}$

$\omega^4 = \cos\dfrac{8\pi}{5} + i\sin\dfrac{8\pi}{5}$

Then, using (a):

$1 + \omega + \omega^2 + \omega^3 + \omega^4 = 0$

$\Rightarrow 1 + \left(\cos \dfrac{2\pi}{5} + \mathrm{i}\sin \dfrac{2\pi}{5} \right) + \left(\cos \dfrac{4\pi}{5} + \mathrm{i}\sin \dfrac{4\pi}{5} \right) + \left(\cos \dfrac{6\pi}{5} + \mathrm{i}\sin \dfrac{6\pi}{5} \right) + \left(\cos \dfrac{8\pi}{5} + \mathrm{i}\sin \dfrac{8\pi}{5} \right) = 0$

$\Rightarrow 1 + \left(\cos \dfrac{2\pi}{5} + \cos \dfrac{4\pi}{5} + \cos \dfrac{6\pi}{5} + \cos \dfrac{8\pi}{5} \right) + \mathrm{i}\left(\sin \dfrac{2\pi}{5} + \sin \dfrac{4\pi}{5} + \sin \dfrac{6\pi}{5} + \sin \dfrac{8\pi}{5} \right) = 0$

$\Rightarrow 1 + \left(\cos \dfrac{2\pi}{5} + \cos \dfrac{4\pi}{5} + \cos \dfrac{6\pi}{5} + \cos \dfrac{8\pi}{5} \right) + \mathrm{i}\left(\sin \dfrac{2\pi}{5} + \sin \dfrac{4\pi}{5} + \sin \left(\dfrac{-4\pi}{5} \right) + \sin \left(\dfrac{-2\pi}{5} \right) \right) = 0$

$\Rightarrow 1 + \left(\cos \dfrac{2\pi}{5} + \cos \dfrac{4\pi}{5} + \cos \dfrac{6\pi}{5} + \cos \dfrac{8\pi}{5} \right) + \mathrm{i}\left(\sin \dfrac{2\pi}{5} + \sin \dfrac{4\pi}{5} - \sin \dfrac{4\pi}{5} - \sin \dfrac{2\pi}{5} \right) = 0$

$\Rightarrow 1 + \left(\cos \dfrac{2\pi}{5} + \cos \dfrac{4\pi}{5} + \cos \dfrac{6\pi}{5} + \cos \dfrac{8\pi}{5} \right) + 0\mathrm{i} = 0$

$\Rightarrow \cos \dfrac{2\pi}{5} + \cos \dfrac{4\pi}{5} + \cos \dfrac{6\pi}{5} + \cos \dfrac{8\pi}{5} = -1$

8. (a) $z^n - \dfrac{1}{z^n} = z^n - z^{-n}$

$= \left(\cos\theta + \mathrm{i}\sin\theta \right)^n - \left(\cos\theta + \mathrm{i}\sin\theta \right)^{-n}$

$= \cos n\theta + \mathrm{i}\sin n\theta - \cos(-n\theta) - \mathrm{i}\sin(-n\theta)$ (by de Moivre)

$= \cos n\theta + \mathrm{i}\sin n\theta - \cos n\theta + \mathrm{i}\sin n\theta$

$= 2\mathrm{i}\sin n\theta$

(b) $\left(z - \dfrac{1}{z} \right)^5 = z^5 + 5z^4\left(-\dfrac{1}{z} \right) + 10z^3\left(-\dfrac{1}{z} \right)^2 + 10z^2\left(-\dfrac{1}{z} \right)^3 + 5z\left(-\dfrac{1}{z} \right)^4 + \left(-\dfrac{1}{z} \right)^5$

$= z^5 - 5z^3 + 10z - \dfrac{10}{z} + \dfrac{5}{z^3} - \dfrac{1}{z^5}$

$= \left(z^5 - \dfrac{1}{z^5} \right) - 5\left(z^3 - \dfrac{1}{z^3} \right) + 10\left(z - \dfrac{1}{z} \right)$

$= 2\mathrm{i}\sin 5\theta - 5(2\mathrm{i}\sin 3\theta) + 10(2\mathrm{i}\sin\theta)$ (by part (a))

$= \mathrm{i}(2\sin 5\theta - 10\sin 3\theta + 20\sin\theta)$

But also $\left(z - \dfrac{1}{z} \right)^5 = (2\mathrm{i}\sin\theta)^5 = 32\,\mathrm{i}\sin^5\theta$

Therefore

$32\mathrm{i}\sin^5\theta = \mathrm{i}(2\sin 5\theta - 10\sin 3\theta + 20\sin\theta)$

$\Rightarrow 32\sin^5\theta = 2\sin 5\theta - 10\sin 3\theta + 20\sin\theta$

$\therefore A = -10, B = 20$

(c) $\displaystyle\int_0^{\pi/3} 32\sin^5\theta\,\mathrm{d}\theta = \int_0^{\pi/3} 2\sin 5\theta - 10\sin 3\theta + 20\sin\theta\,\mathrm{d}\theta$

$= \left[-\dfrac{2}{5}\cos 5\theta + \dfrac{10}{3}\cos 3\theta - 20\cos\theta \right]_0^{\frac{\pi}{3}}$

$= \left(-\dfrac{2}{5} \times \dfrac{1}{2} + \dfrac{10}{3}(-1) - 20 \times \dfrac{1}{2} \right) - \left(-\dfrac{2}{5} + \dfrac{10}{3} - 20 \right)$

$= \left(-\dfrac{203}{15} \right) - \left(-\dfrac{256}{15} \right)$

$= \dfrac{53}{15}$

9. (a) (i) $|z| = \sqrt{\left(\dfrac{1}{2}\cos\theta\right)^2 + \left(\dfrac{1}{2}\sin\theta\right)^2}$

$\qquad = \sqrt{\dfrac{1}{4}\cos^2\theta + \dfrac{1}{4}\sin^2\theta}$

$\qquad = \sqrt{\dfrac{1}{4}\left(\cos^2\theta + \sin^2\theta\right)}$

$\qquad = \sqrt{\dfrac{1}{4}} = \dfrac{1}{2} < 1$

(ii) This is an infinite geometric series with $u_1 = 1$ and $r = \dfrac{1}{2}e^{i\theta}$, and from part (i) we know that $|r| < 1$, so

$S_\infty = \dfrac{1}{1 - \frac{1}{2}e^{i\theta}}$

$\quad = \dfrac{2}{2 - e^{i\theta}}$

(iii) $1 + \dfrac{1}{2}e^{i\theta} + \dfrac{1}{4}e^{2i\theta} + \dfrac{1}{8}e^{3i\theta} + \ldots = \dfrac{2}{2 - e^{i\theta}}$

$\Rightarrow 1 + \dfrac{1}{2}\left(\cos\theta + i\sin\theta\right) + \dfrac{1}{4}\left(\cos\theta + i\sin\theta\right)^2 + \dfrac{1}{8}\left(\cos\theta + i\sin\theta\right)^3 + \ldots = \dfrac{2}{2 - \left(\cos\theta + i\sin\theta\right)}$

$\Rightarrow 1 + \dfrac{1}{2}\left(\cos\theta + i\sin\theta\right) + \dfrac{1}{4}\left(\cos 2\theta + i\sin 2\theta\right) + \dfrac{1}{8}\left(\cos 3\theta + i\sin 3\theta\right) + \ldots = \dfrac{2}{2 - \cos\theta - i\sin\theta}$

$\Rightarrow 1 + \dfrac{1}{2}\cos\theta + \dfrac{1}{4}\cos 2\theta + \ldots + i\left(\dfrac{1}{2}\sin\theta + \dfrac{1}{4}\sin 2\theta + \ldots\right) = \dfrac{2}{\left(2 - \cos\theta - i\sin\theta\right)} \times \dfrac{\left(2 - \cos\theta + i\sin\theta\right)}{\left(2 - \cos\theta + i\sin\theta\right)}$

$\Rightarrow 1 + \dfrac{1}{2}\cos\theta + \dfrac{1}{4}\cos 2\theta + \ldots + i\left(\dfrac{1}{2}\sin\theta + \dfrac{1}{4}\sin 2\theta + \ldots\right) = \dfrac{4 - 2\cos\theta + 2i\sin\theta}{4 - 4\cos\theta + \cos^2\theta + \sin^2\theta}$

$\Rightarrow 1 + \dfrac{1}{2}\cos\theta + \dfrac{1}{4}\cos 2\theta + \ldots + i\left(\dfrac{1}{2}\sin\theta + \dfrac{1}{4}\sin 2\theta + \ldots\right) = \dfrac{4 - 2\cos\theta}{5 - 4\cos\theta} + i\left(\dfrac{2\sin\theta}{5 - 4\cos\theta}\right)$

Equating imaginary parts:

$\dfrac{1}{2}\sin\theta + \dfrac{1}{4}\sin 2\theta + \dfrac{1}{8}\sin 3\theta + \ldots = \dfrac{2\sin\theta}{5 - 4\cos\theta}$

(b) (i) $\dfrac{1}{z} = z^{-1}$

$\qquad = \left(\cos\theta + i\sin\theta\right)^{-1}$

$\qquad = \cos(-\theta) + i\sin(-\theta)$ (by de Moivre)

$\qquad = \cos\theta - i\sin\theta$

(iii) $z^4 - 3z^3 + 4z^2 - 3z + 1 = 0$

Dividing through by z^2 (since $z \neq 0$):

$z^2 - 3z + 4 - \dfrac{3}{z} + \dfrac{1}{z^2} = 0$

$\Leftrightarrow \left(z^2 + \dfrac{1}{z^2}\right) - 3\left(z + \dfrac{1}{z}\right) + 4 = 0$

$\Leftrightarrow \left(2\cos 2\theta\right) - 3\left(2\cos\theta\right) + 4 = 0$ (by part (ii))

$\Leftrightarrow \cos 2\theta - 3\cos\theta + 2 = 0$

$\Leftrightarrow \left(2\cos^2\theta - 1\right) - 3\cos\theta + 2 = 0$

$\Leftrightarrow 2\cos^2\theta - 3\cos\theta + 1 = 0$

$\Leftrightarrow \left(2\cos\theta - 1\right)\left(\cos\theta - 1\right) = 0$

$\Leftrightarrow \cos\theta = \dfrac{1}{2}$ or $\cos\theta = 1$

(ii) $z^n + \dfrac{1}{z^n} = z^n + z^{-n}$

$\qquad = \left(\cos\theta + i\sin\theta\right)^n + \left(\cos\theta + i\sin\theta\right)^{-n}$

$\qquad = \cos n\theta + i\sin n\theta + \cos(-n\theta) + i\sin(-n\theta)$

$\qquad\qquad\qquad\qquad$ (by de Moivre)

$\qquad = \cos n\theta + i\sin n\theta + \cos n\theta - i\sin n\theta$

$\qquad = 2\cos n\theta$

$\therefore \cos n\theta = \dfrac{1}{2}\left(z^n + \dfrac{1}{z^n}\right)$

When $\cos\theta = \dfrac{1}{2}$,

$$\sin\theta = \pm\sqrt{1-\cos^2\theta}$$

$$= \pm\sqrt{1-\left(\dfrac{1}{2}\right)^2} = \pm\sqrt{1-\dfrac{1}{4}} = \pm\dfrac{\sqrt{3}}{2}$$

When $\cos\theta = 1$,
$$\sin\theta = \pm\sqrt{1-\cos^2\theta} = \pm\sqrt{1-1^2} = 0$$

So

$$z = \cos\theta + i\sin\theta$$

$$= \dfrac{1}{2} \pm i\dfrac{\sqrt{3}}{2} \quad \text{or} \quad 1 \pm i0$$

i.e. the roots are 1 (repeated) and $\dfrac{1}{2} \pm i\dfrac{\sqrt{3}}{2}$.

Going for the top 8

1.　(a)　$1 - 2i$

(b)　The fifth root is $a - bi$.

Using the property of the product of the roots of a polynomial:

$$3(1+2i)(1-2i)(a+bi)(a-bi) = (-1)^5\left(\dfrac{-150}{1}\right)$$

$$\Rightarrow 3(1+4)(a^2+b^2) = 150$$

$$\Rightarrow 15(a^2+b^2) = 150$$

$$\Rightarrow a^2+b^2 = 10$$

(c)　By the property of the sum of the roots of a polynomial:

$$3+(1+2i)+(1-2i)+(a+bi)+(a-bi) = -\dfrac{-7}{1}$$

$$\Rightarrow 5+2a = 7$$

$$\Rightarrow a = 1$$

So, from part (b),

$$1^2 + b^2 = 10$$

$$\therefore b = 3 \quad (b > 0)$$

(d)　From part (c), the fourth and fifth roots are $1 \pm 3i$. So

$$z^5 - 7z^4 + pz^3 + qz^2 + rz - 150$$
$$= (z-3) \times (z-(1+2i)) \times (z-(1-2i))$$
$$\qquad \times (z-(1+3i)) \times (z-(1-3i))$$
$$= (z-3)(z^2-2z+5)(z^2-2z+10)$$
$$= (z-3)(z^4-4z^3+19z^2-30z+50)$$
$$= z^5 - 7z^4 + 31z^3 - 87z^2 + 140z - 150$$

$$\therefore p = 31,\ q = -87,\ r = 140$$

2.　(a)　$w = \dfrac{2}{z-i}$

$$\Rightarrow wz - iw = 2$$
$$\Rightarrow wz = 2 + iw$$
$$\Rightarrow z = \dfrac{2+iw}{w}$$

(b)　$|z| = \left|\dfrac{2+iw}{w}\right|$

When $|z| = 1$:

$$1 = \left|\dfrac{2+iw}{w}\right|$$
$$\Rightarrow |w| = |2+iw|$$
$$\Rightarrow |w|^2 = |2+iw|^2$$

Then, letting $w = u + iv$:

$$|u+iv|^2 = |2+i(u+iv)|^2$$
$$\Rightarrow |u+iv|^2 = |2-v+iu|^2$$
$$\Rightarrow u^2+v^2 = (2-v)^2 + u^2$$
$$\Rightarrow v^2 = 4 - 4v + v^2$$
$$\Rightarrow 4v = 4$$
$$\Rightarrow v = 1$$

i.e. $\operatorname{Im}(w) = 1$

3.　(a)　$\dfrac{e^{i\theta}+e^{-i\theta}}{2} = \dfrac{(\cos\theta+i\sin\theta)+(\cos(-\theta)+i\sin(-\theta))}{2}$

$$= \dfrac{\cos\theta+i\sin\theta+\cos\theta-i\sin\theta}{2}$$

$$= \dfrac{2\cos\theta}{2}$$

$$= \cos\theta$$

(b)　$\cos(3i) = \dfrac{e^{i(3i)}+e^{-i(3i)}}{2} = \dfrac{e^{-3}+e^3}{2}$

(c)　$\cos(\pi+3i) = \dfrac{e^{i(\pi+3i)}+e^{-i(\pi+3i)}}{2}$

$$= \dfrac{e^{i\pi}e^{-3}+e^{-i\pi}e^3}{2}$$

$$= \dfrac{-e^{-3}-e^3}{2}$$

$$= -\left(\dfrac{e^{-3}+e^3}{2}\right)$$

Note that this is the same as $-\cos(3i)$.

4.　(a)　Let $z = a + bi$. Then

$$z^2 + z = k$$

$$\Leftrightarrow (a+bi)^2 + a + bi = k$$

$$\Leftrightarrow a^2 + 2abi - b^2 + a + bi = k$$

$$\Leftrightarrow a^2 - b^2 + a + (2ab+b)i = k \quad \cdots (*)$$

Equating imaginary parts:

$$2ab + b = 0$$

$$\Leftrightarrow b(2a+1) = 0$$

$$\Leftrightarrow b = 0 \ \text{ or } \ a = -\frac{1}{2}$$

i.e. $\text{Im}(z) = 0$ (so that z is real) or $\text{Re}(z) = -\frac{1}{2}$

(b) If z is not real (i.e. $b \neq 0$), then $a = -\frac{1}{2}$.

Equating real parts in (*):

$$a^2 - b^2 + a = k$$

$$\left(-\frac{1}{2}\right)^2 - b^2 - \frac{1}{2} = k$$

$$\therefore \ b^2 = \frac{1}{4} - k$$

Since z is not real, there must be (non-zero real) solutions to this equation for b.

Therefore, $-\frac{1}{4} - k > 0$, i.e. $k < -\frac{1}{4}$.

5. $|i| = 1$ and $\arg i = \frac{\pi}{2}$, so $i = e^{i\frac{\pi}{2}}$.

Therefore $i^i = \left(e^{i\frac{\pi}{2}}\right)^i = e^{-\frac{\pi}{2}}$, which is real.

9 DIFFERENTIATION

Mixed practice 9

1. $A = \pi r^2 \Rightarrow \dfrac{dA}{dr} = 2\pi r$

It is given that $\dfrac{dr}{dt} = 3$

$$\therefore \ \frac{dA}{dt} = \frac{dA}{dr} \times \frac{dr}{dt}$$
$$= 2\pi r \times 3$$
$$= 6\pi r \ \text{cm}^2\,\text{s}^{-1}$$

When $r = 20$: $\dfrac{dA}{dt} = 6\pi \times 20 = 120\pi \ \text{cm}^2\,\text{s}^{-1}$

2. $h'(x) = \lim\limits_{t \to 0} \dfrac{h(x+t) - h(x)}{t}$

$$= \lim_{t \to 0} \frac{\left[f(x+t) + g(x+t)\right] - \left[f(x) + g(x)\right]}{t}$$

$$= \lim_{t \to 0} \frac{\left[f(x+t) - f(x)\right] + \left[g(x+t) - g(x)\right]}{t}$$

$$= \lim_{t \to 0} \frac{f(x+t) - f(x)}{t} + \lim_{t \to 0} \frac{g(x+t) - g(x)}{t}$$

$$= f'(x) + g'(x)$$

3. (a) Perimeter $= 2x + 2y$

$$40 = 2x + 2y$$

$$\therefore \ y = 20 - x$$

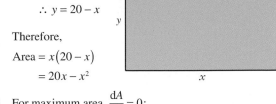

Therefore,

Area $= x(20 - x)$

$$= 20x - x^2$$

(b) For maximum area, $\dfrac{dA}{dx} = 0$:

$$A = 20x - x^2 \Rightarrow \frac{dA}{dx} = 20 - 2x$$

$$20 - 2x = 0 \Rightarrow x = 10$$

$$\frac{d^2 A}{dx^2} = -2 < 0 \quad \therefore \ \text{maximum}$$

When $x = 10$, $y = 20 - x = 20 - 10 = 10$, i.e. a square.

4. $\dfrac{dy}{dx} = 5(\cos 3x)3 + 2x$

$$= 15\cos 3x + 2x$$

When $x = \pi$, $y = 5\sin 3\pi + \pi^2 = \pi^2$ and

$$\frac{dy}{dx} = 15\cos 3\pi + 2\pi = -15 + 2\pi$$

Gradient of normal is $m = \dfrac{-1}{-15 + 2\pi} = \dfrac{1}{15 - 2\pi}$

So equation of the normal is:

$$y - y_1 = m(x - x_1)$$

$$y - \pi^2 = \frac{1}{15 - 2\pi}(x - \pi)$$

$$\therefore \ y = \frac{1}{15 - 2\pi}x + \pi^2 - \frac{\pi}{15 - 2\pi}$$

5. (a) $s = at^2 + bt$

So $v = \dfrac{ds}{dt} = 2at + b \quad \cdots (*)$

and acceleration $= \dfrac{dv}{dt} = 2a$, a constant

(b) Substituting the given information into (*):

$$t = 1, v = 1 \ \Rightarrow 1 = 2a + b \ \cdots (1)$$

$$t = 2, v = 5 \ \Rightarrow 5 = 4a + b \ \cdots (2)$$

$(2) - (1)$ gives $4 = 2a$

So $a = 2$

and then, from (1), $b = 1 - 2a = 1 - 4 = -3$

6. Applying implicit differentiation to $x^3 + y^3 = 3$:

$$\frac{\mathrm{d}}{\mathrm{d}x}(x^3 + y^3) = \frac{\mathrm{d}}{\mathrm{d}x}(3)$$

$$\Rightarrow 3x^2 + 3y^2 \frac{\mathrm{d}y}{\mathrm{d}x} = 0$$

$$\Rightarrow \frac{\mathrm{d}y}{\mathrm{d}x} = -\frac{x^2}{y^2}$$

$$= -\left(\frac{x}{y}\right)^2 < 0 \text{ for all } x \text{ and } y$$

So the curve is always decreasing.

7. (a) Every non-constant polynomial has at least one (possibly complex) root; or equivalently, every polynomial of degree n has n roots (some of which may be repeated).

(b) Stationary points occur where the derivative is zero. Differentiating a polynomial of degree n gives a polynomial of degree $n - 1$, which has at most $n - 1$ distinct roots by the Fundamental Theorem of Algebra. Hence there are at most $n - 1$ distinct points where the derivative is zero, or at most $n - 1$ stationary points.

(c) $\dfrac{\mathrm{d}y}{\mathrm{d}x} = 3ax^2 + 2bx + c$

If $3ax^2 + 2bx + c = 0$ has only one root, then the discriminant is zero:

$$\Delta = (2b)^2 - 4(3a)c$$

$$0 = 4b^2 - 12ac$$

$$\therefore b^2 - 3ac = 0$$

8. (a) The zeros are where $f(x) = 0$:

$$x^4 - x = 0$$

$$\Leftrightarrow x(x^3 - 1) = 0$$

$$\Leftrightarrow x = 0 \text{ or } x^3 - 1 = 0$$

$$\Leftrightarrow x = 0,\ 1$$

(b) $f(x)$ is decreasing where $f'(x) < 0$:

$$f'(x) < 0$$

$$\Leftrightarrow 4x^3 - 1 < 0$$

$$\Leftrightarrow x < \frac{1}{\sqrt[3]{4}}$$

(c) $f''(x) = 12x^2$

$$f''(x) = 0$$

$$\Leftrightarrow 12x^2 = 0$$

$$\Leftrightarrow x = 0$$

(d) $f(x)$ is concave up where $f''(x) > 0$:

$$f''(x) > 0$$

$$\Leftrightarrow 12x^2 > 0$$

$$\Leftrightarrow x^2 > 0$$

$$\Leftrightarrow x \in \left]-\infty, 0\right[\cup \left]0, \infty\right[$$

(e) At a point of inflexion, $f''(x) = 0$, so from (c) the only possibility is $x = 0$. However, there must also be a change in concavity from one side of the point to the other; and since, by (d), $f(x)$ is concave up on both sides of $x = 0$, this cannot be a point of inflexion.

(f)

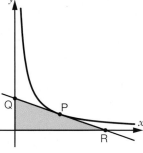

9. (a) $y = x^{-1} \Rightarrow \dfrac{\mathrm{d}y}{\mathrm{d}x} = -x^{-2}$

So, at $x = p$, $\dfrac{\mathrm{d}y}{\mathrm{d}x} = -p^{-2} = -\dfrac{1}{p^2}$ and $y = \dfrac{1}{p}$

Therefore, the equation of the tangent is:

$$y - y_1 = m(x - x_1)$$

$$y - \frac{1}{p} = -\frac{1}{p^2}(x - p)$$

$$p^2 y - p = -(x - p)$$

$$p^2 y + x = 2p$$

(b) At Q, $x = 0$:

$$p^2 y + 0 = 2p$$

$$\Rightarrow y = \frac{2}{p}$$

At R, $y = 0$

$$p^2 \times 0 + x = 2p$$

$$\Rightarrow x = 2p$$

So the area of triangle OQR is

$$A = \frac{1}{2}bh = \frac{1}{2}(2p)\left(\frac{2}{p}\right) = 2, \text{ which is independent of } p.$$

(c) Since Q $= \left(0, \dfrac{2}{p}\right)$ and R $= (2p, 0)$,

$$QR = \sqrt{(2p - 0)^2 + \left(0 - \frac{2}{p}\right)^2}$$

$$= \sqrt{4p^2 + \frac{4}{p^2}}$$

$$= 2\sqrt{p^2 + p^{-2}}$$

(d) The value of p that minimises QR is the same as the value which minimises QR^2. For a minimum, $\frac{d}{dp}(QR^2) = 0$:

$$\frac{d}{dp}(4p^2 + 4p^{-2}) = 0$$

$$\Rightarrow 8p - 8p^{-3} = 0$$

$$\Rightarrow p^4 - 1 = 0$$

$$\Rightarrow p = \pm 1$$

But we know $p > 0$, so $p = 1$.

To verify that this is gives a minimum, check the second derivative at $p = 1$:

$$\frac{d^2}{dp^2}(QR^2) = 8 + 24p^{-4}$$

$$= 8 + 24(1)^{-4}$$

$$= 32 > 0 \quad \therefore \text{ minimum}$$

Going for the top 9

1. For stationary points, $\frac{dy}{dx} = 0$. Using implicit differentiation:

$$\frac{d}{dx}(y^2 + 4xy - x^2) = \frac{d}{dx}(20)$$

$$2y\frac{dy}{dx} + 4y + 4x\frac{dy}{dx} - 2x = 0$$

$$\frac{dy}{dx} = 0 \Rightarrow 4y - 2x = 0 \Rightarrow x = 2y$$

Substituting this into the original equation:

$$y^2 + 4(2y)y - (2y)^2 = 20$$

$$\Rightarrow y^2 + 8y^2 - 4y^2 = 20$$

$$\Rightarrow 5y^2 = 20$$

$$\Rightarrow y^2 = 4$$

$$\Rightarrow y = \pm 2$$

When $y = 2$, $x = 2 \times 2 = 4$.

When $y = -2$, $x = 2 \times (-2) = -4$.

So the stationary points are $(4, 2)$ and $(-4, -2)$.

2. Applying implicit differentiation to $x^2 + y^2 = 9$:

$$\frac{d}{dx}(x^2 + y^2) = \frac{d}{dx}(9)$$

$$\Rightarrow 2x + 2y\frac{dy}{dx} = 0$$

$$\Rightarrow \frac{dy}{dx} = -\frac{x}{y}$$

Then, differentiating again:

$$\frac{d^2y}{dx^2} = -\frac{y - x\frac{dy}{dx}}{y^2}$$

$$= -\frac{y - x\left(-\frac{x}{y}\right)}{y^2}$$

$$= -\frac{y^2 + x^2}{y^3}$$

$$= -\frac{9}{y^3} \quad \text{(using the original equation)}$$

3. By Pythagoras' theorem, the distance d between a general point on the curve, (x, x^2), and the point $(0, 9)$ satisfies:

$$d^2 = (x - 0)^2 + (x^2 - 9)^2$$

$$= x^2 + x^4 - 18x^2 + 81$$

$$= x^4 - 17x^2 + 81$$

The distance will be minimised when d^2 is minimised, and this will occur where $\frac{d}{dx}(d^2) = 0$.

$$\frac{d}{dx}(x^4 - 17x^2 + 81) = 0$$

$$\Leftrightarrow 4x^3 - 34x = 0$$

$$\Leftrightarrow 2x(2x^2 - 17) = 0$$

$$\Leftrightarrow x = 0 \text{ or } x = \pm\sqrt{\frac{17}{2}}$$

To check which point gives a minimum, consider the second derivative:

$$\frac{d^2}{dx^2}(d^2) = 12x^2 - 34$$

When $x = 0$, $\frac{d^2}{dx^2}(d^2) = -34 < 0 \quad \therefore \text{ maximum}$

When $x = \pm\sqrt{\frac{17}{2}}$,

$$\frac{d^2}{dx^2}(d^2) = 12\left(\pm\sqrt{\frac{17}{2}}\right)^2 - 34 = 68 > 0 \quad \therefore \text{ both minima}$$

Therefore, the closest points to $(0, 9)$ on the curve $y = x^2$ are $\left(\sqrt{\frac{17}{2}}, \frac{17}{2}\right)$ and $\left(-\sqrt{\frac{17}{2}}, \frac{17}{2}\right)$.

4. Consider the general cubic $y = ax^3 + bx^2 + cx + d$, where $a \neq 0$. Taking successive derivatives:

$$y' = 3ax^2 + 2bx + c$$

$$y'' = 6ax + 2b$$

$$y''' = 6a$$

At point(s) of inflexion, $y'' = 0$, i.e. $0 = 6ax + 2b$

$$\Leftrightarrow x = -\frac{b}{3a}$$

But there must also be a change in concavity for this to be a point of inflexion, which means that $y''' \neq 0$. This is the case here as $y''' = 6a \neq 0$ since $a \neq 0$.

Hence, every cubic has a (single) point of inflexion (and this occurs at $x = -\dfrac{b}{3a}$).

5.
$$a = \frac{dv}{dt}$$
$$= \frac{d}{dt}\left(s^2 + s\right)$$
$$= 2s\frac{ds}{dt} + \frac{ds}{dt}$$
$$= 2sv + v$$
$$= (2s+1)v$$
$$= (2s+1)(s^2+s)$$

6. It is given that $\dfrac{dl}{dt} = 0.4$ and $\dfrac{d\theta}{dt} = -0.01$.

The area is $A = \dfrac{1}{2}ab\sin C = \dfrac{1}{2}l^2\sin\theta$

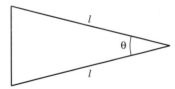

$$\therefore \frac{dA}{dt} = \frac{1}{2}\left(2l\frac{dl}{dt}\sin\theta + l^2\cos\theta\frac{d\theta}{dt}\right) \quad \text{(by product rule and chain rule)}$$
$$= \frac{1}{2}\left(2l \times 0.4 \times \sin\theta + l^2\cos\theta \times (-0.01)\right)$$
$$= \frac{l}{2}\left(0.8\sin\theta - 0.01l^2\cos\theta\right)$$

So, when $l = 4$ and $\theta = \dfrac{\pi}{4}$:

$$\frac{dA}{dt} = \frac{4}{2}\left(0.8\sin\frac{\pi}{4} - 0.01 \times 4^2\cos\frac{\pi}{4}\right)$$
$$= 2\left(0.8 \times \frac{\sqrt{2}}{2} - 0.01 \times 4^2 \times \frac{\sqrt{2}}{2}\right)$$
$$= 0.64\sqrt{2} = 0.905 \text{ m}^2\text{s}^{-1} \text{ (3 SF)}$$

7. By the product rule:

$$\frac{d}{dx}\left(x \times x^{-1}\right) = 1 \times x^{-1} + x\frac{d}{dx}\left(x^{-1}\right)$$

But also $\dfrac{d}{dx}\left(x \times x^{-1}\right) = \dfrac{d}{dx}(1) = 0$

$$\therefore x^{-1} + x\frac{d}{dx}\left(x^{-1}\right) = 0$$
$$\Rightarrow x\frac{d}{dx}\left(x^{-1}\right) = -x^{-1}$$
$$\Rightarrow \frac{d}{dx}\left(x^{-1}\right) = -x^{-2}$$

8. **(a)** The point P has coordinates (p, p^2)

$$\tan\alpha = \frac{e^p}{p}$$
$$\therefore \alpha = \arctan\left(\frac{e^p}{p}\right)$$

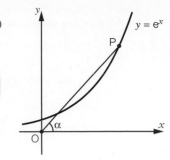

(b) $y = e^x \Rightarrow \dfrac{dy}{dx} = e^x$

Therefore, at (p, e^p) the gradient of the tangent is $m = e^p$.

So the equation is

$$y - y_1 = m(x - x_1)$$
$$y - e^p = e^p(x - p)$$
$$\Rightarrow y = e^p x + e^p(1 - p)$$

(c) At Q, $y = 0$. So

$$0 = e^p x + e^p(1 - p)$$
$$\Leftrightarrow x = p - 1$$

Therefore, the coordinates of Q are $(p - 1, 0)$.

(d) $\tan\beta = \dfrac{e^p}{p - (p-1)} = e^p$

$$\therefore \beta = \arctan\left(e^p\right)$$

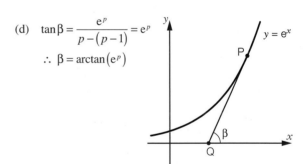

(e) Let $O\hat{P}Q = \gamma$

Then, in triangle OPQ,

$$\alpha + (\pi - \beta) + \gamma = \pi$$
$$\Rightarrow \gamma = \beta - \alpha = \arctan\left(e^p\right) - \arctan\left(\frac{e^p}{p}\right)$$

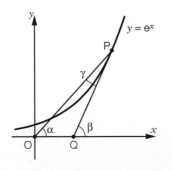

So

$$\tan\gamma = \tan\left[\arctan\left(e^p\right) - \arctan\left(\frac{e^p}{p}\right)\right]$$

$$= \frac{e^p - \frac{e^p}{p}}{1 + e^p \times \frac{e^p}{p}} \quad \text{(using the } \tan(A - B) \text{ identity)}$$

$$= \frac{pe^p - e^p}{p + e^{2p}}$$

$$= \frac{e^p(p-1)}{p + e^{2p}}$$

Hence $\gamma = \arctan\left|\frac{e^p(p-1)}{p + e^{2p}}\right|$

From GDC, the graph is:

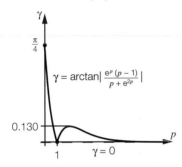

(f) From GDC, maximum value of γ for $p > 1$ is $\gamma = 0.130$ radians (3 SF).

(g) For the equation $e^x = kx$ to have exactly one solution, the line $y = kx$ must be a tangent to the curve $y = e^x$ at the solution point (p, e^p).

This will occur when $\gamma = 0$, which we see from the graph in part (e) is when $p = 1$, i.e. at the point $(1, e)$.

So, since $y = kx$,

$$k = \frac{y}{x} = \frac{e}{1} = e$$

10 INTEGRATION

Mixed practice 10

1. (a) $\int \sqrt{e^x}\, dx = \int \left(e^x\right)^{\frac{1}{2}}\, dx$

    $= \int e^{\frac{x}{2}}\, dx$

    $= 2e^{\frac{x}{2}} + c$

   (b) $\int_0^{\ln 2} \frac{e^x}{\sqrt{e^x + 1}}\, dx = \int_0^{\ln 2} e^x(e^x + 1)^{-\frac{1}{2}}\, dx$

    $= \left[2\left(e^x + 1\right)^{\frac{1}{2}}\right]_0^{\ln 2}$

    $= 2\left(e^{\ln 2} + 1\right)^{\frac{1}{2}} - 2\left(e^0 + 1\right)^{\frac{1}{2}}$

    $= 2\left(\sqrt{3} - \sqrt{2}\right)$

(*Note*: Here the integration has been done by the reverse chain rule, but you may find it clearer to use the substitution $u = e^x + 1$.)

2. Use the cosine double angle identity to rewrite the integral:

$$\int_0^\pi \cos^2 5x\, dx = \frac{1}{2}\int_0^\pi (\cos 10x + 1)\, dx \quad \text{(from } \cos 2\theta = 2\cos^2\theta - 1)$$

$$= \frac{1}{2}\left[\frac{1}{10}\sin 10x + x\right]_0^\pi$$

$$= \frac{1}{2}\left[\left(\frac{1}{10}\sin(10\pi) + \pi\right) - \left(\frac{1}{10}\sin 0 + 0\right)\right]$$

$$= \frac{\pi}{2}$$

3. Let $u = 4 - x$. Then $x = 4 - u$

and $\frac{du}{dx} = -1$ so that $dx = -du$. Hence

$$\int x\sqrt{4 - x}\, dx = \int (4 - u)\sqrt{u}\,(-du)$$

$$= \int u\sqrt{u} - 4\sqrt{u}\ du$$

$$= \int u^{\frac{3}{2}} - 4u^{\frac{1}{2}}\ du$$

$$= \frac{2}{5}u^{\frac{5}{2}} - \frac{8}{3}u^{\frac{3}{2}} + c$$

$$= \frac{2}{5}(4 - x)^{\frac{5}{2}} - \frac{8}{3}(4 - x)^{\frac{3}{2}} + c$$

4. (a) $\int \tan x\, dx = \int \frac{\sin x}{\cos x}\, dx$

   Let $u = \cos x$

   Then $\frac{du}{dx} = -\sin x \implies dx = -\frac{du}{\sin x}$

   $$\int \frac{\sin x}{\cos x}\, dx = \int \frac{\sin x}{u}\left(-\frac{du}{\sin x}\right)$$

   $$= \int -\frac{1}{u}\, du$$

   $$= -\ln|u| + c$$

   $$= \ln|u^{-1}| + c$$

   $$= \ln\left|(\cos x)^{-1}\right| + c$$

   $$= \ln|\sec x| + c$$

   (b) (i) Using the identity $\sec^2 x = 1 + \tan^2 x$:

   $$\int \tan^2 x\, dx = \int \sec^2 x - 1\, dx$$

   $$= \tan x - x + c$$

   (ii) $\int \sec x \tan x\, dx = \sec x + c$

   (iii) $\int \sec^2 x \tan x\, dx = \frac{1}{2}\tan^2 x + c$ (by the reverse

   chain rule, since $\frac{d}{dx}(\tan x) = \sec^2 x$, or by using the substitution $u = \tan x$).

5. (a) $x^2 - 4x + 5 = (x-2)^2 - (-2)^2 + 5 = (x-2)^2 + 1$

(b) $s = \int v \, dt$

$$= \int \frac{1}{t^2 - 4t + 5} \, dt$$

$$= \int \frac{1}{(t-2)^2 + 1} \, dt \quad \text{by part (a)}$$

$$= \arctan(t-2) + c$$

When $t = 0$, $s = 5$:

$$5 = \arctan(0-2) + c$$

$$\Rightarrow 5 = -\arctan 2 + c$$

$$\Rightarrow c = \arctan 2 + 5$$

Therefore $s = \arctan(t-2) + \arctan 2 + 5$

(c) $a = \dfrac{dv}{dt}$

$$= \frac{d}{dt}(t^2 - 4t + 5)^{-1}$$

$$= -(t^2 - 4t + 5)^{-2}(2t - 4)$$

$$= \frac{4 - 2t}{(t^2 - 4t + 5)^2}$$

(d) Velocity will reach a maximum when the denominator of $v = \dfrac{1}{t^2 - 4t + 5}$ is minimum (the denominator is always positive).

By (a), $t^2 - 4t + 5 = (t-2)^2 + 1$, and this has a minimum of 1 (when $t = 2$).

So $v_{max} = \dfrac{1}{1} = 1 \text{ ms}^{-1}$

6. Solving simultaneously for the intersection points of the two curves:

$$\frac{1}{1+x^2} = \frac{1}{2}x^2$$

$$\Leftrightarrow 2 = x^2 + x^4$$

$$\Leftrightarrow x^4 + x^2 - 2 = 0$$

$$\Leftrightarrow (x^2 + 2)(x^2 - 1) = 0$$

$$\Leftrightarrow x^2 = -2 \quad \text{or} \quad x^2 = 1$$

$x^2 = -2$ does not give real solutions, $\therefore x = \pm 1$

Then

$$\text{Area} = \int_{-1}^{1} \frac{1}{1+x^2} - \frac{1}{2}x^2 \, dx$$

$$= \left[\arctan x - \frac{1}{6}x^3 \right]_{-1}^{1}$$

$$= \left(\arctan 1 - \frac{1}{6}(1)^3 \right) - \left(\arctan(-1) - \frac{1}{6}(-1)^3 \right)$$

$$= \left(\frac{\pi}{4} - \frac{1}{6} \right) - \left(-\frac{\pi}{4} + \frac{1}{6} \right)$$

$$= \frac{\pi}{2} - \frac{1}{3}$$

7. From GDC:

$$\int_0^1 e^{\sin x} \, dx = 1.63187$$

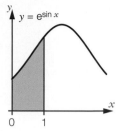

8. (a) $s = \int v \, dt = \int t \sin t \, dt$

By parts:

Let $u = t$ and $\dfrac{dv}{dt} = \sin t$

Then $\dfrac{du}{dt} = 1$ and $v = -\cos t$

$$\int_0^{3\pi/2} t \sin t \, dt = \left[t(-\cos t) \right]_0^{3\pi/2} - \int_0^{3\pi/2} 1(-\cos t) \, dt$$

$$= \left[-t \cos t \right]_0^{3\pi/2} + \int_0^{3\pi/2} \cos t \, dt$$

$$= \left[-t \cos t + \sin t \right]_0^{3\pi/2}$$

$$= \left(-\frac{3\pi}{2}\cos\frac{3\pi}{2} + \sin\frac{3\pi}{2} \right)$$

$$\quad - \left(-0\cos 0 + \sin 0 \right)$$

$$= -1 \text{ m}$$

(b) At maximum displacement, $\dfrac{ds}{dt} = 0$, i.e. $v = 0$:

$$v = t \sin t = 0$$

$$\Leftrightarrow t = 0 \quad \text{or} \quad \sin t = 0$$

$$\therefore t = 0, \pi \quad \text{(for } 0 \le t \le \frac{3\pi}{2}\text{)}$$

To check that $t = \pi$ is a local maximum (clearly $t = 0$ isn't), consider $\dfrac{d^2 s}{dt^2}$.

$$\frac{d^2 s}{dt^2} = \frac{dv}{dt}$$

$$= \frac{d}{dt}(t \sin t)$$

$$= \sin t + t \cos t$$

When $t = \pi$:

$$\frac{d^2 s}{dt^2} = \sin \pi + \pi \cos \pi = -\pi < 0 \quad \therefore \text{ local maximum.}$$

At $t = \pi$, displacement from the initial position (using the integration in part (a)) is

$$s = \left[-t \cos t + \sin t \right]_0^{\pi}$$

$$= (-\pi \cos \pi + \sin \pi) - (-0\cos 0 + \sin 0)$$

$$= \pi \text{ m}$$

This is greater than the displacement in part (a), so the maximum displacement is achieved after π s.

(c) Since $t = \pi$ is a local maximum for displacement, the ball changes direction here and subsequently passes back through the initial point before reaching a displacement of -1 m from the initial position at $t = \dfrac{3\pi}{2}$ (by part (a)). So:

- Distance travelled between $t = 0$ and $t = \pi$ is $d_1 = \pi$ m.

- Distance travelled between $t = \pi$ and $t = \dfrac{3\pi}{2}$ is $d_2 = \pi - (-1) = (\pi + 1)$ m

  Therefore, total distance travelled is $d = d_1 + d_2 = (2\pi + 1)$ m.

(*Note*: The velocity graph is given here for information but is not strictly necessary to answer the question.)

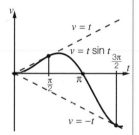

9. $\displaystyle\int_0^a \sin 2x \, dx = \frac{3}{4}$

$\Rightarrow \left[-\dfrac{1}{2}\cos 2x \right]_0^a = \dfrac{3}{4}$

$\Rightarrow \left(-\dfrac{1}{2}\cos 2a \right) - \left(-\dfrac{1}{2}\cos 0 \right) = \dfrac{3}{4}$

$\Rightarrow -\dfrac{1}{2}\cos 2a + \dfrac{1}{2} = \dfrac{3}{4}$

$\Rightarrow \cos 2a = -\dfrac{1}{2}$

$0 < a \le \pi \Rightarrow 0 < 2a \le 2\pi$

$\therefore 2a = \dfrac{2\pi}{3},\ \dfrac{4\pi}{3}$

$\Rightarrow a = \dfrac{\pi}{3}$ or $\dfrac{2\pi}{3}$

10. (a) Let $u = 2^x$

Then $\dfrac{du}{dx} = (\ln 2)2^x$ so $dx = \dfrac{du}{(\ln 2)2^x} = \dfrac{du}{(\ln 2)u}$

$\displaystyle\int 2^x \, dx = \int u \frac{du}{(\ln 2)u}$

$= \displaystyle\int \frac{u}{(\ln 2)u} \, du$

$= \displaystyle\int \frac{1}{\ln 2} \, du$

$= \dfrac{u}{\ln 2} + c$

$= \dfrac{2^x}{\ln 2} + c$

(b) By the product rule:

$\dfrac{d}{dx}\left(x \log_2 x \right) = \log_2 x + x \dfrac{1}{x \ln 2}$

$= \log_2 x + \dfrac{1}{\ln 2}$

(c) $\displaystyle\int \log_2 x \, dx = \int 1 \times \log_2 x \, dx$

So, using integration by parts:

Let $u = \log_2 x$ and $\dfrac{dv}{dx} = 1$

Then $\dfrac{du}{dx} = \dfrac{1}{x \ln 2}$ and $v = x$

$\displaystyle\int 1 \times \log_2 x \, dx = x \log_2 x - \int x \frac{1}{x \ln 2} \, dx$

$= x \log_2 x - \displaystyle\int \frac{1}{\ln 2} \, dx$

$= x \log_2 x - \dfrac{x}{\ln 2} + c$

Alternatively, from part (b),

$\dfrac{d}{dx}\left(x \log_2 x \right) - \dfrac{1}{\ln 2} = \log_2 x;$

that is, $\dfrac{d}{dx}\left[x \log_2 x - \dfrac{1}{\ln 2}x \right] = \log_2 x.$

So $\displaystyle\int \log_2 x \, dx = x \log_2 x - \dfrac{x}{\ln 2} + c$

11. (a) From GDC:

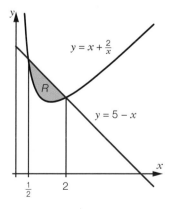

Points of intersection are $x = \dfrac{1}{2}$ and $x = 2$.

Area of $R = \int_{\frac{1}{2}}^{2} 5 - x - \left(x + \frac{2}{x}\right) dx$

$= \int_{\frac{1}{2}}^{2} 5 - 2x - \frac{2}{x} dx$

$= \left[5x - x^2 - 2\ln x\right]_{\frac{1}{2}}^{2}$

$= \left(6 - 2\ln 2\right) - \left(\frac{9}{4} - 2\ln\frac{1}{2}\right)$

$= \frac{15}{4} - \ln 4 + \ln\frac{1}{4}$

$= \frac{15}{4} - \ln 4 - \ln 4$

$= \frac{15}{4} - 2\ln 4$

(b) $V = \pi\int_{\frac{1}{2}}^{2} (5 - x)^2 - \left(x + \frac{2}{x}\right)^2 dx$

$= \pi\int_{\frac{1}{2}}^{2} 25 - 10x + x^2 - \left(x^2 + 4 + \frac{4}{x^2}\right) dx$

$= \pi\int_{\frac{1}{2}}^{2} 21 - 10x - \frac{4}{x^2} dx$

$= \pi\left[21x - 5x^2 + \frac{4}{x}\right]_{\frac{1}{2}}^{2}$

$= \pi\left[(42 - 20 + 2) - \left(\frac{21}{2} - \frac{5}{4} + 8\right)\right]$

$= \frac{27\pi}{4}$

12. By parts:

Let $u = x^2$ and $\frac{dv}{dx} = \cos 2x$

Then $\frac{du}{dx} = 2x$ and $v = \frac{1}{2}\sin 2x$

$\int x^2\cos 2x\, dx = x^2\frac{1}{2}\sin 2x - \int 2x\left(\frac{1}{2}\sin 2x\right) dx$

$= \frac{1}{2}x^2\sin 2x - \int x\sin 2x\, dx$

Then, integrating $\int x\sin 2x\, dx$ by parts again:

Let $u = x$ and $\frac{dv}{dx} = \sin 2x$

Then $\frac{du}{dx} = 1$ and $v = -\frac{1}{2}\cos 2x$

$\int x\sin 2x\, dx = x\left(-\frac{1}{2}\cos 2x\right) - \int 1\times\left(-\frac{1}{2}\cos 2x\right) dx$

$= -\frac{1}{2}x\cos 2x + \frac{1}{2}\int\cos 2x\, dx$

$= -\frac{1}{2}x\cos 2x + \frac{1}{4}\sin 2x + c$

So, substituting this into the first expression gives

$\int_{0}^{\pi/4} x^2\cos 2x\, dx = \left[\frac{1}{2}x^2\sin 2x\right]_{0}^{\frac{\pi}{4}} - \int_{0}^{\pi/4} x\sin 2x\, dx$

$= \left[\frac{1}{2}x^2\sin 2x\right]_{0}^{\frac{\pi}{4}}$

$- \left[-\frac{1}{2}x\cos 2x + \frac{1}{4}\sin 2x\right]_{0}^{\frac{\pi}{4}}$

$= \frac{1}{4}\left[2x^2\sin 2x + 2x\cos 2x - \sin 2x\right]_{0}^{\frac{\pi}{4}}$

$= \frac{1}{4}\left[\left(\frac{\pi^2}{8} + 0 - 1\right) - \left(0 + 0 - 0\right)\right]$

$= \frac{1}{4}\left(\frac{\pi^2}{8} - 1\right)$

13. (a) By observation,

$x^2 + 3 = (x + 2)(x - 2) + 7$

So $\frac{x^2 + 3}{x + 2} = x - 2 + \frac{7}{x + 2}$

i.e. $A = 1$, $B = -2$, $C = 7$

(Alternatively, you can do this by polynomial long division or by formally comparing coefficients.)

(b) $\int\frac{x^2 + 3}{x + 2} dx = \int x - 2 + \frac{7}{x + 2} dx$

$= \frac{1}{2}x^2 - 2x + 7\ln|x + 2| + c$

14. (a) $V_A = \pi\int_{0}^{9} x^2\, dy$

$= \pi\int_{0}^{9} y\, dy$

$= \pi\left[\frac{1}{2}y^2\right]_{0}^{9}$

$= \frac{81\pi}{2}$

(b) When the rectangle made up of regions A and B together is rotated 2π radians about the y-axis, it forms a cylinder of radius 3 and height 9. The volume of the cylinder is

$V_{AB} = \pi r^2 h$

$= \pi\times 3^2\times 9$

$= 81\pi$

So

$V_B = V_{AB} - V_A$

$= 81\pi - \frac{81\pi}{2}$

$= \frac{81\pi}{2}$

15. (a) Using the double angle identity
$\cos 2x = 1 - 2\sin^2 x$:

$$\int 2\sin^2 x \, dx = \int 1 - \cos 2x \, dx$$

$$= x - \frac{1}{2}\sin 2x + c$$

$$= x - \frac{1}{2}\left(2\sin x \cos x\right) + c$$

$$= x - \sin x \cos x + c$$

(b) At points of intersection:

$$\sin x = 2\sin^2 x$$

$$\Leftrightarrow 2\sin^2 x - \sin x = 0$$

$$\Leftrightarrow \sin x \left(2\sin x - 1\right) = 0$$

$$\Leftrightarrow \sin x = 0 \quad \text{or} \quad \sin x = \frac{1}{2}$$

$$\therefore x = 0, \frac{\pi}{6} \quad \text{in the domain} \left[0, \frac{\pi}{2}\right]$$

$x = 0: \quad y = \sin 0 = 0$

$x = \frac{\pi}{6}: \quad y = \sin\frac{\pi}{6} = \frac{1}{2}$

So the coordinates of the points of intersection are $(0, 0)$ and $\left(\frac{\pi}{6}, \frac{1}{2}\right)$.

(c) $A = \displaystyle\int_0^{\pi/6} \sin x - 2\sin^2 x \, dx$

$$= \left[-\cos x - \left(x - \sin x \cos x\right)\right]_0^{\frac{\pi}{6}} \quad \text{(using part (a))}$$

$$= \left[\sin x \cos x - \cos x - x\right]_0^{\frac{\pi}{6}}$$

$$= \left(\sin\frac{\pi}{6}\cos\frac{\pi}{6} - \cos\frac{\pi}{6} - \frac{\pi}{6}\right)$$
$$- \left(\sin 0 \cos 0 - \cos 0 - 0\right)$$

$$= \frac{\sqrt{3}}{4} - \frac{\sqrt{3}}{2} - \frac{\pi}{6} - 1$$

$$= -\frac{\sqrt{3}}{4} - \frac{\pi}{6} - 1$$

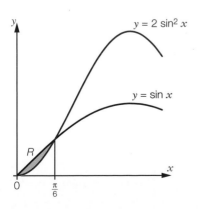

(d)

$$V = \pi \int_0^{\pi/6} (\sin x)^2 - (2\sin^2 x)^2 \, dx$$

$$= \pi \int_0^{\pi/6} \sin^2 x - (1 - \cos 2x)^2 \, dx \qquad \text{(using } \cos 2\theta = 1 - 2\sin^2\theta\text{)}$$

$$= \pi \int_0^{\pi/6} \frac{1}{2}(1 - \cos 2x) - (1 - \cos 2x)^2 \, dx$$

$$= \pi \int_0^{\pi/6} \frac{1}{2}(1 - \cos 2x) - (1 - 2\cos 2x + \cos^2 2x) \, dx$$

$$= \pi \int_0^{\pi/6} -\frac{1}{2} + \frac{3}{2}\cos 2x - \cos^2 2x \, dx$$

$$= \pi \int_0^{\pi/6} -\frac{1}{2} + \frac{3}{2}\cos 2x - \frac{1}{2}(\cos 4x + 1) \, dx \quad \text{(using } \cos 2\theta = 2\cos^2\theta - 1\text{)}$$

$$= \pi \int_0^{\pi/6} -1 + \frac{3}{2}\cos 2x - \frac{1}{2}\cos 4x \, dx$$

$$= \pi \left[-x + \frac{3}{4}\sin 2x - \frac{1}{8}\sin 4x\right]_0^{\frac{\pi}{6}}$$

$$= \pi \left[\left(-\frac{\pi}{6} + \frac{3}{4}\sin\frac{\pi}{3} - \frac{1}{8}\sin\frac{2\pi}{3}\right) - \left(-0 + \frac{3}{4}\sin 0 - \frac{1}{8}\sin 0\right)\right]$$

$$= \pi \left(-\frac{\pi}{6} + \frac{3\sqrt{3}}{8} - \frac{\sqrt{3}}{16}\right)$$

$$= \pi \left(-\frac{\pi}{6} + \frac{5\sqrt{3}}{16}\right)$$

(e) $\displaystyle\int \arcsin x \, dx = \int 1 \times \arcsin x \, dx$, so by parts:

Let $u = \arcsin x$ and $\dfrac{dv}{dx} = 1$

Then $\dfrac{du}{dx} = \dfrac{1}{\sqrt{1 - x^2}}$ and $v = x$

$$\int 1 \times \arcsin x \, dx = x \arcsin x - \int x \frac{1}{\sqrt{1 - x^2}} \, dx$$

$$= x \arcsin x + \sqrt{1 - x^2} + c$$

(*Note*: The integration $\displaystyle\int x \frac{1}{\sqrt{1 - x^2}} \, dx$ has been done by the reverse chain rule here, but you could also do this with the substitution $u = 1 - x^2$.)

(f) When $y = 1$:

$$1 = 2\sin^2 x$$

$$\Leftrightarrow \sin^2 x = \frac{1}{2}$$

$$\Leftrightarrow \sin x = \pm\frac{1}{\sqrt{2}}$$

So the smallest positive value of x is $x = \dfrac{\pi}{4}$.

The area we want is the area of region A in the diagram.

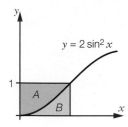

Area of A = area of rectangle − area of B

$$= \left(\frac{\pi}{4} \times 1\right) - \int_0^{\pi/4} 2\sin^2 x \, dx$$

$$= \frac{\pi}{4} - \left[x - \sin x \cos x\right]_0^{\pi/4} \quad \text{(by part (a))}$$

$$= \frac{\pi}{4} - \left[\frac{\pi}{4} - \frac{1}{\sqrt{2}} \times \frac{1}{\sqrt{2}}\right]$$

$$= \frac{1}{2}$$

(g) Similarly to (f), when $y = p$:

$$p = 2\sin^2 x$$

$$\Leftrightarrow \sin^2 x = \frac{p}{2}$$

$$\Leftrightarrow \sin x = \pm\sqrt{\frac{p}{2}}$$

So the smallest positive value of x is $x = \arcsin\sqrt{\frac{p}{2}}$

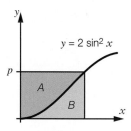

Area of A = area of rectangle − area of B

$$= \left(p\arcsin\sqrt{\frac{p}{2}}\right) - \int_0^{\arcsin\sqrt{p/2}} 2\sin^2 x \, dx$$

$$= p\arcsin\sqrt{\frac{p}{2}} - \left[x - \sin x \cos x\right]_0^{\arcsin\sqrt{p/2}}$$

$$= p\arcsin\sqrt{\frac{p}{2}} - \left[x - \sin x\sqrt{1 - \sin^2 x}\right]_0^{\arcsin\sqrt{p/2}}$$

$$= p\arcsin\sqrt{\frac{p}{2}} - \left[\left(\arcsin\sqrt{\frac{p}{2}} - \sqrt{\frac{p}{2}}\sqrt{1 - \frac{p}{2}}\right) - (0)\right]$$

$$= p\arcsin\sqrt{\frac{p}{2}} - \arcsin\sqrt{\frac{p}{2}} + \frac{1}{2}\sqrt{2p - p^2}$$

(h) Since the area of the shaded region A in (g) is also given by $\int_0^p x \, dy = \int_0^p \arcsin\left(\sqrt{\frac{y}{2}}\right) dy$, we have

$$\int_0^p \arcsin\left(\sqrt{\frac{y}{2}}\right) dy = p\arcsin\sqrt{\frac{p}{2}} - \arcsin\sqrt{\frac{p}{2}} + \frac{1}{2}\sqrt{2p - p^2}$$

So

$$\int \arcsin\left(\sqrt{\frac{y}{2}}\right) dy = y\arcsin\sqrt{\frac{y}{2}} - \arcsin\sqrt{\frac{y}{2}} + \frac{1}{2}\sqrt{2y - y^2} + c$$

Let $x = \frac{y}{2}$ so that $y = 2x$

Then $\frac{dx}{dy} = \frac{1}{2}$ and $dy = 2\,dx$

Substituting this into the formula for $\int \arcsin\left(\sqrt{\frac{y}{2}}\right) dy$ gives

$$\int \arcsin\left(\sqrt{x}\right)(2\,dx) = 2x\arcsin\sqrt{x}$$

$$- \arcsin\sqrt{x} + \frac{1}{2}\sqrt{2(2x) - (2x)^2} + c$$

$$\Rightarrow 2\int \arcsin\left(\sqrt{x}\right) dx = 2x\arcsin\sqrt{x}$$

$$- \arcsin\sqrt{x} + \frac{1}{2}\sqrt{4x - 4x^2} + c$$

$$\Rightarrow \int \arcsin\left(\sqrt{x}\right) dx = x\arcsin\sqrt{x}$$

$$- \frac{1}{2}\arcsin\sqrt{x} + \frac{1}{4}\sqrt{4x - 4x^2} + c$$

$$= x\arcsin\sqrt{x} - \frac{1}{2}\arcsin\sqrt{x} + \frac{1}{2}\sqrt{x - x^2} + c$$

Going for the top 10

1.   Let $x = \sin\theta$

Then $\frac{dx}{d\theta} = \cos\theta \Rightarrow dx = \cos\theta\,d\theta$

$$\int \sqrt{1 - x^2} \, dx = \int \sqrt{1 - \sin^2\theta}\,\cos\theta\,d\theta$$

$$= \int \sqrt{\cos^2\theta}\,\cos\theta\,d\theta$$

$$= \int \cos^2\theta\,d\theta$$

$$= \int \frac{1}{2}(\cos 2\theta + 1)\,d\theta$$

$$= \frac{1}{2}\left(\frac{1}{2}\sin 2\theta + \theta\right) + c$$

$$= \frac{1}{2}(\sin\theta\cos\theta + \theta) + c$$

$$= \frac{1}{2}\left(\sin\theta\sqrt{1 - \sin^2\theta} + \theta\right) + c$$

$$= \frac{1}{2}\left(x\sqrt{1 - x^2} + \arcsin x\right) + c$$

2. **(a)** $C - S = \int \dfrac{\cos x}{\cos x + \sin x}\,dx - \int \dfrac{\sin x}{\cos x + \sin x}\,dx$

$$= \int \dfrac{\cos x - \sin x}{\cos x + \sin x}\,dx$$

$$= \ln|\cos x + \sin x| + c$$

(*Note*: Here the integration has been done by the reverse chain rule, but you could also use the substitution $u = \cos x + \sin x$.)

(b) $C + S = \int \dfrac{\cos x}{\cos x + \sin x}\,dx + \int \dfrac{\sin x}{\cos x + \sin x}\,dx$

$$= \int \dfrac{\cos x + \sin x}{\cos x + \sin x}\,dx$$

$$= \int 1\,dx$$

$$= x + c$$

Then $S = \dfrac{1}{2}\left[(C + S) - (C - S)\right]$

$$= \dfrac{1}{2}\left(x - \ln|\cos x + \sin x|\right) + \tilde{c}$$

i.e. $\displaystyle\int \dfrac{\sin x}{\cos x + \sin x}\,dx = \dfrac{1}{2}\left(x - \ln|\cos x + \sin x|\right) + c$

3. $\displaystyle\int \cos^3 x\,dx = \int \cos x \cos^2 x\,dx$

$$= \int \cos x \left(1 - \sin^2 x\right)dx$$

$$= \int \cos x - \cos x \sin^2 x\,dx$$

$$= \sin x - \dfrac{1}{3}\sin^3 x + c$$

4. **(a)** $V = \pi\displaystyle\int_{\pi/3}^{2\pi/3} \sin^2 x - \left(\dfrac{1}{2}\right)^2 dx$

$$= \pi\int_{\pi/3}^{2\pi/3} \dfrac{1}{2}(1 - \cos 2x) - \dfrac{1}{4}\,dx$$

$$= \dfrac{\pi}{4}\int_{\pi/3}^{2\pi/3} 1 - 2\cos 2x\,dx$$

$$= \dfrac{\pi}{4}\left[x - \sin 2x\right]_{\pi/3}^{2\pi/3}$$

$$= \dfrac{\pi}{4}\left[\left(\dfrac{2\pi}{3} - \sin\dfrac{4\pi}{3}\right) - \left(\dfrac{\pi}{3} - \sin\dfrac{2\pi}{3}\right)\right]$$

$$= \dfrac{\pi}{4}\left(\dfrac{\pi}{3} + \sqrt{3}\right)$$

$y = \sin x$

$y = \dfrac{1}{2}$

(b) The volume of revolution of the curve $y = \sin x$ around the line $y = \dfrac{1}{2}$ is the same as that of the curve $y = \sin x - \dfrac{1}{2}$ around the x-axis (i.e. translating everything down by $\dfrac{1}{2}$).

$$V = \pi\int_{\pi/3}^{2\pi/3}\left(\sin x - \dfrac{1}{2}\right)^2 dx$$

$$= \pi\int_{\pi/3}^{2\pi/3}\sin^2 x - \sin x + \dfrac{1}{4}\,dx$$

$$= \pi\int_{\pi/3}^{2\pi/3}\dfrac{1}{2}(1 - \cos 2x)$$

$$- \sin x + \dfrac{1}{4}\,dx$$

$$= \dfrac{\pi}{4}\int_{\pi/3}^{2\pi/3} 3 - 2\cos 2x - 4\sin x\,dx$$

$$= \dfrac{\pi}{4}\left[3x - \sin 2x + 4\cos x\right]_{\pi/3}^{2\pi/3}$$

$$= \dfrac{\pi}{4}\left(2\pi - \sin\dfrac{4\pi}{3} + 4\cos\dfrac{4\pi}{3}\right) - \left(\pi - \sin\dfrac{2\pi}{3} + 4\cos\dfrac{2\pi}{3}\right)$$

$$= \dfrac{\pi}{4}\left(\pi + \sqrt{3} - 4\right)$$

$y = \sin x - \dfrac{1}{2}$

5. By parts:

Let $u = e^x$ and $\dfrac{dv}{dx} = \sin x$

Then $\dfrac{du}{dx} = e^x$ and $v = -\cos x$

$\displaystyle\int e^x \sin x\,dx = -e^x \cos x - \int -e^x \cos x\,dx$

$$= -e^x \cos x + \int e^x \cos x\,dx$$

For $\displaystyle\int e^x \cos x\,dx$, use parts again:

Let $u = e^x$ and $\dfrac{dv}{dx} = \cos x$

Then $\dfrac{du}{dx} = e^x$ and $v = \sin x$

$\displaystyle\int e^x \cos x\,dx = e^x \sin x - \int e^x \sin x\,dx$

Substituting this into the expression for $\int e^x \sin x\,dx$ above:

$\displaystyle\int e^x \sin x\,dx = -e^x \cos x + \int e^x \cos x\,dx$

$$= -e^x \cos x + \left(e^x \sin x - \int e^x \sin x\,dx\right)$$

$\therefore 2\displaystyle\int e^x \sin x\,dx = -e^x \cos x + e^x \sin x$

Hence $\displaystyle\int e^x \sin x\,dx = \dfrac{1}{2}e^x(\sin x - \cos x) + c$

6. (a) (i) $$\sqrt{\frac{1-3x}{1+3x}} = \sqrt{\frac{1-3x}{1+3x}} \times \sqrt{\frac{1-3x}{1-3x}}$$

$$= \frac{\left(\sqrt{1-3x}\right)^2}{\sqrt{(1+3x)(1-3x)}}$$

$$= \frac{1-3x}{\sqrt{1-9x^2}}$$

(ii) $$\int\sqrt{\frac{1-3x}{1+3x}}\,dx = \int\frac{1-3x}{\sqrt{1-9x^2}}\,dx$$

$$= \int\frac{1}{\sqrt{1-9x^2}}\,dx - \int\frac{3x}{\sqrt{1-9x^2}}\,dx$$

$$= \frac{1}{3}\int\frac{1}{\sqrt{\left(\frac{1}{3}\right)^2 - x^2}}\,dx$$

$$-\left(\frac{1}{-6}\right)\int\frac{-18x}{\sqrt{1-9x^2}}\,dx$$

$$= \frac{1}{3}\arcsin\left(\frac{x}{\frac{1}{3}}\right) + \frac{2}{6}\sqrt{1-9x^2} + C$$

$$= \frac{1}{3}\left(\arcsin(3x) + \sqrt{1-9x^2}\right) + C$$

(b) (i) $$\int\sec^3 x\,dx = \int\sec x\,\sec^2 x\,dx$$

Let $u = \sec x$ and $\dfrac{dv}{dx} = \sec^2 x$

Then $\dfrac{du}{dx} = \sec x\tan x$ and $v = \tan x$

$$\int\sec x\,\sec^2 x\,dx = \sec x\tan x - \int\sec x\tan x\tan x\,dx$$

$$= \sec x\tan x - \int\sec x\tan^2 x\,dx$$

$$= \sec x\tan x - \int\sec x\left(\sec^2 x - 1\right)dx$$

$$= \sec x\tan x - \int\sec^3 x - \sec x\,dx$$

$$= \sec x\tan x - \int\sec^3 x\,dx + \int\sec x\,dx$$

$$= \sec x\tan x - \int\sec^3 x\,dx$$

$$+ \ln|\sec x + \tan x| + C$$

$\therefore 2\int\sec^3 x\,dx = \sec x\tan x + \ln|\sec x + \tan x| + C$

Hence $\int\sec^3 x\,dx = \dfrac{1}{2}\left(\sec x\tan x + \ln|\sec x + \tan x|\right) + C$

(ii) Let $x = \sqrt{3}\tan\theta$

Then $\dfrac{dx}{d\theta} = \sqrt{3}\sec^2\theta \Rightarrow dx = \sqrt{3}\sec^2\theta\,d\theta$

To change the limits:

At $x = 0$, $0 = \sqrt{3}\tan\theta \Rightarrow \theta = 0$

At $x = 1$, $1 = \sqrt{3}\tan\theta \Rightarrow \tan\theta = \dfrac{1}{\sqrt{3}}$

$$\Rightarrow \theta = \frac{\pi}{6}$$

So $\displaystyle\int_0^1\sqrt{x^2+3}\,dx = \int_0^{\pi/6}\sqrt{(\sqrt{3}\tan\theta)^2 + 3}\,\left(\sqrt{3}\sec^2\theta\,d\theta\right)$

$$= \int_0^{\pi/6}\sqrt{3\tan^2\theta + 3}\,\left(\sqrt{3}\sec^2\theta\,d\theta\right)$$

$$= \int_0^{\pi/6}\sqrt{3}\sqrt{\tan^2\theta + 1}\,\left(\sqrt{3}\sec^2\theta\,d\theta\right)$$

$$= 3\int_0^{\pi/6}\sec^3\theta\,d\theta$$

$$= 3\left[\frac{1}{2}\left(\sec\theta\tan\theta + \ln|\sec\theta + \tan\theta|\right)\right]_0^{\frac{\pi}{6}}$$

$$= \frac{3}{2}\left[\left(\sec\frac{\pi}{6}\tan\frac{\pi}{6} + \ln\left|\sec\frac{\pi}{6} + \tan\frac{\pi}{6}\right|\right)\right.$$

$$\left. - \left(\sec 0\tan 0 + \ln|\sec 0 + \tan 0|\right)\right]$$

$$= \frac{3}{2}\left(\frac{2}{3} + \ln\sqrt{3}\right)$$

$$= \frac{3}{2}\left(\frac{2}{3} + \frac{1}{2}\ln 3\right)$$

$$= 1 + \frac{3}{4}\ln 3$$

11 PROBABILITY AND STATISTICS

Mixed practice 11

1. (a) Let $X =$ height of a tree. Then $X \sim \mathrm{N}(26.2, 5.6^2)$.

$$P(X > 30) = 1 - P(X < 30)$$
$$= 1 - 0.75129\ldots \quad\text{(from GDC)}$$
$$= 0.249$$

(b) Let $Y =$ the number of trees out of the 16 that are more than 30 m tall.

Then $Y \sim \mathrm{B}(16, 0.249)$.

$$P(Y \geq 2) = 1 - P(Y \leq 1)$$
$$= 1 - 0.06487\ldots \quad\text{(from GDC)}$$
$$= 0.935$$

2. Probability distribution of X:

x	1	2	3	4
$P(X = x)$	k	$4k$	$9k$	$16k$

$$k + 4k + 9k + 16k = 1 \Leftrightarrow k = \frac{1}{30}$$

$$E(X) = 1(k) + 2(4k) + 3(9k) + 4(16k)$$
$$= 100k = \frac{100}{30} = 3.33$$

$$\text{Var}(X) = \left[1(k) + 4(4k) + 9(9k) + 16(16k)\right] - \left(\frac{100}{30}\right)^2$$

$$= \frac{354}{30} - \left(\frac{100}{30}\right)^2$$

$$= 0.689$$

3. By Bayes' theorem:

$$P(A \mid B) = \frac{P(A)P(B \mid A)}{P(A)P(B \mid A) + P(A')P(B \mid A')}$$

$$\therefore \frac{7}{16} = \frac{0.3 P(B \mid A)}{0.3 P(B \mid A) + 0.7 \times 0.5}$$

$$\Leftrightarrow 2.1 P(B \mid A) + 2.45 = 4.8 P(B \mid A)$$

$$\Leftrightarrow 2.7 P(B \mid A) = 2.45$$

$$\Leftrightarrow P(B \mid A) = \frac{49}{54}$$

4. $\sum p_i = 1$

$$\Rightarrow 0.3 + p + q = 1$$

$$\Rightarrow p + q = 0.7 \quad \cdots (1)$$

$$E(Y) = 3.1$$

$$\Rightarrow 0.1 + 0.4 + 3p + 4q = 3.1$$

$$\Rightarrow 3p + 4q = 2.6 \quad \cdots (2)$$

Solving equations (1) and (2) simultaneously gives
$p = 0.2$, $q = 0.5$.

5. (a) $\int_0^2 k(4 - x^2)\, dx = 1$

$$\Rightarrow k\left[4x - \frac{x^3}{3}\right]_0^2 = 1$$

$$\Rightarrow k\left(\frac{16}{3}\right) = 1$$

$$\Rightarrow k = \frac{3}{16}$$

(b) $\int_0^m \frac{3}{16}(4 - x^2)\, dx = \frac{1}{2}$

$$\Rightarrow \frac{3}{16}\left(4m - \frac{m^3}{3}\right) = \frac{1}{2}$$

$$\Rightarrow 12m - m^3 = 8$$

$$\Rightarrow m^3 - 12m + 8 = 0$$

6. Let X = the number of times the cat visits my garden in one day.
Then $X \sim \text{Po}(4)$.

(a) $P(X \geq 1) = 1 - P(X = 0)$

$$= 1 - 0.018315\ldots$$

$$= 0.98168\ldots \approx 0.982$$

(b) $(0.98168\ldots)^7 = 0.879$

(c) $P(X \geq 5 \mid X \geq 1) = \dfrac{P(X \geq 5)}{P(X \geq 1)}$

$$= \frac{1 - P(X \leq 4)}{0.982}$$

$$= \frac{1 - 0.629}{0.982}$$

$$= 0.378$$

7. (a) (i) $\int_0^2 k e^{-x^2}\, dx = 1$

From GDC, $\int_0^2 e^{-x^2}\, dx = 0.882$

$$\therefore k = \frac{1}{0.882} = 1.13$$

(ii) Let q_1 be the lower quartile; then

$$\int_0^{q_1} k e^{-x^2}\, dx = 0.25$$

From GDC, $q_1 = 0.224$.

(iii) $\mu = E(X) = \int_0^2 k x e^{-x^2}\, dx = 0.556$
(3 SF, from GDC)

(b) (i) $P(X > \mu) = \int_{0.556}^2 k e^{-x^2}\, dx = 0.429$

$$P(X < \mu) = \int_0^{0.556} k e^{-x^2}\, dx = 0.571$$

P(one above and one below the mean)

$$= P\big(\big((X_1 > \mu) \cap (X_2 < \mu)\big)$$

$$\cup \big((X_1 < \mu) \cap (X_2 > \mu)\big)\big)$$

$$= (0.429 \times 0.571) + (0.571 \times 0.429)$$

$$= 0.490$$

(ii) $P(X_1 > \mu \mid \text{one above and one below the mean})$

$$= \frac{P\big((X_1 > \mu) \cap (X_2 < \mu)\big)}{P(\text{one above and one below the mean})}$$

$$= \frac{0.429 \times 0.571}{(0.429 \times 0.571) + (0.571 \times 0.429)} = 0.5$$

8. (a) Let X = number of requests in one day.
Then $X \sim \text{Po}(1.8)$.

Some requests have to be turned down if there are more than 3 requests in a day.

$$P(X > 3) = 1 - P(X \leq 3)$$

$$= 1 - 0.891$$

$$= 0.109$$

(b) $P(X = 4 \mid X > 3) = \dfrac{P\big((X = 4) \cap (X > 3)\big)}{P(X > 3)}$

$$= \frac{P(X = 4)}{P(X > 3)}$$

$$= \frac{0.0723}{0.109} = 0.665$$

(c) Let Y = number in requests in two days. Then $Y \sim \text{Po}(3.6)$.

$$P(Y > 6) = 1 - P(Y \le 6)$$
$$= 1 - 0.9267 = 0.0733$$

(d) Let Z = number of days in a 7-day week with more than 3 requests.

Then $Z \sim \text{B}(7, 0.109)$.

$$P(Z \ge 2) = 1 - P(Z \le 1)$$
$$= 1 - 0.828 = 0.172$$

(e) Let N = number of vans hired out in one day.

When the number of requests is 3 or fewer, $N = X$; when the number of requests is more than 3, $N = 3$. Therefore:

$$P(N = 0) = P(X = 0) = 0.165$$
$$P(N = 1) = P(X = 1) = 0.298$$
$$P(N = 2) = P(X = 2) = 0.268$$
$$P(N = 3) = P(X = 3) + P(X > 3)$$
$$= 0.161 + 0.109 = 0.269$$

So the probability distribution of N is:

N	0	1	2	3
$P(N = n)$	0.165	0.298	0.268	0.269

(f) Let I = the income in one day; then $I = 120N$, so the probability distribution of I is:

I	0	120	240	360
$P(I = i)$	0.165	0.298	0.268	0.269

$E(I) = 0 \times 0.165 + 120 \times 0.298 + 240 \times 0.268 + 360 \times 0.269 = \$197$

(g) Let D = the distance travelled by a van.

Then $D \sim \text{N}(150, \sigma^2)$ and $P(D > 200) = 0.1$.

$$\frac{D - 150}{\sigma} \sim \text{N}(0, 1)$$

$$P\left(\frac{D - 150}{\sigma} > \frac{200 - 150}{\sigma}\right) = 0.1$$

$$\Rightarrow \frac{200 - 150}{\sigma} = 1.28 \quad \text{(from GDC)}$$

$$\Rightarrow \sigma = 39.0 \text{ km}$$

(h) $D \sim \text{N}(150, 39.0^2)$, so $P(D < 100) = 0.100$

P(two vans each travel less than 100 km) = $0.100^2 = 0.0100$

Going for the top 11

1. (a) $\int_0^\pi kx \sin x \, dx = 1$

Using integration by parts:

$$k\left(\left[-x\cos x\right]_0^\pi - \int_0^\pi -\cos x \, dx\right) = 1$$

$$\Rightarrow k\left(-\pi(-1) + \left[\sin x\right]_0^\pi\right) = 1$$

$$\Rightarrow k\pi = 1$$

$$\Rightarrow k = \frac{1}{\pi}$$

(b) Let q_1 = first quartile, q_3 = third quartile. Then:

$$\int_0^{q_1} \frac{1}{\pi} x \sin x \, dx = 0.25$$

$$\Rightarrow \frac{1}{\pi}\left[-x\cos x + \sin x\right]_0^{q_1} = 0.25$$

$$\Rightarrow -q_1 \cos q_1 + \sin q_1 = 0.25\pi$$

$$\Rightarrow q_1 = 1.43 \quad \text{(from GDC)}$$

$$\int_0^{q_3} \frac{1}{\pi} x \sin x \, dx = 0.75$$

$$\Rightarrow \frac{1}{\pi}\left[-x\cos x + \sin x\right]_0^{q_3} = 0.75$$

$$\Rightarrow -q_3 \cos q_3 + \sin q_3 = 0.75\pi$$

$$\Rightarrow q_3 = 2.35 \quad \text{(from GDC)}$$

$$\text{IQR} = q_3 - q_1 = 0.919$$

2. $X \sim \text{Po}(\lambda)$, $P(X = k) = \dfrac{e^{-\lambda}\lambda^k}{k!}$

$$P(X = 0) + P(X = 2) = 3P(X = 1)$$

$$\Leftrightarrow \frac{e^{-\lambda}\lambda^0}{0!} + \frac{e^{-\lambda}\lambda^2}{2!} = 3 \times \frac{e^{-\lambda}\lambda^1}{1!}$$

$$\Leftrightarrow 1 + \frac{\lambda^2}{2} = 3\lambda$$

$$\Leftrightarrow \lambda^2 - 6\lambda + 2 = 0$$

$$\Leftrightarrow \lambda = \frac{6 \pm \sqrt{36 - 8}}{2}$$

$$= \frac{6 \pm \sqrt{28}}{2}$$

$$= \frac{6 \pm 2\sqrt{7}}{2}$$

$$= 3 \pm \sqrt{7}$$

$$\therefore \lambda = 3 + \sqrt{7} \quad (\text{as } \lambda > 1)$$

3. (a) For Annie to win with her second shot, Annie, Brent and Carlos have to miss once and then Annie scores:

$$0.4 \times 0.5 \times 0.2 \times 0.6 = 0.024$$

(b) For Carlos to get a second shot, he has to miss once and Annie and Brent have to miss twice:

$0.4^2 \times 0.5^2 \times 0.2 = 0.008$

(c) (i) For Brent to win with his kth shot, he has to miss $(k-1)$ times and score once, Annie has to miss k times, and Carlos has to miss $(k-1)$ times:

$0.5^{k-1} \times 0.5 \times 0.4^k \times 0.2^{k-1} = (0.5 \times 0.4 \times 0.2)^{k-1}$
$\times (0.5 \times 0.4)$
$= 0.04^{k-1} \times 0.2$

(ii) $P(\text{Brent wins})$

$= \sum_{k=1}^{\infty} P(\text{Brent wins on } k\text{th shot})$

$= \sum_{k=1}^{\infty} 0.2 \times 0.04^{k-1}$

Using the formula for the sum of the geometric series with $u_1 = 0.2$ and $r = 0.04$:

$P(\text{Brent wins}) = \dfrac{0.2}{1 - 0.04} = 0.208$

12 INDUCTION

Mixed practice 12

1. Writing odd numbers as $2r - 1$ for $r \geq 1$, we need to prove that $\sum_{r=1}^{n} 2r - 1 = n^2$.

Let $n = 1$:

LHS $= 2 \times 1 - 1 = 1$

RHS $= 1^2 = 1$

So the statement is true for $n = 1$.

Assume it is true for $n = k$:

$\sum_{r=1}^{k} 2r - 1 = k^2 \quad \cdots (*)$

Let $n = k + 1$:

$\sum_{r=1}^{k+1} 2r - 1 = \left(\sum_{r=1}^{k} 2r - 1 \right) + 2(k+1) - 1$

$= \left(\sum_{r=1}^{k} 2r - 1 \right) + 2k + 1$

$= (k^2) + 2k + 1 \quad \text{(by } (*))$

$= (k+1)^2$

So the statement is true for $n = k + 1$.

The statement is true for $n = 1$, and if true for $n = k$ it is also true for $n = k + 1$. Hence, the statement is true for all $n \geq 1$ by the principle of mathematical induction.

2. Let $n = 0$:

$3^{4n+2} + 2^{6n+3} = 3^2 + 2^3 = 17 = 17 \times 1$

So the statement is true for $n = 0$.

Assume it is true for $n = k$:

$3^{4k+2} + 2^{6k+3} = 17A \quad \text{for some } A \in \mathbb{Z} \quad \cdots (*)$

Let $n = k + 1$:

$3^{4(k+1)+2} + 2^{6(k+1)+3} = 3^{4k+6} + 2^{6k+9}$
$= 3^4 (3^{4k+2}) + 2^{6k+9}$
$= 3^4 (17A - 2^{6k+3}) + 2^{6k+9} \quad \text{(by } (*))$
$= 81 \times 17A - 81 \times 2^{6k+3} + 2^{6k+9}$
$= 81 \times 17A - 2^{6k+3}(81 - 2^6)$
$= 81 \times 17A - 2^{6k+3}(17)$
$= 17(81A - 2^{6k+3})$

So the statement is true for $n = k + 1$.

The statement is true for $n = 0$, and if true for $n = k$ it is also true for $n = k + 1$. Hence, the statement is true for all $n \geq 0$ by the principle of mathematical induction.

3. (a) $3^1 = 3 < 1 + 5$

$3^2 = 9 > 2 + 5$

So the smallest positive integer M is $M = 2$.

(b) The statement is true for $n = 2$ by part (a).

Assume it is true for $n = k$:

$3^k > k + 5 \quad \text{where } k \geq 2 \quad \cdots (*)$

Let $n = k + 1$:

$3^{k+1} = 3(3^k)$
$> 3(k+5) \quad \text{(by } (*))$
$= 3k + 15$
$= (k+1) + 5 + 2k + 9$
$> (k+1) + 5$

So the statement is true for $n = k + 1$.

The statement is true for $n = 2$, and if true for $n = k$ it is also true for $n = k + 1$. Hence, the statement is true for all $n \geq 2$ by the principle of mathematical induction.

4. (a) Differentiating $f(x) = x \cos x$:

$f'(x) = 1 \times \cos x + x(-\sin x)$
$= \cos x - x \sin x$
$f''(x) = -\sin x - (1 \times \sin x + x \cos x)$
$= -2 \sin x - x \cos x$

(b) Let $n = 1$:

LHS $= f^{(2 \times 1)}(x) = f^{(2)}(x) = f''(x)$

RHS $= (-1)^1 (x \cos x + 2 \times 1 \times \sin x) = -x \cos x - 2 \sin x$

So the statement is true for $n = 1$, by part (a).

Assume it is true for $n = k$:

$$f^{(2k)}(x) = (-1)^k (x \cos x + 2k \sin x) \quad \cdots (*)$$

Let $n = k + 1$:

$$f^{(2(k+1))}(x) = f^{(2k+2)}(x)$$

$$= \frac{d^2}{dx^2}\left(f^{(2k)}(x)\right)$$

$$= \frac{d^2}{dx^2}\left((-1)^k (x \cos x + 2k \sin x)\right) \quad \text{(by (*))}$$

$$= \frac{d}{dx}\left((-1)^k (\cos x - x \sin x + 2k \cos x)\right)$$

$$= (-1)^k (-\sin x - \sin x - x \cos x - 2k \sin x)$$

$$= (-1)^k (-x \cos x - (2 + 2k) \sin x)$$

$$= (-1)^{k+1} (x \cos x + 2(k + 1) \sin x)$$

So the statement is true for $n = k + 1$.

The statement is true for $n = 1$, and if true for $n = k$ it is also true for $n = k + 1$. Hence, the statement is true for all $n \geq 1$ by the principle of mathematical induction.

5. (a) $f(n+1) - f(n) = \left[(n+1)^3 - 4(n+1)\right] - \left[n^3 - 4n\right]$

$$= n^3 + 3n^2 + 3n + 1 - 4n - 4 - n^3 + 4n$$

$$= 3n^2 + 3n - 3$$

(b) Let $n = 1$:

$$f(1) = 1^3 - 4 \times 1 = -3 = 3 \times (-1)$$

So the statement is true for $n = 1$.

Assume it is true for $n = k$:

$$f(k) = 3A \quad \text{for some } A \in \mathbb{Z} \quad \cdots (*)$$

Let $n = k + 1$:

$$f(k+1) = f(k) + 3k^2 + 3k - 3 \quad \text{(by part (a))}$$

$$= 3A + 3k^2 + 3k - 3 \quad \text{(by (*))}$$

$$= 3(A + k^2 + k - 1)$$

So the statement is true for $n = k + 1$.

The statement is true for $n = 1$, and if true for $n = k$ it is also true for $n = k + 1$. Hence, the statement is true for all $n \geq 1$ by the principle of mathematical induction.

6. Let $n = 1$:

$$10^{n+1} - 9n - 10 = 10^2 - 9 - 10 = 81 = 81 \times 1$$

So the statement is true for $n = 1$.

Assume it is true for $n = k$:

$$10^{k+1} - 9k - 10 = 81A \quad \text{for some } A \in \mathbb{Z} \quad \cdots (*)$$

Let $n = k + 1$:

$$10^{(k+1)+1} - 9(k+1) - 10 = 10^{k+2} - 9k - 19$$

$$= 10(10^{k+1}) - 9k - 19$$

$$= 10(81A + 9k + 10) - 9k - 19$$

$$\text{(by (*))}$$

$$= 10 \times 81A + 90k + 100 - 9k - 19$$

$$= 10 \times 81A + 81k + 81$$

$$= 81(10A + k + 1)$$

So the statement is true for $n = k + 1$.

The statement is true for $n = 1$, and if true for $n = k$ it is also true for $n = k + 1$. Hence, the statement is true for all $n \geq 1$ by the principle of mathematical induction.

7. As $n > 1$, the base case is $n = 2$:

$$u_2 = \sqrt{1 + 2u_1} = \sqrt{1 + 2 \times 2} = \sqrt{5} < 4$$

So the statement is true for $n = 2$.

Assume it is true for $n = k$:

$$u_k < 4 \quad \cdots (*)$$

Let $n = k + 1$:

$$u_{k+1} = \sqrt{1 + 2u_k}$$

$$< \sqrt{1 + 2 \times 4} \quad \text{(by (*))}$$

$$= 3$$

$$< 4$$

So the statement is true for $n = k + 1$.

The statement is true for $n = 2$, and if true for $n = k$ it is also true for $n = k + 1$. Hence, the statement is true for all $n \geq 2$ (and therefore for all $n \geq 1$ as $u_1 < 4$) by the principle of mathematical induction.

8. Let $n = 1$:

$$u_1 = 5^1 - 2 \times 3^1 = -1, \text{ as given.}$$

So the statement is true for $n = 1$.

Let $n = 2$:

$$u_2 = 5^2 - 2 \times 3^2 = 7, \text{ as given.}$$

So the statement is true for $n = 2$.

Assume it is true for $n = k$ and $n = k + 1$:

$$u_k = 5^k - 2 \times 3^k \quad \cdots (*)$$

$$u_{k+1} = 5^{k+1} - 2 \times 3^{k+1} \quad \cdots (**)$$

Let $n = k + 2$:

$$u_{k+2} = 8u_{k+1} - 15u_k$$

$$= 8(5^{k+1} - 2 \times 3^{k+1}) - 15(5^k - 2 \times 3^k) \quad \text{(by (*) and (**))}$$

$$= 8 \times 5^{k+1} - 15 \times 5^k - 16 \times 3^{k+1} + 30 \times 3^k$$

$$= 5^k(8 \times 5 - 15) - 3^k(16 \times 3 - 30)$$

$$= 5^k(25) - 3^k(18)$$

$$= 5^k(5^2) - 3^k(3^2 \times 2)$$

$$= 5^{k+2} - 2 \times 3^{k+2}$$

So the statement is true for $n = k + 2$.

The statement is true for $n = 1$ and $n = 2$, and if true for $n = k$ and $n = k + 1$ it is also true for $n = k + 2$. Hence, the statement is true for all $n \geq 1$ by the principle of mathematical induction.

9.   Let $n = 1$:

$\text{LHS} = \left[r(\cos\theta + i\sin\theta) \right]^1 = r(\cos\theta + i\sin\theta)$

$\text{RHS} = r^1 \left(\cos(1 \times \theta) + i\sin(1 \times \theta) \right) = r(\cos\theta + i\sin\theta)$

So the statement is true for $n = 1$.

Assume it is true for $n = k$:

$\left[r(\cos\theta + i\sin\theta) \right]^k = r^k(\cos k\theta + i\sin k\theta) \quad \cdots (*)$

Let $n = k + 1$:

$\left[r(\cos\theta + i\sin\theta) \right]^{k+1}$

$= r(\cos\theta + i\sin\theta) \left[r(\cos\theta + i\sin\theta) \right]^k$

$= r(\cos\theta + i\sin\theta) \left[r^k(\cos k\theta + i\sin k\theta) \right] \quad \text{(by (*))}$

$= r^{k+1}(\cos\theta + i\sin\theta)(\cos k\theta + i\sin k\theta)$

$= r^{k+1}\left[\cos\theta\cos k\theta + i\cos\theta\sin k\theta \right.$
$\qquad \left. + i\sin\theta\cos k\theta - \sin\theta\sin k\theta \right]$

$= r^{k+1}\left[\cos\theta\cos k\theta - \sin\theta\sin k\theta \right.$
$\qquad \left. + i(\cos\theta\sin k\theta + \sin\theta\cos k\theta) \right]$

$= r^{k+1}\left[\cos(\theta + k\theta) + i\sin(\theta + k\theta) \right]$

$= r^{k+1}\left[\cos((k+1)\theta) + i\sin((k+1)\theta) \right]$

So the statement is true for $n = k + 1$.

The statement is true for $n = 1$, and if true for $n = k$ it is also true for $n = k + 1$. Hence, the statement is true for all $n \geq 1$ by the principle of mathematical induction.

Going for the top 12

1.   As n is an odd positive integer, let $n = 2m - 1$ for $m \in \mathbb{Z}^+$.

Let $m = 1$:

$\left((2m-1)^2 + 3 \right)\left((2m-1)^2 + 15 \right) = (1^2 + 3)(1^2 + 15)$
$\qquad\qquad\qquad\qquad\qquad = 64 = 32 \times 2$

So the statement is true for $m = 1$.

Assume it is true for $m = k$:

$\left((2k-1)^2 + 3 \right)\left((2k-1)^2 + 15 \right) = 32A$
$\qquad\qquad\qquad\qquad\text{for some } A \in \mathbb{Z} \quad \cdots (*)$

Also, by expanding:

$\left((2k-1)^2 + 3 \right)\left((2k-1)^2 + 15 \right)$

$= (2k-1)^4 + 18(2k-1)^2 + 45$

$= 16k^4 - 32k^3 + 24k^2 - 8k + 1 + 72k^2 - 72k + 18 + 45$

$= 16k^4 - 32k^3 + 96k^2 - 80k + 64 \quad \cdots (**)$

Let $m = k + 1$:

$\left([2(k+1)-1]^2 + 3 \right)\left([2(k+1)-1]^2 + 15 \right)$

$= \left([2k+1]^2 + 3 \right)\left([2k+1]^2 + 15 \right)$

$= (2k+1)^4 + 18(2k+1)^2 + 45$

$= 16k^4 + 32k^3 + 24k^2 + 8k + 1 + 72k^2 + 72k + 18 + 45$

$= 16k^4 + 32k^3 + 96k^2 + 80k + 64$

$= (16k^4 - 32k^3 + 96k^2 - 80k + 64) + 64k^3 + 160k$

$= \left((2k-1)^2 + 3 \right)\left((2k-1)^2 + 15 \right) + 32(2k^3 + 5k) \quad \text{(by (**))}$

$= 32A + 32(2k^3 + 5k) \quad \text{(by (*))}$

$= 32(A + 2k^3 + 5k)$

So the statement is true for $m = k + 1$.

The statement is true for $m = 1$, and if true for $m = k$ it is also true for $m = k + 1$. Hence, the statement is true for all $m \geq 1$ (and thus for all odd $n \geq 1$) by the principle of mathematical induction.

2.   Let $n = 1$:
$\text{LHS} = 1 + 1 = 2$

$\text{RHS} = \left(\frac{1}{2} \times 1 \right)(3 \times 1 + 1) = \frac{1}{2}(4) = 2$

So the statement is true for $n = 1$.
Assume it is true for $n = k$:

$(k+1) + (k+2) + (k+3) + \ldots + (2k) = \frac{1}{2}k(3k+1) \quad \cdots (*)$

Let $n = k + 1$:

$\left((k+1)+1 \right) + \left((k+1)+2 \right) + \ldots + \left(2(k+1) \right)$

$= (k+2) + (k+3) + \ldots + 2k + (2k+1) + (2k+2)$

$= \left[\frac{1}{2}k(3k+1) - (k+1) \right] + (2k+1) + (2k+2) \quad \text{(by (*))}$

$= \frac{1}{2}k(3k+1) + 3k + 2$

$= \frac{1}{2}\left[k(3k+1) + 6k + 4 \right]$

$= \frac{1}{2}\left[3k^2 + 7k + 4 \right]$

$= \frac{1}{2}(k+1)(3k+4)$

$= \frac{1}{2}(k+1)(3(k+1)+4)$

So the statement is true for $n = k + 1$.

The statement is true for $n = 1$, and if true for $n = k$ it is also true for $n = k + 1$. Hence, the statement is true for all $n \geq 1$ by the principle of mathematical induction.

3. (a) (i) Let $n = 1$:

$$\text{LHS} = \cos\theta$$

$$\text{RHS} = \frac{\sin 2\theta}{2\sin\theta} = \frac{2\sin\theta\cos\theta}{2\sin\theta} = \cos\theta$$

So the statement is true for $n = 1$.

Assume it is true for $n = k$:

$$\cos\theta + \cos 3\theta + \cos 5\theta + \ldots + \cos\big((2k-1)\theta\big)$$
$$= \frac{\sin(2k\theta)}{2\sin\theta} \quad \cdots (*)$$

Let $n = k + 1$:

$$\cos\theta + \cos 3\theta + \ldots + \cos\big((2[k+1]-1)\theta\big)$$
$$= \cos\theta + \cos 3\theta + \ldots + \cos\big((2k+1)\theta\big)$$
$$= \Big[\cos\theta + \cos 3\theta + \ldots + \cos\big((2k-1)\theta\big)\Big] + \cos\big((2k+1)\theta\big)$$
$$= \frac{\sin(2k\theta)}{2\sin\theta} + \cos\big((2k+1)\theta\big) \qquad \text{(by $(*)$)}$$
$$= \frac{\sin(2k\theta) + 2\sin\theta\cos\big((2k+1)\theta\big)}{2\sin\theta}$$
$$= \frac{\sin(2k\theta) + 2\sin\theta\cos(2k\theta + \theta)}{2\sin\theta}$$
$$= \frac{\sin(2k\theta) + 2\sin\theta\big(\cos(2k\theta)\cos\theta - \sin(2k\theta)\sin\theta\big)}{2\sin\theta}$$
$$= \frac{\sin(2k\theta) + \big(2\sin\theta\cos\theta\big)\cos(2k\theta) - \big(2\sin^2\theta\big)\sin(2k\theta)}{2\sin\theta}$$
$$= \frac{\sin(2k\theta) + \big(\sin 2\theta\big)\cos(2k\theta) - \big(1 - \cos 2\theta\big)\sin(2k\theta)}{2\sin\theta}$$
$$= \frac{\sin(2k\theta) + \sin 2\theta\cos(2k\theta) - \sin(2k\theta) + \cos 2\theta\sin(2k\theta)}{2\sin\theta}$$
$$= \frac{\sin 2\theta\cos(2k\theta) + \cos 2\theta\sin(2k\theta)}{2\sin\theta}$$
$$= \frac{\sin(2k\theta + 2\theta)}{2\sin\theta}$$
$$= \frac{\sin\big(2(k+1)\theta\big)}{2\sin\theta}$$

So the statement is true for $n = k + 1$.

The statement is true for $n = 1$, and if true for $n = k$ it is also true for $n = k + 1$. Hence, the statement is true for all $n \geq 1$ by the principle of mathematical induction.

(ii) Let $n = 7$ and $\theta = \dfrac{\pi}{7}$. Then

$$\cos\frac{\pi}{7} + \cos\frac{3\pi}{7} + \cos\frac{5\pi}{7} + \ldots + \cos\frac{(2\times 7 - 1)\pi}{7}$$
$$= \frac{\sin\big(2 \times 7 \times \frac{\pi}{7}\big)}{2\sin\frac{\pi}{7}} \qquad \text{(by part (a)(i))}$$

$$\Leftrightarrow \cos\frac{\pi}{7} + \cos\frac{3\pi}{7} + \cos\frac{5\pi}{7} + \ldots + \cos\frac{13\pi}{7} = \frac{\sin(2\pi)}{2\sin\frac{\pi}{7}}$$

$$\therefore \cos\frac{\pi}{7} + \cos\frac{3\pi}{7} + \cos\frac{5\pi}{7} + \ldots + \cos\frac{13\pi}{7} = 0$$

(b) Let $n = 1$:

$$\text{LHS} = \csc\big(2^1\theta\big) = \csc 2\theta$$

$$\text{RHS} = \cot\theta - \cot\big(2^1\theta\big)$$
$$= \cot\theta - \cot 2\theta$$
$$= \frac{\cos\theta}{\sin\theta} - \frac{\cos 2\theta}{\sin 2\theta}$$
$$= \frac{\cos\theta}{\sin\theta} - \frac{\cos 2\theta}{2\sin\theta\cos\theta}$$
$$= \frac{2\cos^2\theta - \cos 2\theta}{2\sin\theta\cos\theta}$$
$$= \frac{2\cos^2\theta - \big(2\cos^2\theta - 1\big)}{2\sin\theta\cos\theta}$$
$$= \frac{1}{2\sin\theta\cos\theta}$$
$$= \frac{1}{\sin 2\theta} = \csc 2\theta$$

So the statement is true for $n = 1$.

Assume it is true for $n = k$:

$$\sum_{r=1}^{k}\csc\big(2^r\theta\big) = \cot\theta - \cot\big(2^k\theta\big) \quad \cdots (*)$$

Let $n = k + 1$:

$$\sum_{r=1}^{k+1}\csc\big(2^r\theta\big) = \sum_{r=1}^{k}\csc\big(2^r\theta\big) + \csc\big(2^{k+1}\theta\big)$$
$$= \cot\theta - \cot\big(2^k\theta\big) + \csc\big(2^{k+1}\theta\big) \qquad \text{(by $(*)$)}$$
$$= \cot\theta - \frac{\cos\big(2^k\theta\big)}{\sin\big(2^k\theta\big)} + \frac{1}{\sin\big(2^{k+1}\theta\big)}$$
$$= \cot\theta - \frac{\cos\big(2^k\theta\big)}{\sin\big(2^k\theta\big)} + \frac{1}{\sin\big(2[2^k\theta]\big)}$$
$$= \cot\theta - \frac{\cos\big(2^k\theta\big)}{\sin\big(2^k\theta\big)} + \frac{1}{2\sin\big(2^k\theta\big)\cos\big(2^k\theta\big)}$$
$$= \cot\theta - \frac{2\cos^2\big(2^k\theta\big) - 1}{2\sin\big(2^k\theta\big)\cos\big(2^k\theta\big)}$$
$$= \cot\theta - \frac{\cos\big(2[2^k\theta]\big)}{2\sin\big(2^k\theta\big)\cos\big(2^k\theta\big)}$$
$$= \cot\theta - \frac{\cos\big(2[2^k\theta]\big)}{\sin\big(2[2^k\theta]\big)}$$
$$= \cot\theta - \cot\big(2[2^k\theta]\big)$$
$$= \cot\theta - \cot\big(2^{k+1}\theta\big)$$

So the statement is true for $n = k + 1$.

The statement is true for $n = 1$, and if true for $n = k$ it is also true for $n = k + 1$. Hence, the statement is true for all $n \geq 1$ by the principle of mathematical induction.

ANSWERS TO PRACTICE QUESTIONS

1 COUNTING PRINCIPLES

1. (a) 40 320 (b) 5040
   (c) 30 240 (d) $\dfrac{1}{1680}$
2. 720
3. (a) 120 (b) $\dfrac{3}{5}$
4. 720
5. (a) 720
   (b) (i) 240 (ii) 480 (iii) 216
   (c) (i) $\dfrac{1}{5}$ (ii) $\dfrac{1}{5}$
6. $\dfrac{1}{126}$
7. (a) 4845 (b) $\dfrac{1}{323}$ (c) 1365 (d) 3844
8. (a) 792 (b) 210 (c) $\dfrac{791}{792}$
9. 60 480
10. (a) 358 800 (b) 62 990 928 000
11. (a) 1 123 200 (b) 1 263 600
12. 144
13. 2904
14. $n = 8$
15. 7
16. $n = 10$
17. $n = 5$
18. $n = 15$

2 EXPONENTS AND LOGARITHMS

1. $\dfrac{\log 3}{\log 125}$
2. $\dfrac{\log 48}{\log\left(\dfrac{4}{9}\right)}$
3. $\dfrac{\log\left(\dfrac{8}{3}\right)}{\log 50}$

4. $x = 0$ or $x = 2$
5. $x = \ln 6$
6. $x = \ln 3$ and $y = \ln 2$, or $x = \ln 2$ and $y = \ln 3$
7. $\log\left(\dfrac{a^3 c}{b^2}\right)$
8. $1 + a + 2b - \dfrac{c}{2}$
9. $a = \dfrac{b^2}{10}$
10. $y = e^2 x^4$
11. (a) $y = \ln(800 - e^{2x})$ and $y = \dfrac{e^5}{x^3}$
    (b) $(2.89, 6.17)$, $(3.30, 4.12)$
12. $x = 8$
13. $x = 4 + 2\sqrt{6}$
14. $x = 2^{\pm\frac{1}{5}}$
15. $x = \dfrac{3}{2}$ or $-\dfrac{5}{4}$
16. (a) 2.13 (b) 2.37 g
17. 43 105

3 POLYNOMIALS

1. $k > 8 + 6\sqrt{2}$ or $k < 8 - 6\sqrt{2}$
2. $0 < k < 24$
3. $-5 < a < 7$
4.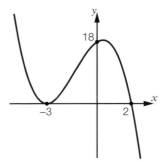
5. $y = 3x^3 - 9x - 6$
6. $2x^2 + 7x + 4 - \dfrac{25x + 35}{x^2 - 2x + 5}$
7. $f(x) = (2x + 1)(3x + 4)(x - 3)$

8. (a) $a = 1, b = 24$ (b) $x = 2, \dfrac{3}{2}, -4$

9. $a = -1, b = -6$

10. $a = -3, b = -1$

11. $b = \dfrac{8}{3}, d = \dfrac{4}{3}$

12. (a) $b + d = 9$ (b) $a = -3, b = -15, c = 5, d = 24$

13. $x^2 - 19x + 9 = 0$

14. $ax^2 + 2bx + 4c = 0$

15. $\alpha = \dfrac{c}{d}$

16. 61 236

17. (a) ± 2 (b) $560x^4$

4 FUNCTIONS, GRAPHS AND EQUATIONS

1. $-3 < x < 3$

2. $x \in \mathbb{R}, x \neq -1, 1$

3. $y \geq -8a^2$

4. $f^{-1}(x) = \dfrac{\ln x - b}{a}$

5. $x = \dfrac{5}{12}$

6. (a) Many to one; 4 and 6 both map to 4.

    (b) 4   (c) 7

7.

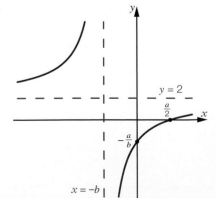

8. (a) Translation by vector $\begin{pmatrix} 2 \\ 0 \end{pmatrix}$ and vertical stretch with scale factor 3.

    (b) Translation by vector $\begin{pmatrix} 0 \\ -2 \end{pmatrix}$ and reflect the part below the x-axis in the x-axis.

9. (a)

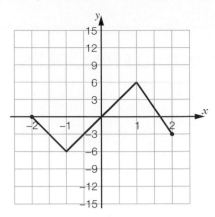

(b)

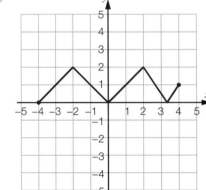

(c)

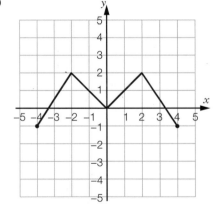

10. $y = -2x^3 - 12x^2 - 19x - 9$

11. $a = 3, b = 2, c = -\dfrac{\pi}{4}$

12.

13. (a) Zeros: $x = -1, 5$. Vertex: $(2, -9)$

(b)
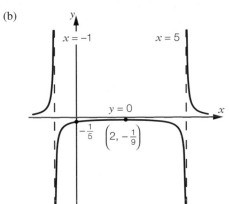

(c)
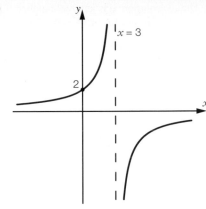

14. (a) $f^{-1}(x) = \dfrac{3x+1}{3-2x}$

(b) (i) Domain: $x \in \mathbb{R}, x \neq -1.5$. Range: $y \in \mathbb{R}, y \neq 1.5$

(ii) Domain: $x \in \mathbb{R}, x \neq 1.5$. Range: $y \subset \mathbb{R}, y \neq -1.5$

15. (a)
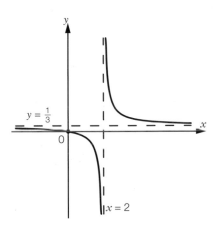

(b)
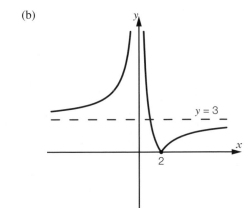

16. $-2 < x < 0$ or $x > 2$

17. $x \geq 2$ or $x \leq -3$

18. (a) $x(x-2)(x-3)$

(b)
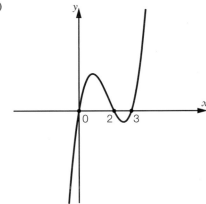

(c) $x < 0$ or $2 < x < 3$

19. (a)
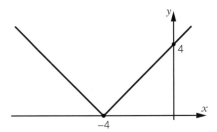

(b) $x > 1$

20. (a)
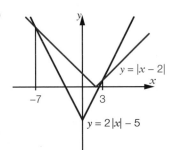

(b) $x > 3$ or $x < -7$

21. (a) Unique solution: a is any real number;
$x = 14 - 2a$, $y = 4a - 15$, $z = 9 - 2a$

(b) Unique solution: $a \neq 3$; $x = -7$, $y = 17$, $z = 0$.
Infinitely many solutions: $a = 3$;

$$\begin{pmatrix} x \\ y \\ z \end{pmatrix} = \begin{pmatrix} -7 \\ 17 \\ 0 \end{pmatrix} + \lambda \begin{pmatrix} 2 \\ -5 \\ 1 \end{pmatrix}$$

5 SEQUENCES AND SERIES

1. (a) −86   (b) 660

2. (a) 6.5   (b) 33rd term

   (c) 24 or 41

3. −0.669

4. 128 or 384

5. $a = 8$, $r = \dfrac{3}{2}$

6. (a) $a = \dfrac{1}{2}$, $r = 4$

   (b) 9th term   (c) 10

7. (a) −3, 7   (b) 54

8. (a) \$32 619   (b) \$1 511 552

   (c) 13th year   (d) 27

9. (a) \$185   (c) 56

10. (a) 1.77147 m

   (b) 11th   (c) 57 m

11. (b) $k = 2.5$ (c) 28 years

6 TRIGONOMETRY

1. $a = 3$, $b = 2$

2. $f(x) \in \left[\dfrac{2}{7}, \dfrac{2}{3}\right]$

3. $\dfrac{3\pi}{4}$

10. $-\sqrt{\dfrac{5}{6}}$

11. $-\dfrac{\sqrt{7}}{4}$

12. $\dfrac{2}{\sqrt{5}}$

13. $x = \dfrac{\pi}{8}, \dfrac{7\pi}{8}$

14. $x = -\dfrac{8\pi}{9}, -\dfrac{5\pi}{9}, -\dfrac{2\pi}{9}, \dfrac{\pi}{9}, \dfrac{4\pi}{9}, \dfrac{7\pi}{9}$

15. $x = \dfrac{\pi}{36}, \dfrac{5\pi}{36}, \dfrac{25\pi}{36}, \dfrac{29\pi}{36}, -\dfrac{23\pi}{36}, -\dfrac{19\pi}{36}$

16. $x = \dfrac{\pi}{6}, \dfrac{\pi}{3}, \dfrac{2\pi}{3}, \dfrac{5\pi}{6}, \dfrac{7\pi}{6}, \dfrac{4\pi}{3}, \dfrac{5\pi}{3}, \dfrac{11\pi}{6}$

17. $\theta = -1.89, -0.464, 1.25, 2.68$

18. $x = \dfrac{2\pi}{3}, \dfrac{4\pi}{3}$

19. $x = \pm\dfrac{\pi}{2}, \dfrac{\pi}{6}, \dfrac{5\pi}{6}$

20. $\theta = \dfrac{\pi}{6}, \dfrac{5\pi}{6}$

21. $R = 2$, $\theta = \dfrac{\pi}{6}$; minimum value $\dfrac{2}{5}$

22. $R = \sqrt{34}$, $\alpha = 0.540$, maximum point $\left(0.540, \sqrt{34}\right)$

23. 6.75 cm

24. 23.2

25. 21.2 m

7 VECTORS

1. (a) $\overrightarrow{MN} = \dfrac{1}{2}(c - a)$ (b) $\overrightarrow{QP} = \dfrac{1}{2}(c - a)$

2. (a) $\begin{pmatrix} -16 \\ -8 \\ 8 \end{pmatrix}$ (b) $4\sqrt{6} \approx 9.80$

3. (a) $\begin{pmatrix} -3 \\ 6 \\ -1 \end{pmatrix}$ (b) $\dfrac{1}{\sqrt{46}}\begin{pmatrix} -3 \\ 6 \\ -1 \end{pmatrix}$

4. (a) $r = \begin{pmatrix} -3 \\ 1 \\ 2 \end{pmatrix} + \lambda\begin{pmatrix} 0 \\ 2 \\ 5 \end{pmatrix}$ (b) $(-3, 5, 12)$

5. The lines do not intersect (they are skew).

6. $x + 5y - 2z = 5$

7. $2x - 13y - 5z = -25$

8. (a) $(0, 5, 13)$ (b) $15x + 6y + z = 43$

9. $r = \begin{pmatrix} 4 \\ -4 \\ 0 \end{pmatrix} + \lambda\begin{pmatrix} 0 \\ 1 \\ 1 \end{pmatrix}$

10. $\left(\dfrac{9}{2}, \dfrac{5}{2}, \dfrac{3}{2}\right)$

11. $(1, -1, 3)$

12. $48.2°$

13. $79.5°$

14. $67.1°$

15. (a) $\Pi_1 : \begin{pmatrix} 1 \\ -2 \\ -5 \end{pmatrix}$, $\Pi_2 : \begin{pmatrix} 3 \\ -7 \\ -1 \end{pmatrix}$

    (b) $58.5°$

16. $\dfrac{\sqrt{230}}{5} \approx 3.03$

17. (a) $r = \begin{pmatrix} 2 \\ -3 \\ 1 \end{pmatrix} + \lambda \begin{pmatrix} 3 \\ -1 \\ 1 \end{pmatrix}$ (b) $\dfrac{7\sqrt{11}}{11} \approx 2.11$

18. $\dfrac{7}{6}\sqrt{6} = 2.86$

19. (a) $\sqrt{53} \approx 7.28\,\mathrm{m\,s^{-1}}$

    (b) $7.90°$ (c) $12\sqrt{53} \approx 87.4\,\mathrm{m}$

20. $\text{Speed} = 5\sqrt{17} \approx 20.6\,\mathrm{km\,h^{-1}}$

8 COMPLEX NUMBERS

1. $z = -3 - 4i$

2. $z = 1 - 2i$

3. $\mathrm{Im}(z) = -\dfrac{1}{2}$

4. (b) $z = 1 + i$ or $z = \dfrac{7}{5} - \dfrac{1}{5}i$

5. $z = 1 - i$ or $z = -\dfrac{5}{3}$

6. (b) $z = \dfrac{25}{13} + \dfrac{60}{13}i$

7. $4\left(\cos\left(-\dfrac{\pi}{2}\right) + i\sin\left(-\dfrac{\pi}{2}\right)\right) = -4i$

8. (a) $z_1 = \sqrt{2}\,e^{-i\frac{\pi}{4}}$, $z_2 = 2e^{i\frac{2\pi}{3}}$ (b) $-\dfrac{1}{4}i$

9. $-2, -3i$

10. $a = 2, b = -3, c = 20$

11. (b) $-2i, 3 + i, 3 - i$

12. $4\cos^3\theta\sin\theta - 4\cos\theta\sin^3\theta$

13. (a) $\cos^5\theta + 5i\cos^4\theta\sin\theta - 10\cos^3\theta\sin^2\theta - 10i\cos^2\theta\sin^3\theta + 5\cos\theta\sin^4\theta + i\sin^5\theta$

    (b) (i) $16\sin^5\theta - 20\sin^3\theta + 5\sin\theta$

       (ii) $16\cos^5\theta - 20\cos^3\theta + 5\cos\theta$

14. (a) $\cos3\theta = \cos^3\theta - 3\cos\theta\sin^2\theta$

        $\sin3\theta = 3\cos^2\theta\sin\theta - \sin^3\theta$

15. $\dfrac{1}{4}(\cos3\theta + 3\cos\theta)$

17. (a) $A = 5, B = 10$

    (b) $\dfrac{1}{16}\left(\dfrac{1}{5}\sin5\theta + \dfrac{5}{3}\sin3\theta + 10\sin\theta\right) + c$

18. (a) $|z| = 8$, $\arg z = -\dfrac{\pi}{3}$

    (b) $2e^{-i\frac{\pi}{9}}, 2e^{-i\frac{7\pi}{9}}, 2e^{i\frac{5\pi}{9}}$

19. $2, -2, 2i, -2i$

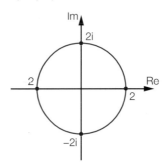

20. $e^{i\frac{\pi}{12}}, e^{i\frac{\pi}{4}}, e^{i\frac{7\pi}{12}}, e^{i\frac{11\pi}{12}}, e^{i\frac{3\pi}{4}}, e^{i\frac{5\pi}{12}}$

9 DIFFERENTIATION

5. $2xe^{x^2} + \dfrac{3x\cos3x - \sin3x}{2x^2}$

6. $x = -4, 3$

7. $\dfrac{12 - 18x^2}{\left(x^2 + 2\right)^3}$

8. (c) $\dfrac{1}{2}\ln3$

9. $y - e^{-12} = \dfrac{e^{12}}{12}(x - 2)$ or $e^{12}x - 12y + 12e^{-12} - 2e^{12} = 0$

10. -1.26

11. $-\dfrac{1}{2}$

12. $(0, 5), (0, -2)$

13. $\dfrac{y - 3 - 2y^2(y-3)^2}{4xy(y-3)^2 + x + 1}$

14. (a) $-\csc y \cot y$ (b) $-\dfrac{1}{x\sqrt{x^2-1}}$

15. $(-1, 10)$ maximum, $(1, 6)$ minimum

16. $(0, 1)$ minimum, $\left(\dfrac{\pi}{2}, \dfrac{\pi}{2}\right)$ maximum,

$\left(\dfrac{3\pi}{2}, -\dfrac{3\pi}{2}\right)$ minimum

17. $\ln(2\pi)$

18. Minimum area $= 48\pi$; $\dfrac{d^2A}{dr^2} = 2\pi + 256\pi r^{-3} > 0$ when $r = 4$

19. $131\,\text{cm}^2$

21. $(4, -121)$

22. $a = -12$; $b = -4$

23. (a) $a \geq -2$ (b) $a = -1$

(c)

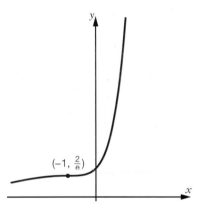

24.

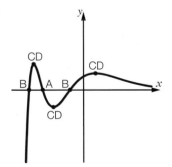

25. (a)

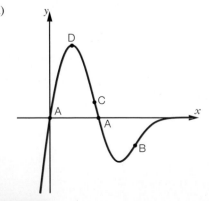

(b) Concave down   (c) Increasing

(d) Minimum as $f'' > 0$

26. $\dfrac{200}{9\pi(500)^{\frac{2}{3}}} = 0.112\,\text{m s}^{-1}$

27. $\dfrac{6}{125}\,\text{rad s}^{-1}$

28. (a) 2 hours   (b) $(-)\dfrac{16\sqrt{3}}{9}\,\text{km}$

(c) $8\,\text{km h}^{-1}$

29. (a) $v = \pi\cos\left(\dfrac{3\pi t}{2}\right)$, $a = -\dfrac{3\pi^2}{2}\sin\left(\dfrac{3\pi t}{2}\right)$

(b) $t = \dfrac{2}{9}, \dfrac{4}{9}$

10 INTEGRATION

1. $-\dfrac{1}{2}\cos(x^2) - x^2\cos x + 2x\sin x + 2\cos x + c$

2. $x + \dfrac{1}{2}x^2\ln x - \dfrac{x^2}{4} + c$

3. $-\dfrac{1}{3}\ln|1 - 3e^x| + c$

4. $-\csc x + c$

5. $\dfrac{\left(\frac{7}{9}\right)^x}{\ln\left(\frac{7}{9}\right)} + c$

6. $2\sqrt{x} + \ln x + c$

7. $\sqrt{2}$

8. $e - 1$

9. 1

10. $\dfrac{\pi}{6}\left(e^{18} - e^6\right)$

11. $\dfrac{\pi^2}{8}$

12. $\dfrac{\pi}{4}$

13. $\dfrac{\pi}{2}$

14. (a) $5\left(t + \dfrac{1}{2}e^{-2t} - \dfrac{1}{2}\right)$

(b) $\dfrac{5}{4}\left(2t^2 - e^{-2t} - 2t + 1\right)$

(c) $\dfrac{5}{2}\left(9 + e^{-10}\right)\,\text{m s}^{-1}$

15. $k = -25$

16. (a) $v = 10 - 2e^{-t}$ (b) $10.2\,\text{s}$

11 PROBABILITY AND STATISTICS

1. Mean 11.5 years; standard deviation 3.31 years

2. $196\,\text{cm}$

3. $0.214\,\text{m}$

4. (a) Median ≈ 53.5; IQR ≈ 29

   (b) $p = 65, q = 5, r = 8$

   (c) Mean 46.3; standard deviation 19.9

5. (a) 7   (b) 19.9

6. 0.33

7. $\dfrac{2}{7}$

8. (a) $\left(\dfrac{7}{8}\right)^5\left(\dfrac{1}{8}\right) = \dfrac{16\,807}{262\,144} \approx 0.0641$

   (b) $\left(\dfrac{7}{8}\right)^{13} \approx 0.176$

9. 0.5

10. (a) 5   (b) $\dfrac{5}{7}$

11. (a)

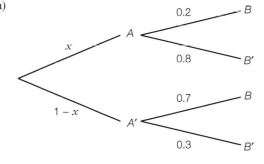

   (b) 0.7

   (c) No; $P(A) \neq P(A \mid B)$

12. $\dfrac{9}{23} \approx 0.391$

13. $\dfrac{1}{3}$

14. $\dfrac{20}{37}$

15. $\text{E}(Z) = 18.2,\ \text{Var}(Z) = 22.56$

16. $c = 0.2, p = 0.2$

17. 0.0378

18. (a) 0.301   (b) 0.919

19. $p = \dfrac{2}{3},\ n = 7$

20. (a) Mean 17.5; variance 12.5

   (b) Not appropriate; mean and variance should be equal for a Poisson distribution.

21. (a) $\dfrac{2}{e^4 - e^{-4}}$ (b) 1.654

22. (b) 0.111

23. (a) 0.233   (b) 0.202

   (c) 7.04

24. 2.47 or 3.93

25. (a) 0.0668   (b) 0.653

26. $14.0\,\text{g}$

27. $152.8\,\text{ml}$

28. (b) $\mu - 1.28155\sigma = 47$; $\mu = 68.12,\ \sigma = 16.48$

13 EXAMINATION SUPPORT

Spot the common errors

1. (i) Tried to integrate a product factor by factor

   (ii) Integrated e^{2x} to $2e^{2x}$ rather than $\dfrac{1}{2}e^{2x}$

   (iii) Missed out '$+ c$'

2. (i) Expanded $\ln(10 - x)$ into two logarithms

   (ii) Sign error in performing the 'expansion' led to $-\ln x$, which then cancelled with the first $\ln x$

   (iii) Tried to undo ln without first getting everything on each side of the equation (including minus signs) inside a ln

   (iv) Obtained an answer which cannot go into the original expression (log of a negative number)

3. 'Cancelled' an expression which is not a factor of the entire denominator